Texas & New Mexico on the Eve of the Civil War

Texas & New Mexico on the Eve of the Civil War

The Mansfield & Johnston Inspections, 1859–1861

Edited and with an Introduction by

JERRY THOMPSON

UNIVERSITY OF NEW MEXICO PRESS

ALBUQUERQUE

First Edition

Library of Congress Cataloging-in-Publication Data

Texas and New Mexico on the eve of the Civil War : the Mansfield and Johnston inspections, 1859–1861 / edited and with an introduction by Jerry Thompson. — 1st ed.
p. cm.
Includes bibliographical references and index.
ISBN 0-8263-2102-X (alk. paper)
1. Texas —History, Military—19th century. 2. New Mexico—History, Military—19th century. 3. Fortification—Inspection—Texas—History—19th century. 4. Fortification—Inspection—New Mexico—History—19th century. 5. Mansfield, Joseph K. F. (Joseph King Fenno), 1803–1862. 6. Johnston, Joseph E. (Joseph Eggleston), 1807–1891. 7. United States. Army—Military life—History—19th century. 8. United States. Army—Operational readiness—History—19th century. 9. Confederate States of America Army—Operational readiness—History. I. Mansfield, Joseph K. F. (Joseph King Fenno), 1803–1862. II. Johnston, Joseph E. (Joseph Eggleston), 1807–1891. III. Thompson, Jerry D. IV. Title.
F391 .T25 2001
355'.00976'09034—dc21
00-011118

Design: *Mina Yamashita*

For Sara,

Loving companion

on the Long Road

to Shambala

CONTENTS

INTRODUCTION

Throughout the history of the antebellum United States Army, only a few officers were able to jump grades by obtaining appointments in new regiments or to high staff positions not covered by the seniority rule.[1] The most striking examples are those of Capt. Joseph King Fenno Mansfield, appointed directly to full colonel and inspector general in 1853, and Capt. Joseph Eggleston Johnston, promoted to lieutenant colonel in the newly formed First Cavalry in 1855, then to brigadier general and quartermaster in 1860. Johnston thus became the first graduate in the history of the United States Military Academy promoted to a general's rank in the regular army.[2] Both Mansfield and Johnston were particularly fortunate and gifted officers and their place in United States military history has been well established.

From 1859 to 1861, Johnston and Mansfield undertook inspections of the Departments of Texas and New Mexico. Their job, briefly stated, was to inspect, investigate, and report on all matters affecting the efficiency, discipline, and welfare of the army. Their inspections covered the troops, officers, quarters, and general administration of units and posts. Johnston, who was four years younger than Mansfield, reported from July to November 1859 not only on the isolated posts in the Department of New Mexico but on those in the Department of Texas that stretched along the San Antonio-El Paso Road (called the Lower Military Road) from Fort Bliss at Franklin (El Paso) to San Antonio. Beginning at Galveston and Indianola in September 1860 and ending with Department Headquarters in San Antonio five months later, Mansfield conducted a comprehensive inspection of most posts, encampments, and depots in the Department of Texas. Together, their reports comprise an important part of Texas history, combining at different times elements of frontier courage, military strategy, and political ambition.

While Mansfield was diplomatic and detailed in his inspection reports, Johnston had a tendency to editorialize. In a bluntness that captured the attention of the adjutant general, Johnston went as far as to urge the War Department not to wage war on the Navajos. "An attack upon this tribe would be very impolitic [and] much opposed to humanity & justice," he wrote from forlorn Fort Defiance. "These people have made more unassisted progress towards civilization than any Indian tribe that I have known," he continued. On the opposite side, both Johnston and Mansfield took note of the rampant alcoholism in the frontier army. As the two frequently noted, temperance was a weak, if not nonexistent, ideal on the frontier, where it was common for soldiers to supplement their rations with spirits purchased from the post sutler or whiskey peddler. Too often, consuming whiskey was one way to cope with a hostile environment and emotional isolation. Such extreme reactions, it would seem, were the inevitable result of an extreme environment. Scholars and general readers alike will find in the inspection reports of Mansfield and Johnston, published here for the first time, a rare and informative glimpse into the army in the Southwest on the eve of the Civil War.

MANSFIELD

Joseph K. F. Mansfield was born to Henry and Mary (Fenno) Mansfield at New Haven, Connecticut, on December 22, 1803, the youngest of six children. A few months after his birth, his mother was granted a divorce on grounds of adultery after she discovered that her merchant-husband was living with a woman at St. Croix in the Virgin Islands. When the family moved to Middletown, Connecticut, an older brother, John, assumed the guardianship of the young lad and saw to his education. Capt. John F. Mansfield died of fever, however, after commanding the Cincinnati Light Infantry during Gen. William Hull's disastrous invasion of Lower Canada in the War of 1812. Joseph was only eleven at the time.

Attempting to gain admission for Joseph to West Point, Jared Mansfield, a lieutenant colonel in the engineers and professor of natural and experimental philosophy at West Point, frequently mentioned John's death in his lengthy letters to both President James Monroe and Secretary of War John C. Calhoun. The lad, Jared Mansfield wrote, was of "fine bodily form & of superior mental endowments" and possessed a good understanding of "Latin, French & German," as well as a "fine taste in painting, drawing & other minor arts."[3] In 1817, two months before his fourteenth birthday, J. K. F. Mansfield

Joseph K. F. Mansfield at the beginning of the Civil War.
(Photograph courtesy of the Library of Congress)

was accepted into the United States Military Academy, the youngest in his class. Mansfield did well at West Point, and, in 1822, he graduated second in a class of forty and was breveted a second lieutenant in the engineers. As was the custom, the Corps of Engineers took the academy's brightest and most energetic graduates. Only weeks later he was promoted to second lieutenant. In March 1832, he was made a first lieutenant and, in July 1838, a captain.[4] Much of Mansfield's early antebellum career was spent constructing fortifications along the South Atlantic and Gulf Coast, especially Fort Pulaski, near Savannah, Georgia.[5]

In 1838 (the same year he was promoted to captain), Mansfield married Louisa Mary Mather, daughter of a wealthy New England shipper. Although theirs was a long courtship, they did not waste time in beginning a family. A son, Samuel Mather, arrived a year after their marriage, and, in 1841, an only daughter, Mary Louisa, joined the three. A second son, Joseph Totten, was born in late 1844 but died at only nine months. Yet another son, Henry L., was born in 1845.[6]

Mansfield knew the Lone Star state well. Only months prior to the commencement of hostilities with Mexico in 1846, he inspected the entire Texas coast for suitable depot locations to supply forts to be established on the Rio Grande. At the beginning of the war, Mansfield was made chief engineer under Gen. Zachary Taylor and supervised the construction of Fort Texas, opposite Matamoros. He also survived the Mexican bombardment of the fort on May 9, 1846, and was breveted a major for gallantry and distinctive service.[7] Following the opening battles of the war, Mansfield observed that Taylor owed "his rank & success more to my opinions before the battles of Palo Alto & Resaca than to any other circumstance."[8]

Along with a squad of Texans at Monterrey, Mansfield successfully reconnoitered the Mexican defenses. During the storming of the city that followed on September 23, 1846, he led a charge armed with only a sword in one hand and a spyglass in the other. Seriously wounded in the leg, he lay in the makeshift American hospital for months.[9] Although he was again breveted for gallantry and meritorious service, the wound he received at Monterrey scarred him physically and psychologically for the rest of his life.[10] Visited daily by General Taylor, he recovered sufficiently to act as an advisor at the Battle of Buena Vista on February 23, 1847. In anticipation of his own death, he carefully showed First Lt. Henry Washington Benham, a Connecticut-born engineer, "the peculiarities of his teeth to recognize him even in decay."[11] After the battle he wrote his wife Louisa back in Middletown, Connecticut, "Thank God that I have come safely out of a tremendous battle. The greatest ever fought in America."[12] Yet again he would be breveted for gallantry and meritorious service, this time to colonel.[13] In fact, Mansfield was one of the few American officers to receive three brevets in the war. Five years later, Secretary of War Jefferson Davis, impressed with Mansfield's performance during the war and his service on the army's Board of Engineers for Fortifications afterward, recommended him for inspector general and colonel. While the other inspector general, Col. Sylvester Churchill, operated in the area east of the Mississippi River, Mansfield was sent into the vast expanses of the Trans-Mississippi.

Mansfield's inspection of the Department of Texas in 1860–1861 was only one of several inspections he completed in the Trans-Mississippi. Promoted to colonel and named inspector general of the army on May 28, 1853, he had seen as much of the West as anyone, with the possible exception of some fur trappers and traders such as Jedediah Smith. When he was first named inspector general, Mansfield had examined the Ninth Military Department, consisting at the time of the Territory of New Mexico, including Fort Massachusetts in what is today southern Colorado, as well as Fort Bliss, a newly established post in far west Texas opposite the Mexican town of El Paso del Norte.

The following year, Mansfield undertook an exhausting inspection of the vast Department of the Pacific, which included posts in California and the territories of Oregon and Washington. A year later, in April 1856, he undertook an equally fatiguing examination of the Department of Texas, landing at Galveston and making his way down the coast to depots at Indianola and Corpus Christi. From Corpus Christi, Mansfield continued along the coast to Fort Brown. The peripatetic inspector then turned up the Rio Grande to inspect Ringgold Barracks at Rio Grande City, Fort McIntosh at Laredo, and Fort Duncan at Eagle Pass, eventually heading north and west to visit Forts Clark, Lancaster, and Davis. Back along the San Antonio-El Paso Road, he went north to visit Forts Mason, McKavett, Chadbourne, and Belknap, as well as Camp Cooper. The following year he traveled across the Great Plains to examine the army in Utah. In 1858 and 1859, he inspected the Department of Oregon and the Department of California.

Scholars have referred to Mansfield as an "exceedingly energetic and productive inspector general," noting that in the years from 1853 to 1857, control of the office of inspector general was the subject of a power struggle between the commanding general, Winfield Scott, and the secretary of war, Jefferson Davis.[14] Mansfield, they conclude, was his own man, and managed to avoid the bitter political struggle by remaining constantly in the field. Although he lacked literary gifts and the "sense of controlled outrage when something affronted his sensibilities, he compensated with his greater diligence and sobriety."[15]

JOHNSTON

Joseph Eggleston Johnston had much in common with Mansfield. Both were intelligent and highly ambitious. Johnston's grandfather had emigrated from Scotland in 1726 and had entered the mercantile trade in Virginia much as Mansfield's father had become a New England trader.[16] Settling near Petersburg, Virginia, Johnston's father served during the American Revolution in the brigade of "Light Horse Harry" Lee, the father of Robert E. Lee. Johnston was also proud that his mother, Mary Valentine Wood, was the niece of Patrick Henry. It was on the family estate at Farmville, southwest of Richmond, that Joseph Eggleston Johnston was born the seventh son of Mary and Peter Johnston on February 3, 1807. When Peter Johnston became a circuit court judge on the eve of the War of 1812, the family moved to the Appalachian frontier town of Abingdon in the mountains of southwest Virginia, not far from the Tennessee border. In his childhood, the boy loved to reenact the victory over the Tories at the Battle of King's Mountain. Inspired by such activities and trained at Abingdon Academy, Johnston obtained the education that would take him to West Point.[17]

In 1829, Johnston graduated thirteenth in a class of forty-six that included Robert E. Lee, who ranked second, and the brilliant Charles Mason, who was first. Unable to get into the prestigious engineers as Mansfield had done, Johnston was commissioned a second lieutenant in the Fourth Artillery. His first assignment was at Fort Columbus in New York Harbor. In the years that followed, he served in the Black Hawk War and the First Seminole War. Impatient with the slow process of promotion and seeking greater financial rewards in the civilian world, Johnston resigned from the military shortly thereafter. With his engineering skills he was certain to earn three, four, or even five times more than the 750 dollars he made each year in the army.[18] Returning to Virginia, he took a job with the Topographical Bureau in Washington, D.C., and was promptly sent back to Florida in the midst of a Second Seminole War to explore and survey some 450 miles of the Florida coast.[19] In a fight with the Seminole on the Jupiter River in January 1836, Johnston narrowly escaped death when he received a scalp wound and had several rifle balls pass through his clothing, including two through his cap.[20] Back in Washington in 1838, he reentered the military, this time

Joseph E. Johnston shortly after the Civil War.
(Photograph courtesy of the Library of Congress)

as a first lieutenant in the newly formed topographical engineers.

In July 1845, Johnston married Lydia McLane from the gentility of Maryland's eastern shore. Regardless, he was soon off to war in Mexico, appointed to Gen. Winfield Scott's staff and participating in the siege of Vera Cruz. Just as Mansfield had been wounded at Monterrey, Johnston, while reconnoitering the Mexican artillery at Cerro Gordo, was hit by grapeshot and severely wounded.[21] In the confusion of the war, he was breveted a lieutenant colonel for gallantry and meritorious conduct, skipping over the rank of major.[22] Recovering from his wounds just as the American army moved against Mexico City, Johnston commanded a battalion in the assault on Chapultepec for which he received another brevet, this time to colonel.[23] As had been the case in the Seminole Wars, Johnston was consistently praised for his heroism in Mexico. The euphoria over victory, however, was tempered by the death of a nephew, Preston Johnston.[24]

After the war, Johnston had his first look at Texas when, from 1848 to 1853, he served as chief topographical engineer of the Eighth Military Department. While in San Antonio, he undertook the task of exploring a potential route for a proposed transcontinental railroad route that would stretch west through the *terrae incognitae* of the Texas Trans-Pecos to the Pacific. In 1849, with a company of infantry and twenty civilian laborers, Johnston constructed what the army would call the Lower Military Road, a rough wagon road that stretched some 670 miles west from San Antonio to El Paso. "The road is generally excellent with abundance of grass and fuel," Johnston wrote.[25] Although his party was totally exhausted by the time they reached El Paso, Johnston went on to explore the conifer-crowned Sacramento Mountains in southeastern New Mexico Territory and then to survey the Texas-New Mexico boundary line.

In March 1855, Johnston was promoted to lieutenant colonel in the newly established First Cavalry. Under the hard-nosed Lt. Col. Edwin Vose "Bull" Sumner, he served ably in the political turmoil that was "Bleeding Kansas." Two years later, he again took up his former capacity as explorer and topographical engineer when he surveyed the southern boundary of Kansas.[26] By early 1859, he was back in Mexico, this time as an aid to his brother-in-law, Robert McLane, who had been named Minister to Mexico. Arriving in Vera Cruz, Johnston undertook the delicate task of examining military routes across Mexico.[27] When it was learned that the Mexicans would not tolerate further American adventurism, he returned to the United States. He requested permission to conduct an inspection tour of European fortifications but was sent instead to New Mexico Territory as acting inspector general.

THE INSPECTIONS

Inspecting the frontier was not a light undertaking. Indeed, Mansfield's initial departure provides a suitable image for our own trek through this historic episode. At 8 A.M. on October 8, 1859, in a spring wagon pulled by four mules, the fifty-five-year-old Mansfield departed San Antonio on the El Paso Road to report on the Department of Texas. Among those accompanying the inspector general were an Irish-born servant, a ten-year veteran of the Texas frontier army, and an escort of ten men and a sergeant.[28] The ponderous caravan consisted of three canvas-covered wagons carrying provisions, including tents, two hams, flour, hard bread, coffee, sugar, and tea for the men and corn for the six mules needed to pull each wagon.[29] What lay in store no one could have entirely predicted, but that very uncertainty, after all, was the very premise for the inspection.

As inspector general of the army, Mansfield went from post to post, often on the road from sunrise to sunset, traveling up to twenty-five miles a day.[30] At one of the many forts, he would take detailed notes in a small leather notebook and draw rough sketches of the post and the environs. The inspector general would then ride on to places such as Dead Man's Hole, Escondido Creek, Howard Spring, California Spring, or Noria de los Federales, where he would compile his official report and draw a more complete plat based on his preliminary sketches. At these isolated watering holes, he was able to escape the distractions and politics of post life and complete his reports with a greater measure of objectivity.

In his inspection reports that were sent to Adjutant General Samuel Cooper, Mansfield not only recorded the efficiency of post sutlers and officers but made several pleas for improving the circumstances of individual veterans. He always emphasized military readiness, noting soldiers who were present, absent, and even those who were in the guardhouse. In addition, he offered detailed recommendations for specific congressional funding projects, carefully noting the costs of leasing land and buildings at both department headquarters in San Antonio and various posts. Of interest is the fact that Mansfield, aware that Secretary of War John B. Floyd was probably on his way out, addresses his comments directly to General-in-Chief Winfield Scott.[31] In all, Mansfield and Johnston's copious reports, filed individually as letters to the office of the adjutant general, are a rich and unique historical window, combining travelogue, inspection commentary, and delving into the morale, training, equipment, and daily lives of soldiers in the vast and remote Southwest on the eve of the Civil War.

NEW MEXICO AND TEXAS

Mansfield and Johnston found in the vast expanses of the Southwest a defense system that had evolved in the years following the war with Mexico. The army had assumed not only the responsibility of protecting isolated settlements but building and maintaining roads, guarding survey parties, and subduing hostile tribes.[32] In New Mexico Territory, defenses were established to guard "lines of settlement and the arteries of travel, commerce, and communications," a formidable mission in a spacious land.[33] In practice, these tasks meant that most of the newly established posts, although widely scattered, hugged the Rio Grande, the region's historic lifeline. For example, in 1846, Gen. Stephen Watts Kearny had established Fort Marcy at Santa Fe, adjacent to the historic Palace of the Governors. The post was later moved to a location on a small mesa some six-hundred yards north of the plaza. By the time of Mansfield's 1853 inspection, the post had been abandoned and the troops were living in public quarters in the town. Remembering the bloody uprising against American rule at Taos in 1847, Mansfield recommended that a garrison be retained in the territorial capital "to preserve order and sustain the authorities in cases of domestic excitement."[34]

Most of the New Mexico posts that Mansfield inspected in 1853 and Colonel Johnston visited in 1859 had been established when Lt. Col. Edwin V. Sumner assumed command of Military Department No. 9 in April 1851.[35] Sumner, who had been with General Kearny in the conquest of New Mexico five years earlier, was a tough campaigner and exemplary field commander; all the same, he may have inherited the most difficult mission in the Trans-Mississippi West. Secretary of War Charles M. Conrad directed Sumner to "revise the whole system of defence" within the department and get "the troops out of the towns . . . and station them more towards the frontier and nearer to the Indians."[36]

One of the provisions of the Treaty of Guadalupe Hidalgo was the prevention of Indians from committing depredations in Mexico, and this objective was also one of those for the new defense system. The main priority remained defending the frontier and protecting the citizens of the territory. Sumner arrived in the territorial capital on July 19, 1851, and immediately undertook a sweeping revision of the defenses of the territory. "My first step," he wrote, "was to break up the post at Santa Fe, that sink of vice and extravagance," by removing the troops, department headquarters, and public property to Fort Union.[37] Despite the objections of townsmen in the territory, Sumner broke up not only the garrisons at Santa Fe, but also those at Albuquerque, Doña Ana, Socorro, Las Vegas, Rayado, Abiquiu, Seboyeta, and, in Texas, San Elizario and Coons' Ranch near Franklin. In blaming low troop morale on the evil influences of such small communities, Sumner aimed to establish nine new posts, six of them designed to be permanent.[38] During his administration, the posts of Fort Union, Fort Massachusetts, Cantonment Burgwin, Fort Defiance, Fort Conrad, Fort Webster, Fort Fillmore, and Los Lunas were established. In his final analysis, Sumner decided to retain Fort Marcy at Santa Fe.[39] Although the headquarters was moved to Albuquerque, it was returned to Santa Fe.

In July 1851, work began on Fort Union, some twenty-four miles northeast of Las Vegas in the Lone Wolf Valley where the two branches of the Santa Fe Trail converged. Although the post, located on a small tributary of the Mora River, was to become, as Sumner hoped, one of the most important in the Southwest, throughout the 1850s Fort Union consisted of little more than a collection of shabby log buildings. "The place looks like a log village," an officer in the Mounted Rifles wrote. "The houses are scattered in every direction. The quarters are all of logs but are very comfortable."[40] On the line of communications with the Missouri frontier, the fort was also to serve as a deterrent to the Utes and Jicarilla Apaches, the two tribes posing a continuing threat to the Santa Fe Trail and the small settlements in the area.[41] In 1853, Mansfield found that, because Fort Union was too closely situated to the foot of a small mesa, it could not be defended against "an enterprising enemy, unless the heights can be occupied by a block house."[42]

Shortly after the conquest of New Mexico, military officials recognized the strategic significance of the Taos Valley, sixty miles to the west of Fort Union.[43] Located east of a deep, imposing gorge of the Rio Grande and west of the towering Sangre de Cristo range of the Rockies, the valley had long provided easy access from Santa Fe north into Colorado and was a haven for fur traders and trappers. In June 1852, Sumner sent Lt. Robert Ransom, Jr., with Company I of the First Dragoons to establish a new post at a picturesque site near the convergence of two small streams, the Rito de la Olla (Pot Creek) and the Rio Grande del Rancho, some ten miles south of Taos, fifteen miles east of the Rio Grande, and three miles upstream from the gristmill of Ceran St. Vrain.[44] The new post would be along the difficult yet main wagon road between Santa Fe and Taos.[45] The nearest settlement was Talpa, three miles to the northwest.

Cantonment Burgwin was named for Capt. John Henry K. Burgwin, who had died during the 1847 Taos uprising. Poorly constructed of logs, the post became so dilapidated that, when Johnston arrived in 1859, many of the soldiers had been forced to seek housing in the nearby villages. After a "four days' march from Santa Fe, over a frightful road" where in places "wagons had to be let down with ropes," Lydia Spencer Lane, the wife of First Lt. William Bartlett Lane of the Mounted Rifles, recalled being surprised to see the quarters at Fort Burgwin constructed of "rough pine logs . . . old and out of repair." Nevertheless, the post was "most beautifully situated," she continued, "being surrounded by high mountains."[46]

As part of his reorganization of the department, Sumner sent the bluecoats north into the barren San Luis Valley. Fort Massachusetts became the northernmost post in the department and the first military post in the present state of Colorado (Sumner was a native of Boston, Massachusetts; hence the post's name).[47] At long last, the post was established by Maj. George A. H. Blake of the First Dragoons on June 22, 1852, some eighty-five miles north of Taos and six miles north of the present town of Fort Garland at the base of 14,345-foot Blanca Peak. The trail to get there from Taos was so difficult that the fort had to be supplied by pack mule rather than ox train.[48] The post's mission, in the meantime, was to guard the western approach to La Veta Pass in the imposing Sangre de Cristo Mountains and protect the growing number of settlers on the Culebra River to the south.[49] James Bennett, a young dragoon, observed that Fort Massachusetts was "situated in a niche of the mountains" where "snow is seen within a mile . . . the whole year." The post was "surrounded by wolves, bears, and Indians."[50] In 1853, Mansfield concluded that Fort Massachusetts was "too near the spur of the mountain for a good defense against an enterprising enemy," and he recommended that it be relocated on the Culebra River, twenty miles to the south.[51] Moreover, the post was also located in a swampy, unhealthy area where, at more than eight thousand feet, the summers were short and the winters intensely cold. As Mansfield had suggested, the fort was abandoned and reestablished by Capt. Andrew W. Bowman and men of the Third Infantry on June 24, 1858, not on the Culebra River as Mansfield had hoped, but near the Trinchera River some six miles to the south. The new post was named Fort Garland in honor of Col. John Garland of the Eighth Infantry, who was commanding the Department of New Mexico at the time.[52]

Fort Defiance was established in the heart of the Navajo country on September 1851, by Maj. Electus Backus of the Third Infantry on a site selected by Lieutenant Colonel Sumner.[53] Standing at the mouth of picturesque Cañon Bonito, thirty-five miles northwest of present-day Gallup, New Mexico, the isolated post was difficult and expensive to maintain. It was the first United States Army fort in what is today Arizona and the first in the department west of the Continental Divide. Fort Defiance stood on the doorstep of the Navajo sanctuaries of Cañon de Chelly, Black Mesa, and the Chuska Mountains. Lt. William Woods Averell of the Mounted Rifles wrote that Fort Defiance was "simply a rectangle three hundred yards long and two hundred wide enclosed with log houses and without [a] stockade or other defensive works."[54] In 1853, Mansfield, who was impressed with the romantic wilderness of the area, described Fort Defiance as "the most beautiful and interesting post as a whole in New Mexico."[55] The fort, however, had the "disadvantage of being commanded within musketry range by a rocky ridge on the east."[56] Mansfield thus recommended that two small blockhouses be erected, and one was, in fact, built in 1858.[57]

Fort Conrad was established by Sumner's orders on September 8, 1851, by Maj. Marshall S. Howe of the Second Dragoons. Situated on a small rise on the right bank of the Rio Grande, the post was named for Secretary of War Charles M. Conrad. It was located twenty-four miles south of the windswept village of Socorro and ten miles above the northern end of the dreaded *Jornada del Muerto*, a ninety-mile route with little water and shelter that circumvented a big western bend of the Rio Grande.[58] Built across the river from the crumbling adobe ruins of Valverde and the ranch of Robert H. Stapleton, Fort Conrad was designed to protect a large part of the El Paso-Santa Fe segment of the old Camino Real and ward off Apache raids in the Rio Grande Valley. In 1853, Mansfield found the post to be in an advanced state of dilapidation with its buildings "falling down." He recommended the post be vacated and another post constructed farther south, nearer the northern end of the dreaded *Jornada del Muerto*. On March 31, 1854, Fort Conrad was abandoned.[59] Nine miles to the south, Capt. Daniel T. Chandler and troops of the Third Infantry established Fort Craig, which was strategically located just above Paraje de Fra Cristobal, as Mansfield had recommended.[60] Solidly built of rock and adobe, the post was named for Capt. Louis S. Craig of the Third Infantry, who had been killed in June 1852 by deserters in the desert west of Fort Yuma. Not only was Fort Craig one of the largest army posts in the territory, many officers and men also thought it was one of the most attractive. Lieutenant Averell remembered the fort as "an imposing object in the country of small houses."[61] In March 1855, a young dragoon wrote that Fort Craig was "the best and prettiest fort in New Mexico."[62]

Six miles south of Mesilla on the east bank of the Rio Grande, Fort Fillmore was established by Sumner's orders on September 23, 1851, by Lt. Col. Dixon S. Miles of the Third Infantry and named for President Millard Fillmore.[63] Constructed from an estimated 500,000 adobes, the post helped to guard the

Located six miles south of Mesilla on the east side of the Rio Grande, Fort Fillmore was established in September 1851 to guard the Mesilla Valley and a portion of the overland trail that stretched west through the heart of Apacheria to Tucson. Fort Fillmore, Lydia Lane wrote, was "dreary-looking" and "uninviting." (Illustration from Illustrated London News, *Dec. 2, 1854)*

Mesilla Valley and a portion of the overland trail that stretched west through the heart of Apacheria to Tucson. Fort Fillmore was, according to Lydia Lane, a "dreary-looking" and "uninviting" place."[64] Nonetheless, the nearby community of Mesilla, on the west bank of the Rio Grande before the river later changed course and in Mexican territory prior to the Gadsden Purchase, offered a bustling atmosphere. Mesilla was also the largest settlement on the overland trail between San Antonio, Texas, and San Diego, California.

As early as September 14, 1848, a new post, which the army called the "Post Opposite Paso del Norte," emerged in the desert near the village of Franklin, Texas. The post was established when Maj. Jefferson Van Horne led 257 soldiers, including the regimental staff, six infantry companies, and a howitzer battery, west from San Antonio. Four of the companies were quartered at Coons' Rancho at what is now downtown El Paso, while the remaining troops occupied the old Spanish presidio of San Elizario, twenty miles downriver.[65]

The new boundary needed defending as settlers were continually asking for protection from raiding Apaches, and the area was desperate for some semblance of law and order. Undermined by constant desertions and chronic drunkenness, the post was closed in September 1851, and the troops removed to Fort Fillmore, forty miles up the Rio Grande. In 1853, however, Mansfield recommended that the fort be reestablished. A military presence

Originally constructed by Francisco Manuel Elguea in 1803, Fort Webster, a triangular structure, was located at the Santa Rita Copper Mines. In 1852, the garrison was moved to the Rio Mimbres but, due to Mansfield's recommendation, abandoned in December 1853. (Illustration from Bartlett, Narrative of Explorations and Incidents*)*

in the area would not only protect the area from raiding Apaches but also from "any excitement in El Paso, where there is a Mexican population of 7,000 souls."[66] On January 11, 1854, Lt. Col. Edmund Brooke Alexander, with four companies of the Eighth Infantry, set up camp at Magoffinsville, a hacienda three miles east of Coons' Rancho. On March 8, 1854, the official name of the post became Fort Bliss, after Lt. Col. William Wallace Smith Bliss, Gen. Zachary Taylor's chief-of-staff during the Mexican War and his son-in-law. To Lydia Lane, Fort Bliss was poetically named, for she described it as "the most delightful station" in the entire Southwest.[67]

On March 4, 1855, Gen. John Garland and men of the Eighth Infantry located Camp Garland on the Rio Bonito on the eastern slope of the Sacramento Mountain, just south of Capitan Mountain.[68] The camp was later moved two miles to the north and named for Capt. Henry W. Stanton of the First Dragoons, who had died in January 1855 in a fight with the Mescalero Apaches near the Peñasco River. Although far from the region's lines of communications, the post was in the very heart of the Mescalero homeland. Fort Stanton "was a beautiful post," Lydia Lane wrote, "with the best quarters in the army at that time, but it was like being buried alive to stay there. Nothing ever passed that way, and it was seldom a stranger came among us."[69]

Fort Webster was actually inherited rather than established when the United States Boundary Commission and men of the Third Infantry built Cantonment Dawson at the Santa Rita Copper Mines in April 1851. The triangular rock and adobe fort, which was constructed by Francisco Manuel Eluea in 1803, was abandoned by the army after only four months. On January 23, 1852, Capt. Israel Bush Richardson and Company K of the Third Infantry established a camp at "Las Minas del Cobre" and named the encampment for Secretary of War Daniel Webster.[70] A month later, a dragoon arrived at the copper mines to find fifty soldiers, having recently been attacked by the Apaches, fearful of a second attack and almost "frightened out of their wits."[71] The soldiers, he concluded, had "old wagons, logs, barrels, rocks, and other articles too numerous to mention, piled around their fort, making it almost impossible to get to it."[72] On September 9, 1852, a new post was constructed under the guidance of Maj. Gouverneur Morris of the Third Infantry some fifteen miles to the east on the Rio Mimbres.[73] When Mansfield inspected the new post in October 1853, he found the buildings at the post, made of logs and mud, in need of repair. Realizing the post was serving no meaningful purpose, Mansfield recommended that it be relocated to the Gila River forty miles to the west. In December 20, 1853, Fort Webster was abandoned and a new post established, not on the Gila River but on the Rio Grande. Fort Thorn was built near present-day Hatch, New Mexico, on the right bank of the Rio Grande at the small village of Santa Barbara.[74] The fort was named for First Lt. Herman Thorn of the Second Infantry, who had drowned in the Colorado River on October 16, 1849.[75] The post guarded the old Camino Real along the river and was built to deter Apache raids in the upper Mesilla Valley. Unfortunately, the post was built adjacent to a large marsh and consequently was abandoned in March 1859, only six months prior to Colonel Johnston's inspection.

With the signing of the Gadsden Purchase on December 30, 1853, not only Mesilla but some 29,640 square miles of rugged mountains and sun-blistered deserts, including all of present-day Arizona south of the Gila River and a large swath of southwestern New Mexico, passed into the hands of the United States. As a consequence, the military quickly recognized the need to protect the small number of citizens in the area from raiding Apaches. Although Mexican authorities continued to exercise control over Mesilla until October 1854, Colonel Mansfield recommended that a chain of forts

Fort Thorn was established on the right bank of the Rio Grande near the small village of Santa Barbara, near present-day Hatch. The health at the post was never good, probably due to a large adjacent marsh, and by the time of Johnston's 1859 inspection, the post had been abandoned. (Illustration from Davis, El Gringo*)*

be constructed along the trail stretching west from the Rio Grande at Mesilla to the Yuma Crossing on the Colorado River. Having entered the territory in the same party as Mansfield, Gen. John Garland agreed. Precise locations were to be chosen after suitable reconnaissance. At any rate, General Garland, who assumed command of the Department of New Mexico in July 1853, was less concerned with detail, less egotistical than Sumner, and more inclined to delegate authority. Hoping for a more central location, Garland transferred the commissary, quartermaster, and medical stores to Albuquerque, even though he found the town to be the "dirtiest hole in New Mexico."[76]

Responding to residents of Tucson who demanded protection from Apache raids, in November 1856, Maj. Enoch Steen, along with four companies of the First Dragoons, established Camp Moore nine miles north of the Mexican border near the Calabasas Ranch. There, grain, beef, and other supplies could be obtained from Sonora. The camp was named after Lt. Isaiah N. Moore of the First Dragoons, who had died during the war with Mexico in the Battle of San Pasqual, California. Col. Benjamin L. E. Bonneville, who took control of the Department of New Mexico on January 1, 1854, ordered Steen to move the post closer to Tucson. When the area around Tucson and the Mission of San Xavier del Bac a few miles to the south, proved unsatisfactory, Capt. Richard S. Ewell, a bald-headed, bold Indian fighter, along with Company G of the Third Dragoons, was sent on a scouting expedition to the southeast in hopes of finding a location that would offer better grazing.

Captain Ewell was impressed with Ojos Calientes, a place near the head of the Sonoita Valley where thermal springs provided a good water supply and the grass was far better than in the desert around Tucson. Ewell, however, eventually chose a second site some twenty-five miles northeast of Calabasas.[77] Although this location was forty miles from Tucson, Assistant Inspector Gen. N. H. Davis reported the area to be "one of the most beautiful" he had "ever seen for a post," particularly because of "its commanding position of the adjacent country" and the fact that it was situated astride one of the "great thoroughfares of the Apaches."[78] Work on Fort Buchanan, which was almost a mile high in altitude, began in March 1857. The post was constructed on the western slope of a small irregular plateau surrounded by small mesas and hills, ten miles east of 9,453-foot Mt. Wrightson and the lesser spires of the Santa Rita Mountains. Named for James Buchanan, fifteenth president of the United States, the post took fifty thousand adobes to construct. In time, the fort would turn out to be extremely unhealthful, badly situated, and poorly constructed.[79] Similar to Fort Defiance, Fort Buchanan was also among the most difficult and expensive to supply in not only the Department of New Mexico but the entire United States.[80]

In 1860, 3,104 officers and enlisted men were assigned to the Department of New Mexico. At the same time, the army garrisoned, including Fort Bliss and several wandering detachments, 3,009 bluecoats in the Department of Texas.[81] Thus, on the eve of the Civil War, one-third of the army's complement of 17,500 officers and enlisted men was stationed in these two departments. Two-thirds of the men were immigrants, particularly desperate Irish youth who had fled the Emerald Isle and the calamitous potato famine for a better life in America. The second largest foreign contingent was German, of which many could not speak enough English to be understood by their officers. In addition, a sprinkling of disillusioned English, Scottish, and Scandinavian youth had enlisted. A few recruits were deserters from the British army in Canada. Some of the Americans were society's riffraff, including paupers, drunkards, reprobates, the chronically unemployed and shiftless, and even the mentally retarded or incompetent. At least one-fourth were illiterate.[82] Few had any idea of the rigors and dangers that awaited them in the frontier army.

In Texas, the army constructed a frontier defense line that stretched from the Rio Grande to the Red River. In the north, Capt. Ripley A. Arnold and Company F of the Second Dragoons established Fort Worth on June 6, 1849, at the confluence of the Clear Fork and the West Fork of the Trinity River on the site of what is today the city of Fort Worth.[83] On March 27, 1849, at the Waco Indian village of José María on the east bank of the Brazos River, west of what is today Hillsboro, Arnold and two companies of the Second Dragoons began construction of Fort Graham.[84] Other garrisons on the northwestern Texas frontier included Fort Gates, on the north bank of the Leon River, east of present Gatesville, and Fort Crogan, erected by Bvt. Second Lt. Charles H. Tyler and men of the Second Dragoons near present Burnet, northwest of Austin. Farther south, Fort Martin Scott offered protection to the German immigrant community of Fredericksburg, as Fort Lincoln, west of San Antonio, provided security to the small Alsatian village of D'Hanis. Elsewhere, on March 1, 1850, Capt. Samuel M. Plummer and Companies H and K of the First Infantry occupied what became Fort Merrill on the south bank of the Nueces River in Live Oak County. The post, named for Capt. Moses E. Merrill, who died at the Battle of Molino del Rey, was abandoned on December 1, 1855.

South of San Antonio on the right bank of the Nueces River, where the Laredo-San Antonio wagon road crossed the river, Lt. Col. William Wing Loring and three companies of Mounted Rifles set up camp at what would become Fort Ewell on May 18, 1852. The post was named for Lt. Thomas Ewell, who was killed at Cerro Gordo.[85] Inspecting the post a year later, Brevet Lt. Col. William Grigsby Freeman reported that "suitable timber or stone for buildings" could not be found in the vicinity nor "good grazing" for animals. Every attempt to establish a "kitchen garden" had "been unsuccessful."[86] Most of the officers and men were living in tents and exhibiting the "greatest repugnance" for constructing adobe quarters.[87] Lacking fresh fruits and vegetables, as many as thirty-five of the men were suffering from scurvy.[88] "Indeed a less inviting spot," Freeman went on to write, "cannot well be conceived."[89] Poorly built, desolate, and in an area where only scrubby mesquite was available for wood, the post, at the urging of department commander Maj. Gen. Persifor Frazer Smith, was abandoned in October 1854.

To the west of San Antonio, Capt. Seth Eastman of the First Infantry arrived on March 13, 1849, to build Fort Inge on the east bank of the Leona River in Uvalde County. The post was named for Lt. Zebulon M. P. Inge of the Second Dragoons, who was killed at Resaca de la Palma. In his inspection of the Eighth Military Department in 1853, Lieutenant Colonel Freeman found Maj. George B. Crittenden and two companies of the Mounted Rifles, as well as the regimental band at Fort Inge. The soldiers were housed in "two buildings constructed of upright poles chinked up, with thatched roofs" that were "in a wretched state of dilapidation."[90] In his 1855 journey through Texas, Frederick Law Olmsted, the noted architect and writer of travel books, found at Fort Inge "a dozen building, of various sizes."[91] The buildings "were scattered along the border of a convenient parade ground," Olmsted noted, "pleasantly shaded by hackberries and elms." The structures, he continued, "were all very rough and temporary, some of the officers' lodgings being mere *jacals* of sticks and mud. But all were white-washed and neatly kept by taste and discipline."[92] Likewise, Lydia Lane recalled her stay at Fort Inge as exceedingly pleasant, reporting that "butter, eggs, and chickens were brought to the post sometimes from the ranches, eighteen or twenty miles away" and "game was very abundant . . . deer, turkeys, partridges, and ducks right round the post, while the lovely clear stream than ran just back of the house filled with magnificent black bass, which were easily caught."[93]

With the rapid development of communities on the Texas frontier in the early 1850s, the older line of military posts became unnecessary, and a second cordon of forts, some ninety miles to the west, was established. Fort Belknap in Young County secured the northern end of this second tier of posts and became the largest and most important military establishment in North Texas. On November 14, 1851, Maj. John J. Abercrombie with Companies C and G of the Fifth Infantry established a post on the rolling prairie fifteen miles north of present Abilene. The post, which was abandoned four years later, was christened Fort Phantom Hill but commonly called the "Post on the Clear Fork of the Brazos." A year later, farther south in Menard County near the old San Sabá Mission, the army built Fort McKavett. The post was probably named for Capt. Henry McKavett, who was killed at Monterrey in 1846.[94] Capt. John Beardsley and two companies of the Eighth Infantry began construction of Fort Chadbourne on October 28, 1852, on a small tributary of the Colorado River, eleven miles northeast of present Bronte in what became Coke County. The post was named for Lt. Theodore L. Chadbourne, who fell at Resaca de la Palma.[95]

Other posts followed. In August 1856, Companies A and F of the Second Cavalry under Maj. Earl Van Dorn established Camp Colorado on Mukewater Creek about six miles north of the Colorado River and on the route between Fort Belknap and Fort Mason.[96] In July 1857, as a result of many of the soldiers becoming ill, the post was moved about twenty-two miles north to Jim Ned Creek, where adobe quarters were constructed. Lumber for roofs, floors, and doors were hauled by ox teams from East

Texas.[97] In January 1856, Col. Albert Sidney Johnston and men of the Second Cavalry established Camp Cooper on the Clear Fork of the Brazos River in south central Throckmorton County.[98] The post, named for Adjutant General Samuel Cooper, became the headquarters for the Second Cavalry. Lt. Col. Robert E. Lee, who kept a rattlesnake for a pet at the post, commanded the post for fifteen months in 1856 and 1857. Quarters were constructed of adobes and were similar to those at Camp Colorado. During the last years of the 1850s, the post served to deter Indian raids on the northwestern frontier of the state.

On July 8, 1855, in the heart of the picturesque Texas hill country, on the north bank of Verde Creek and three miles north of Bandera Pass, the army established Camp Verde.[99] Blessed with abundant water and shade, as well as mild summers, the post quickly became one of the most desirable in Texas, if not the entire Trans-Mississippi. In 1856, thirty-three camels, nine swift dromedaries, twenty burden camels, and four others of mixed breed arrived at the post that became known as "Little Egypt."[100] Another shipment of forty other camels arrived later. Despite a nasty habit of biting and sometimes spitting at their riders and handlers, the camels demonstrated a capacity to travel longer distances and to carry heavier loads. One camel trek pushed west into the vast expanses of the Big Bend, and, when forty-one additional camels arrived, the army sent some of the animals to California. Although considered a success, the military abandoned the Camel Corps in 1861 with the outbreak of the Civil War.

To protect the southern borders of the state from Indian attacks and Mexican revolutionaries, the War Department also initiated a chain of posts along the Rio Grande, just as Mansfield had suggested in 1846. At the southeastern end of this line of defense was Fort Brown, which the army had established as Fort Texas at the beginning of the Mexican War. The original fort, largely designed by Mansfield, was an earthen works eight hundred yards in perimeter, with six bastions, walls more than nine feet high, a parapet of fifteen feet, and a surrounding ditch fifteen feet deep and twenty feet wide. The post was named for Maj. Jacob Brown, who died on May 9, 1846, from wounds received in the Mexican bombardment of the fort. At the end of the war, quarters for officers and enlisted men were established a quarter mile upriver from the first site on the banks of the river near a large lagoon. In 1853, Lieutenant Colonel Freeman found the soldiers at Fort Brown quartered in "framed houses." The post would have to "be maintained," he concluded, "as long as the opposite bank is Mexican soil."[101]

Soldiers preferred Fort Brown over other posts in Texas largely because

The mild winters in southern Texas made Fort Brown a post favored by army personnel and their dependents in the Department of Texas. In 1856, Captain Randolph B. Marcy found Fort Brown to be "one of the most beautiful and comfortable posts . . . on the frontier," but service at the post could be deadly. Epidemics of yellow fever, cholera, malaria, and dengue fever were common in the Lower Rio Grande Valley. (Illustration from Harper's Weekly*)*

of its mild winters. Helen Chapman, wife of Capt. William W. Chapman, who oversaw the construction of the new post, wrote that Fort Brown was a "comfortable place to live."[102] Capt. Randolph B. Marcy wrote that Fort Brown was "one of the most beautiful and comfortable posts . . . on the frontier." The post was built in a square "with cottages all around for the officers and their families."[103] To Captain Marcy, the Lower Rio Grande Valley was delightful in late autumn. "Everything is beautiful now," he wrote in November 1856, "the trees are in full foliage, the grass is deep green, flowers are all in blossom and the orange trees are covered with fruit while the temperature is mild and the atmosphere balmy."[104] After "being deprived of vegetables at Laredo," Marcy was delighted to find at Fort Brown not only "the finest oranges" but "tomatoes, beans, lettuce, radishes & potatoes in abundance."[105] The post could be deadly, however, as epidemics of yellow fever, cholera, malaria, and the dengue fever were common.[106] Nevertheless, Fort Brown helped stimulate the growth of the adjacent thriving commercial center, Brownsville, which became the administrative seat of Cameron County and the largest town on the Texas bank of the Rio Grande.

Upriver at Davis's Ranch, or what became Rio Grande City, Maj. Joseph H. LaMotte and two companies of the First Infantry established Ringgold Barracks on October 26, 1848.[107] Arriving at Ringgold Barracks by steamer in the spring of 1851, Teresa Griffin Vielé, the young and well-educated wife of Lt. Egbert Vielé and one of the first women to publish an account of army life in the Trans-Mississippi, vividly recalled her first impressions of the post. From the landing on the Rio Grande, the post "rose before us on a high sandy bluff, its rows of long, low, whitewashed modern buildings, placed at regular intervals around a level drill ground, in the centre of which rose the flag-staff, with its colors hanging droopingly, unstirred by the sultry air," Viele wrote.[108] With the help of the army, Rio Grande City and the village of Roma, a few miles upriver, became not only the head of navigation on the Rio Grande but distribution centers for the conveyance of goods sold and smuggled into Mexico. During his 1853 inspection, Freeman found the post to be "in excellent condition in all respects" and "decidedly healthy"[109] At the post, Freeman was "pleased to notice a good reading room with a number of well selected books and newspapers."[110] Three years later, Colonel Mansfield found the post "sickly" but indispensable, largely because of the chaotic political conditions then existing in Mexico and the "unsettled state of Indian difficulties."[111] Still, because the United States and Mexico were at peace, he felt that plans to build a field fort, similar to what he had constructed at Fort Brown, would serve no real purpose.[112] Mansfield did recommend, though, that a depot be established at the fort or upriver at Roma to supply Fort McIntosh and Fort Duncan better.[113]

On March 3, 1849, Lt. Egbert L. Viele rode upriver from Ringgold Barracks to establish Camp Crawford in a big bend of the Rio Grande, one mile above the small village of Laredo, just below a favorite Indian crossing on the river, Paso de los Indios. Nine months later, the post was renamed for Lt. Col. James Simmons McIntosh, a bespectacled Georgian who had died of wounds received at Molino del Rey in 1847. Fort McIntosh became one of few posts in Texas to boast of field fortification when Maj. Richard Delafield of the engineers and First Lt. James Slaughter of the First Artillery, using local laborers and men of the Fifth Infantry, built a star-shaped earthwork at the post in 1853 and 1854.[114]

All the officers who came to the Southwest, especially those from the North and fresh out of West Point, remembered the scorching summer heat in Texas and nowhere was it hotter than at Fort McIntosh. Lydia Lane arrived at the post in 1854 after a trip from Corpus Christi "through a dreary, desolate country, where nothing lived but Indians, snakes, and other venomous reptiles," just in time for one of the hot and dreadful Laredo summers.[115] "The houses were mere shells, entirely exposed to the baking sun all day long," she wrote. "Not a green thing was to be seen but a few ragged mesquite trees. Here and there a blade of grass attempted to grow in the scorching, sandy soil, but it was soon burned up by the hot sun," she

The road between Ringgold Barracks and Fort McIntosh plunged into the impressive Arroyo Zacate two miles below Laredo, Texas. The intense summer heat and inadequate quarters made Fort McIntosh, originally established as Camp Crawford in 1849, an unpopular post with soldiers and their families. "It is difficult to say what sustains this town," Mansfield wrote of Laredo during his December 1860 inspection of Fort McIntosh. (Illustration from William H. Emory, Report on the United States and Mexican Boundary Survey*)*

complained.[116] "Back of our quarters was quite a large yard, but there was not a living thing in it, except tarantulas, scorpions, and centipedes, with an occasional rattlesnake for variety."[117] One officer confessed to Olmsted that, by the end of July at Laredo, "no green thing was to be found within a radius of thirty miles from the town."[118]

In late May 1856, with the thermometer at 99 degrees, Mansfield arrived to find Fort McIntosh "indispensable to secure the peaceable occupation of the country and to destroy the murderous Indians and highwaymen."[119] The men of the Fifth Infantry and First Artillery were exposed "to the heat in their tents & out of them," he reported. "The partial shades that were erected" consisted of little more than "posts set in the ground & cross pieces overhead with bushes thrown thereon."[120] Writing from the fort in July 1856, with the temperature at 110 degrees, Captain Marcy described his unpleasantness in a letter to his daughter: "I am perspiring from every pore although I have neither coat or vest on, and there are ten thousand flies annoying me so that between fighting flies and trying to keep cool my time is pretty well occupied."[121] With gardens impossible, few vegetables were available and these were usually onions that were brought from Mexico. As a result, the men were suffering from scurvy. Despite the dire conditions, Mansfield was complimentary of the men's stamina, perseverance, and, on one occasion, culture—at a theatrical production he found the soldiers' performance "very creditable to them."[122] Regardless, in 1857, Lt. James E. Slaughter, quartermaster at the post, complained of the number of filibusters in Laredo who were threatening the stability on the border. The filibusters had gone as far as to assault one of the officers at the post and threaten to kill another.[123] Capt. Albert Gallatin Brackett of the Second Cavalry wrote his brother, in June 1857, that Fort McIntosh was "too far out on the frontier for people at a distance to feel much interest in our position."[124] The thermometer in the daytime, Brackett wrote, "stands generally at from 102° to 108° in the shade and 125° in the sun. This is the truth and no romance. We have no rain, no grass and corn is worth $1.50 cents per bushel."[125]

On March 27, 1849, Capt. Sidney Burbank with companies A, B, and F of the First Infantry established Fort Duncan at Eagle Pass. The post was named for Col. James Duncan, a hero of the Mexican War. Four years later, Freeman recommended the post be relocated downriver some thirty miles,

Fort Duncan was established by three companies of the First Infantry at Eagle Pass in March 1849. The post "was a wretched place to live," Lydia Lane wrote, but a number of officers reported the post to be one of the best in Texas. (Illustration from William H. Emory, Report on the United States and Mexican Boundary Survey*)*

opposite the Mexican town of Presidio del Rio Grande, at a site where the old Camino Real crossed the Rio Grande. The new site, Freeman argued, would be better situated about halfway between Fort McIntosh and Fort Clark.[126] Three years later, however, Mansfield reported the post to be "well placed and indispensable for some time to come."[127] Lt. Richard W. Johnson of the First Infantry remembered the buildings at the post as being "constructed with little reference to each other, or to the points of the compass" but were "deposited on the ground as the result of a cyclone."[128] Fort Duncan, Lydia Lane wrote, "was a wretched place to live," and those who were sent there "looked on their future station with sinking hearts when they saw it for the first time."[129] Yet Assistant Surgeon Albert J. Myer said Fort Duncan had the reputation for being "one of the best posts in Texas."[130] Nevertheless, he complained of his "queer quarters" that resembled little more than "a grass house."[131] Although he found the winter climate delightful, Myer wrote, "there had been no rain" and "the whole earth is parched and every little breeze drives it in clouds."[132] Arriving at Eagle Pass in 1855, Olmsted found "half a dozen tottering shanties, mere confused piles of poles, brushwood, and rushes, with hides hung over the apertures for doors," but when he heard the notes of a bugle, he looked up to see at Fort Duncan "rows and blocks of white tents, and brown thatched sheds and cabins, and a broad flat surface of green turf, with here and there a blue dot, and a twinkling musket."[133] A few days later, he watched as "a fine band played upon a terrace at the close of evening, and a bevy of fashionably-dressed ladies added a strange feature to the remote scene."[134] Maj. Samuel Peter Heintzelman, who had previously spent four years at Fort Yuma, found Fort Duncan "one of the pleasantest places in Texas . . . where there were gardens, grass, vegetables & springs, with a stream of water close to the quarters."[135] However, after recording a temperature of 106 degrees in late May 1859, Heintzelman had to confess, "I do not like this post, although it is called the finest post in Texas."[136] New York-born Lt. Abner Doubleday confirmed the feeling, telling of his stay at the fort and how the thermometer read "104 in the shade day after day," making it "necessary to suspend all work from 12 to 4 P.M."[137]

To protect travelers, commerce, and communication along the San Antonio-El Paso Road, the army also built a network of posts across the vast expanses of the rugged and desolate Trans-Pecos. Forty-two miles west of Fort Inge, at the head of Las Moras Creek in Kinney County, on June 20, 1852, Maj. Joseph H. LaMotte and Companies C and E of the First Infantry began construction of Fort Riley or what became Fort Clark on a high limestone ridge just west of Las Moras Springs, a desert oasis shaded by

On June 22, 1862, Albert B. Peticolas, a young Texas volunteer in the Confederate Sibley Brigade, sketched Fort Davis, which had changed little since the United States Army abandoned it the previous year. (Photograph no. 60305 courtesy of the Arizona Historical Society, Tucson)

large oak and pecan trees.[138] The post was named for Maj. John B. Clark, a deceased officer who had served in the Mexican War. Besides protecting travelers on the San Antonio-El Paso Road, the post was designed to safeguard the region west of San Antonio from Indian depredations and guard the Mexican border. Fort Clark was at "a point of primary importance . . . from its salient position looking both to the Rio Grande and Indian frontiers," Freeman wrote in 1853.[139] Three years later, Mansfield found Fort Clark "to be in a locality much exposed to Indians marauding."[140] Without the post, he concluded, it would be impossible for small parties to traverse the region.

On October 7, 1854, Lt. Col. Washington Seawell and six companies of the Eighth Infantry began construction of Fort Davis near Limpia Creek in the heart of the scenic Davis Mountains and the homeland of the Mescalero Apaches.[141] Named for Secretary of War Jefferson Davis, the post was situated where wood, water, wild game, and forage abounded. Although the quarters at Fort Davis were bad, Lydia Lane found the "surroundings very beautiful."[142] With "no rain, no cloudy weather, no snow, no mud," Assistant Surgeon Myer said the climate at Fort Davis was "probably the finest in the world."[143] Moreover, Fort Davis was of "great importance to prevent depredations across the River Grande by the wild Indians and as a security to travelers," Mansfield

Adjacent to Live Oak Creek, one-half mile east of the Pecos River, Fort Lancaster was established in August 1855 by two companies of the First Infantry. Lydia Lane said the post was "the worst of all the posts in Texas." Both Johnston and Mansfield found the fort to be critical in guarding the San Antonio-El Paso Road. (Illustration from Harper's Weekly*)*

told the adjutant general in 1856.[144] Although the soldiers of the Eighth Infantry were all living in temporary log quarters that were about to fall down, Mansfield noted that Colonel Seawell had plans to construct an "entire new post, of good stone . . . on the open prairie near the fine springs," just southeast of the post nearer the mouth of the canyon.[145]

One hundred fifty-seven miles to the east on August 20, 1855, one year after Fort Davis was established, Capt. Stephen D. Carpenter with Companies H and K of the First Infantry marked off the location of Fort Lancaster, adjacent to Live Oak Creek, one-half mile east of the Pecos River.[146] To Lydia Lane, Fort Lancaster was "the worst of all the posts in Texas."[147] The post, said Mansfield, was "indispensable to travelers and in a locality often visited by the wild Indians."[148] In addition, it provided travelers an opportunity to "rest and recruit their animals and repair their wagons with safety." The fort, the inspector general concluded, "has and will save many valuable lives."[149] Other posts were just the opposite. For instance, Camp Hudson, located on the Devil's River on one of the most isolated segments of the San Antonio-El Paso Road, was never more than a few crudely built huts. Established by Lt. Theodore Fink and one company of the Eighth Infantry, the post was named for Lt. Walter W. Hudson, who died at Fort McIntosh of wounds he received in a fight with a war party of Tonkawas on the Nueces River in 1850.[150]

Mansfield recommended a post be constructed where the San Antonio-El Paso Road left the Rio Grande some seventy miles below El Paso, before winding its way through the rocky and rugged twists and turns of Quitman Canyon. Such a post "would add very much to the security of the traveller, and no doubt aid the . . . transmission of the mail."[151] As a result, Capt. Arthur T. Lee and Companies C and H of the Eighth Infantry established Fort Quitman on a mesquite-infested arid plain four hundred yards east of the Rio Grande and near the mountains of the same name on September 28, 1858.[152] The post was named after Gen. John Quitman, Mexican War hero and former expansionist governor of Mississippi, who had died two months earlier. The post guarded the San Antonio-El Paso Road and settlers in the valley below El Paso, but was built, much to Mansfield's disgust, five miles upriver from where he had recommended. No one liked the solitude and loneliness of Fort Quitman. Lydia Lane said it was "forlorn and tumble-down."[153] Lt. Zenas R. Bliss of the Eighth Infantry remembered Fort Quitman as "the worst post at which I ever served."[154] There was "no hunting or fishing near the Post," Bliss recalled, "and it was too risky to go into the mountains without an escort."[155] Elsewhere, on March 23, 1859, Lt. Walter Jones and a company of the First Infantry established a camp at Comanche Springs, the largest natural spring in the region, where the San Antonio-El Paso Road intersected the Comanche Trail. The post was named for Lt. Edward Dorsey Stockton, a Kentuckian who had died two years earlier.

RETROSPECT

In the 1850s, the officers and men, especially those who had not served in the Mexican War, found Texas a harsh and unforgiving land inhabited by a rough and hardy people. Arriving in Texas, Lt. Edward L. Hartz, a young officer in the Eighth Infantry only six months out of West Point, was astonished while "walking through the streets of Corpus Christi to find almost every individual . . . wearing a six shooter or an immense knife."[156] Lieutenant Hartz observed that "shooting is as common here as boxing one's ears is up North." In time, Hartz came to look upon his six-shooter "as indispensable an article of dress in Texas as pantaloons."[157] Captain Marcy found the citizenry of Corpus Christi "from all parts of the world and . . . about as lawless a set of scamps as can be found."[158] At Fort Duncan, Lieutenant Doubleday discovered, matters were "not regulated by law to any very great extent for the pistol and the Bowie Knife were still the code of a good many of the population."[159] Shortly after his arrival in Texas, Assistant Surgeon Myer boasted to a future brother-in-law that he was "already quite a Texan" and that he was carrying his revolver "with an air which would astonish you."[160]

The ruggedness of the Texas frontier was perhaps best exemplified by the observations of Frederick Law Olmsted. While at Fort Duncan, the Connecticut-born Olmsted was told by John Woodland, whom he had hired as guide, that, because it would be another day before they could cross the river to visit the Mexican garrison at Piedras Negras, Woodland would attend a funeral. When the frontiersman returned, he informed the noted architect that it was the "most respectable funeral he ever saw on the Rio Grande." Olmsted inquired if a sermon had been preached. "Oh, no, there ain't no parson here," Woodland responded, "there weren't no ceremonies, but they had a coffin fixed up for him; first time I ever saw a coffin out in this country."[161] Lt. Richard W. Johnson wrote that "someone was murdered in Eagle Pass or in its vicinity every day in the year."[162] Horse stealing was "the greatest crime a man could commit," Johnson wrote, while murder was "by no means a serious offence against the dignity of the state."[163] How people handled the isolation of the posts in Texas and New Mexico was also telling. It was seldom any one came to Fort McIntosh, Lydia Lane recalled. "No one travelled in that direction for amusement in those days. Nothing but stern necessity and duty took people to such a desolate place, so, when strangers did arrive, they were kindly welcomed and entertained."[164]

Despite the millions of dollars that the United States Army poured into the Texas economy in the decade prior to the Civil War and the protection the army brought to settlers on the frontier, some Texans resented the presence of the bluecoats. William Robertson "Big Bill" Henry, the grandson of Patrick Henry and sheriff of Bexar County, wrote the Galveston *Tri-Weekly News* in November 1859 that the regulars in Texas were known for little more than their "tidy uniforms" and their inability to protect the Texas frontier. The "dirty shirt Texas Rangers," Henry wrote, were far more effective than "the dashing military officers on prancing steeds."[165] To Henry, "government ambulances, filled with champagne and all the luxuries of life, thronged the roads leading to the various military establishments."[166] Nonetheless, some military outposts became permanent fixtures on the landscape, around which centers of frontier society congregated. Dusty and dingy frontier shantytowns, where whiskey and violence flourished, sprang up in close proximity to most of the forts. In Texas, a few of these primitive communities grew to become towns and cities.

JOHNSTON'S & MANSFIELD'S INSPECTIONS

Lieutenant Colonel Joseph E. Johnston at the time of his inspection of the Departments of New Mexico and Texas. (Photograph courtesy of the United States Military History Institute, Carlisle Barracks, Pa.)

Lt. Col. Joseph E. Johnston's Inspection of the Departments of Texas and New Mexico

1859

Fort Union was the first post Johnston inspected in New Mexico Territory. Consisting of little more than a collection of shabby low buildings, the post was abandoned during the Civil War and moved across Lone Wolf Valley to the east. Fort Union would eventually become one of the most important posts and supply depots in the Southwest. (Illustration from W. W. H. Davis, El Gringo*)*

FORT UNION

Santa Fe
July 11th 1859

Sir:

I have the honor to report that I reached Fort Union on the 7th instant & immediately examined the points compared by the board of officers instituted by Col. Bonneville.[1] The site recommended by that board is in every respect preferable to that now occupied & if limited to those two points, I would not hesitate to confirm the selection of the board. As far as public economy & the comfort of the garrison are concerned, the position is excellent. But for the protection of the position it is useless to occupy either. The favorite grazing grounds of the people of that region are much in advance of them. The most exposed part of that frontier lies to the southeast of Fort Union & about the Pecos—where the Comanches commit most of their depredations. This seems to me a favorable opportunity to remove the garrison of Fort Union to that neighbourhood. It will have a better influence there I think than at any other point on the eastern frontier. Several detachments will meet in that neighbourhood about the 20th instant, which I shall then inspect. An opportunity will at the same time be given me to look for a site for a post near the road from Fort Smith to Albuquerque & beyond the settlements. It will no doubt be easy to find a point, the communications of which with the rest of the department are as good as those of Fort Union, &

nearer to the sources of supply in the east.

I have not regarded a slight delay in this matter because both Maj. Donaldson & Capt. Van Bokkelen told me that it was too late to do more this year than prepare lumber for building during the next. It was too late, they said, to make adobes & put up & cover walls before the coming winter.

Should the General-in-Chief think it better to keep the garrison in its present position, there will be abundant time to prevent from your office any harm or inconvenience from my course.

Most respectfully,
Your obt. servt.
J. E. Johnston
Lt. Col., 1st Cavalry

FORT UNION

Fort Defiance
August 24th 1859

Sir:

I have the honor to report that I inspected Fort Union on the 7th & 8th ulto. As more than half of each company of the garrison was in the Navajoe Country, this report has been postponed until now.

The buildings of the post are, quarters for three companies & a hospital, two large store houses, guard house & prison, three crude company stables, two of which were made by the companies themselves, quarter master's workshops & stables, & the ordinance depot, which contains a new magazine of adobe, store houses, workshops for repairing small arms & quarters for the mil. store keeper & enlisted men of ordnance. Besides the usual proportion of officers quarters, there are five houses which were made for the command of the department & his staff. All of these houses except the magazine & qr. m's store were built of green pine logs. They are now much decayed, so much so that none of them are worth repairing, except that the roofs might be so improved as to make the quarters habitable until next summer. Capt. Morris, commanding the post, has just had a part of his company quarters pulled down—thinking it dangerous to its occupant.

Cos. G. H. & K, Regt. of Mounted Riflemen, form the usual garrison. Capt. Morris, the A.Q.M., Capt. Van Bokkelen & the A.C.S., Lt. May, are the only officers left with 83 enlisted men, 40 of whom are on extra duty, 11 sick & 2 undergoing sentences of Cts. Md. The Non. Comd. Staff & band also remained. I found the other portion of the garrison encamped a mile from this post. Capt. Walker commanding, 3 other officers & 103 enlisted men including 4 of the band—9 are sick & 2 in confinement, with 93 horses. All the arms & accoutrements of the three companies were in good order. Those of the men left at Fort Union, as handsome as possible, & their clothing remarkably neat. The party encamped here left their post on what was supposed to be an expedition for three months & brought a corresponding supply of clothing. It is therefore a good deal worn. The men of the three companies are generally respectable looking & well behaved, healthy & sufficiently muscular in appearance. They are sufficiently instructed on foot. In firing at 200 yards, about a fourth of the shots struck a target 6 ft. by 44 inches. Their pistol firing on horseback was also unsatisfactory. Capt. Walker's being the only company of the three that had practiced. Some of the officers of their regiment regard it as mounted infantry, & therefore do not teach the men to use their arms on horseback. Many of the men hit their horses firmly, but few manage them quickly & steadily as soldiers should. The horses are imperfectly broken, too. This criticism is applicable to all our mounted troops. The remedy would be the institution of a good course of instruction at the cavalry school. Most of the officers prefer the rifle of cal. .54 of an inch to that just adopted—thinking it a more accurate weapon. As there are but 4 horses fit to be ridden at Ft. Union, the troops there were seen only on foot.

The horses (99) are in better condition than could have been expected. Many of them are worn out & unfit for military service. 13 of them have served 8 years; 3, 7 years; 9, 6 years; 1, 5 years; 48, 3½ years; 15, 2 years; & 4, 1 year.

The records of the post & company G (Capt. Morris's) were complete. The Hd. Qrs. of the other two companies being in the Navajoe Country & their books & papers at Fort Union, I was unable to see them.

The hospital is altogether unfit for the lodging of sick men. There is no surgeon at present. Dr. Anderson makes occasional visits from Fort Burgwin.

There is a chaplain at the post, but no school.

The post bakery—each company having its own—No post fund—Nor has Capt. Morris a company fund, the company being in his debt.

All the qr. m. stores camp equipage & clothing for the troops in New Mexico are consigned to the qr. m. of Fort Union. As soon as new trains can be furnished (by the same contractor) they are sent to the depot at Albuquerque. Some of the property just received seems to have been carelessly packed for transportation & damaged in consequence. The store house is comparatively new—but from careless construction or bad materials it is an unfit depository for valuable property. 20 wagons, 5 of which are for post service & the other 15 for transportation, 6 ambulances, 122 mules (in excellent order) & 10 horses, 4 of which are worthless, are kept at the post.

The office contains all the required books & papers neatly kept, & the accounts seem to be accurate. They show a debt of $1163.39. The monthly pay of 14 soldiers on extra duty & 30 men hired as clerk, mechanics, teamsters etc. amounts to about $1040.

From Albuquerque the qr. m. property is distributed to the other posts of the department—including Fort Union, where it usually spends several days, or even weeks, on its way to the depot. From Fort Union the direct distance to Forts Garland, Burgwin, Marcy & Stanton are respectively 147, 65, 99, & 204 miles. The distances between the same points—via Albuquerque are, 402, 310, 320, & 227 miles. The double distance from Fort Union to Albuquerque is 320. The sum of the first distances is 516 of the second, 1579.

The books & accounts of the coms. are apparently correct. The "amount of money is his hands" is $2100. He has a six months' supply of provision for the post & orders to retain an equal quantity of the stores now arriving. The store house is utterly unfit for the purpose, from its decayed condition. Lieut. May seems to be well acquainted with the affairs of his department. He reports that the stores consigned to him are much damaged in transportation especially sugar & such other articles as are not protected by strong boxes. He complains also of the quality & condition of the hams—200 of those last furnished the post were condemned. A large quantity of sugar was spoiled last year, by being brought out under bacon.

The provision for all the posts of the department except Forts Bliss & Fillmore are consigned to the com. of Fort Union. He is usually directed to send supplies for six months to each of the posts north of Albuquerque & the remainder to that depot.

A mil. storekeeper has charge of the ordnance depot. The Magazine, which contains a large quantity of powder, is too near the post. 15 enlisted men of ordnance & 3 hired mechanics are employed in the depot. The Magazine is a good, tho' very cheap building. The others are all temporary. There are several prices of articles here, which can never be of use in this department, especially two 24 pdr. howitzers. There are about 650,000 old musket cartridges & 120,000 of the new. Mr. Shoemaker has on hand $2026.75.[2] Ordinary repairs of small arms are very well executed in his workshop.

This post was probably established to control the Jacarilla Apaches, who frequent the mountainous country between it & Taos. Those Indians no longer require watching. They are so reduced in numbers & so thoroughly subdued.[3]

Most respectfully
Your obt. servt.
J. E. Johnston
Lt. Col., 1st Cavalry

Endorsement: Attention will be called to the want of skill in the use of weapons and in horsemanship. It is expected that the Rifle Regiment will not be inferior in any respect to the other mounted troops. Also to the request of the Chaplain to keep up a school, also to the non compliance with the regulations in regard to the post and company funds. Also to the non compliance with General Orders No. 13 in regard to transportation and employees. The sending [of] supplies from Fort Union to Albuquerque for distribution to posts which are far nearer the former place, and even for that post itself, will be instantly discontinued.

J. B. Floyd
Sec. of War
Jany 11/60

FORT MARCY

Santa Fe, N.M.
July 16th 1859

Sir:

I have inspected during the week the post of Fort Marcy & the offices of the Actg. Asst. Adj. Gen., Chief Quarter Master, Chief Com., Medical Director, and Actg. Ord. Officer of this department, & Adjutant of the 3d Infantry. The books & papers of these offices are kept in the manner prescribed in the Army regulations & their condition indicate that the several officers perform their duties with punctuality & correctness.

The accounts & papers of Major Donaldson, the Chief Quarter Master, show an expenditure in his department of $482,130 since the 1st of October 1858. The extraordinary expenses of the Navajo war, estimated at about $105,000, are included in this sum but not the cost of transporting military stores into New Mexico. The latter varies from $3.50 per hundred pounds per hundred miles in January to $1.25 in May & June & $4.50 in December. This to Fort Union, thence to the other posts in New Mexico the rates range from $2.20 to $1.50. The minimum to Albuquerque is $11.22 per hundred pounds. The merchants of the country, I am informed, pay from $8.00 to $10.00. Stores are frequently carried from Fort Union to the depot at Albuquerque, 165 miles, & brought back for use at the former. Major Donaldson's disbursements at Head Quarters amount to about $1200 per month for hire of men & offices & fuel & quarters for officers. He had 5 wagons & 3 ambulances with their teams, 40 mules, & 6 express horses. It appears from his accounts that the funds on hand are $6805.95 in specie, a deposit of $5362.16 with the Asst. Treasurer in New York & one of $19.76

The army built Fort Marcy in Santa Fe, the New Mexico provincial capital, during the Mexican War. "My first step," Lieutenant Colonel Edwin V. Sumner wrote when he assumed command of Military Department No. 9 in April 1851, "was to break up the post at Santa Fe, that sink of vice and extravagance." Mansfield, however, urged its retention in 1853, and, by the time of Johnston's July 1859 inspection, Fort Marcy was firmly established as departmental headquarters. (Illustration from W. W. H. Davis, El Gringo*)*

with the Asst. Treasurer in St. Louis. Major Donaldson left Santa Fe on leave of absence the morning after my arrival so that I had less opportunity than I desired, of conversing with him of the affairs of his department.

From the contracts & other papers in Lt. Col. Grayson's office, it appears that beef, flour, beans, salt & vinegar for the troops are purchased in New Mexico.[4] All other articles of the ration are sent from Fort Leavenworth except to Forts Bliss & Fillmore, which are supplied from Indianola. By the present contract beef cattle cost $32.50 each. They are herded by contract in a designated district from which they are driven by contract, about monthly, to the several posts where, in winter, they receive half rations of forage. Better beef at cheaper rates could, no doubt, be procured in the manner practiced every where to the east of New Mexico & since my inspection Col. Bonneville has directed Lt. Col. Grayson to order the commissaries of posts to make such contracts. His summary statements & accounts, current & vouchers dated in July, show the balance for which Lt. Col. Grayson is accountable to be $67,765 of which $27,811 are deposited in the Sub Treasury in New York & the remainder is in his safe.

The disbursing officers of the several posts are supplied with funds by drafts on the Asst. Treasurer in New York or St. Louis which they cash in their neighbourhoods.

There is no officer of the Adjutant General's department in the territory & altho' Lt. Wilkins proves himself to be well qualified for the office in which he is acting, its duties might be those appropriately performed, I respectfully suggest, by an Assistant Adjutant General.

Dr. Sloan, besides being Medical Director of the department, is surgeon of the post. He is accountable, according to his papers, for $808.82, which is in his office, except $75.90 in the Sub Treasury in New York.

1st Lt. Jones, R.M.R., is acting ordnance officer. It appears from the papers in his office that all the troops in the department have the new arms except one company of the 3d Infantry, which retains the rifled musket (cal. .69) & that there is, in the ordnance depot, a very large supply of ammunition for the old arms, but a very scanty one for the new & that the Chief of Ordnance has fixed the annual allowance at less than 60 rounds. A quantity insufficient for the instruction of the troops to say nothing of what may be required for field service.

Col. Bonneville is certainly very much interested in his duties & seems to be especially anxious to reduce the expenses of the department & thinks that he has already done so materially. I have no means of judging of this, as there are no accounts here [relevant] to Major Donaldson.[5]

The strength of the company stationed here is a 1st Lieutenant & 40 enlisted men (it is Bvt. Major Sprague's Company E, 8th Infantry). Since my inspection it has left the post as Capt. Macomb's escort. The men are healthy looking, but several seemed to feel the effects of their recent payment. Their commanding officer Lt. Cogswell complains of the bad effect of this station upon these habits & discipline, from the demoralizing influence of the class of Mexicans with which they associate. Their performance as a platoon was respectable. In firing, they have practiced ten times, from 50 to 200 yards. 24 of 60 shots fired at 300 yards, before me, struck a target 5½ feet high & 2 wide. The arms & accoutrements of the company are new & good. The men are well clothed too. The messing is now probably at its worst for the beef is not in very good order, the pasturage being very poor in all this section of country & the garden tho' apparently well cultivated, does not yet furnish vegetables enough even for a platoon. The barracks, which are sufficient for two companies, are in good preservation. The rooms are too large & high, however, to be comfortable in this climate. The bake house is large enough to supply two companies. Another building containing the Comm. Officer's office, guard room, & prison is in good condition. The prison, in an adobe building, is of course insecure. Four other long adobe houses containing the Comd. Officer's quarters, those of the band of the 3d Infantry, & the carpenter's, blacksmith's, & saddler's shops, is almost worthless. The hospital is quite a comfortable one & is kept in excellent order. Sickness is very rare among the troops. Only one of the 4 invalids belong to the garrison. All these buildings & the stables & enclosures for horses & mules are on ground belonging to the United States. There is neither post nor company fund nor saving from the bakehouse or rations, except at the season when the garden furnishes vegetables abundantly.

The principal duties of the quarter master & commissary are to supply & refit parties visiting Head Quarters or passing near & these make his principal expenditures & furnish most of the employment of his mechanics. His books & papers are correct in form & seem to be accurate. According to them the balances for which he is accountable are $1923.10 belonging to the Quarter Master's Department & $1052.34 commissary's funds. Both these sums were counted in my presence. The means of transportation of the post are 5 wagons, much worn, & 59 mules. The latter now in Lt. Cogswell's possession.

This company seems to me to be out of position. It would be more useful, I think, on the frontier.

Most respectfully,
Your obt. servt.
J. E. Johnston
Lt. Col., 1st Cavalry

FORT GARLAND

Fort Garland, N.M.
August 8th 1859

Sir:

I have just inspected Fort Garland. This post is about 15 miles above the Culebra, the northern circuit of the inhabited country & at the base of the Sangre de Christo Mountains; between two bold streams, the Utah & Sangre de Christo, some 600 yards from each. The post is supplied with cool & pure water from the Utah, thro' a small ditch. The distance to the Rio Grande, across a level plain, is about 20 miles. It is 147 miles to Fort Union & 242 to Albuquerque, the two points from which military stores are received—by roads in many places barely practicable. By a road across the Sangre de Christo range, it is nearer than Fort Union to Fort Leavenworth. The post was designed for two companies, but is occupied by but one—Capt. Bowman's A, 3d Infy. It is still unfinished—but the erection of two mess rooms & kitchens & roofing a building intended for laundresses would complete the original plan. The buildings in use as quarters, hospital, guard house, prison, store houses & work shops, are all adequate, altho' none have floors except the officers quarters & comm. store.

There are present a 1st & 2d Lt. & 74 enlisted men including the Hospital Steward. The surgeon is a civilian. 2 corporals & 20 privates are kept on extra & daily duty—4 privates are in confinement by sentence of a general court martial, & 3 are sick. The arms & accoutrements have been in use less than a year & are in good condition—except that on most of the locks "Maynard's attachment" impedes the motion of the hammer & interferes with putting the cap on the cone.[6] Our infantry officers generally are opposed to this "attachment" & their objections seem to me well founded. The supply of clothing is good in quality & quantity. The men are able bodied & healthy looking & in a good state of discipline. Military offenses are rare, drunkenness is almost the only one & is usually punished by confinement under the comd. officers authority. The instruction of the company in military exercises is much behind its discipline. It does not move with accuracy in close order or readiness as skirmishers. Less than a seventh of the shots fired struck the target at 200 yards. There are, probably, two causes of this want of military instruction. One, that the company is alone. The other, that the men have been employed more as laborers, in building, than as soldiers. I am informed that target practice was ordered for the first time in this department, last Spring. It is needless to add that the bayonet exercise is not taught. Lieut. Steck, who has been in command since Capt. Bowman left the post on leave of absence a month ago, has been on detached service the greater part of that time.

The records in the commanding officer's office seem to be complete, except those of councils of administration & accounts of post & company funds. There seems to have been no post fund. That of the company now amounts to $20. It is used to supply the table with mess furniture & condiments.

In the office of the post quartermaster & commissary the books & papers seem to be complete & the accounts correct. The means of transportation at the Qr. Ms' disposal are 2 horses (Mexican & broken down), 35 mules, 4 wagons (one worthless), 36 sets of harness, & 25 pack-saddles. Corn costs $6 per fanega & hay $22 per ton. The expenditures in the last quarter amounted to $3855. The sum on hand is $1.77, against a debt of $422 contracted in July.

In the commissary's store there is a supply of provision for about a year, none of which has been in the department less than a year—the bacon at least two. Most of this supply was brought to Taos last fall or winter by the contractor & left there because the road was bad. About half this quantity was brought up from time to time, when absolutely needed, in the post

Established in June 1852 in what is today southern Colorado, Fort Massachusetts was the northernmost post in Military Department No. 9. The garrison was moved six miles to the south near the Trinchera River in June 1858 and renamed Fort Garland. (Sketch by Robert H. Kern in Edward G. Beckwith, Upon the Route Near the Thirty-eighth and Thirty-ninth Parallel*)*

wagons. 133 hams, just received, have been condemned by a board of survey. They are so offensive that I directed their removal from the store house. Flour of good quality is delivered by the contractor, as required. The amount of expenditures in the last quarter was $430. The sum on hand is $415.

The bake house can supply about 300 rations daily. The bread is very good. There have been no sales nor tax on the latter.

The company has a small library & a garden which will furnish vegetables enough for the year.

The hospital is large enough for a two company post & is quite comfortable, tho' not sufficiently ventilated. It is as clean as its unfinished condition allows. The patients of whom there are four, are well provided & attended. One of them is insane. His removal to an asylum for such cases is much to be desired. There is an ample supply of medicines & hospital stores. The surgical instruments, tho' old, seem to be effective.

In the room used as an ordnance store, there are 17 boxes of mountain howitzer ammunition, altho' there are no such guns at the post & 5500 cartridges for the discarded musket (cal. 69). The company has 4000 cartridges for the rifle musket.

I should have mentioned above, that after three rounds had been fired, most of the muskets retained lead enough to be felt with the rammer. Want of grease on the balls was, I think, the cause.

Most respectfully,
Your obt. Servt.
J. E. Johnston
Lt. Col., 1st Cavalry

FORT BURGWIN

Fort Defiance
August 25th 1859

Sir:

I inspected Fort Burgwin on the 11th & 12th of this month—but postponed this report until I had seen the part of its garrison which is on duty in the Navajoe Country.

The usual garrison consists of Capt. Duncan's Company E, R.M.R., & Capt. Schroeder's Company D, 3d Inf. Capt. Duncan, Lt. Tilford, Qr. M. & Com. & Asst. Surgeon Anderson, 33 enlisted men of Capt. Duncan's Company & 25 of Capt. Schroeder's form the actual one.

I found Capt. Schroeder's Co, a Capt., 2d Lieut. & 45 enlisted men for duty, being temporarily at this post & the detachment of Capt. Duncan's under Capt. Walker's command & in his camp of bivouac, rather—for the men have no other shelter than blankets stretched like tents. Capt. Schroeder's men occupy tents when at the post. Their appearance under arms was soldierly—the arms & accoutrements in good order—their dress appropriate to field service & sufficient for the period, three months, for which they were ordered to supply themselves. Their proficiency in "field exercise," both in close order & as skirmishers, is respectable. They want practice in firing, however. The Capt. left his compy. books & papers at his station. The detachment of Capt. Duncan's Compy., 38 enlisted men with the same number of horses, in commander by a Lt. of Capt. Walker's. What I have said of the three companies belonging to Fort Union, in regard to appearance, condition of arms & accoutrements & proficiency in military exercises is applicable to this one. Many of the company horses are unfit for military service—12 of them have served 7 years; 2, 6 years; 2, 5 years; 19, 4 years; & 4, 2 years.

The records in the office of the Comd. Officer, Qr. M. Comm. & Asst. Surgeon are all complete, except that Dr. Anderson keeps no "case book." Nor, I believe, does any other surgeon in the department.

The quarters (for two companies) hospital, store houses, company & qr. m. stables, guard house & prison, & workshops, were built of green pine

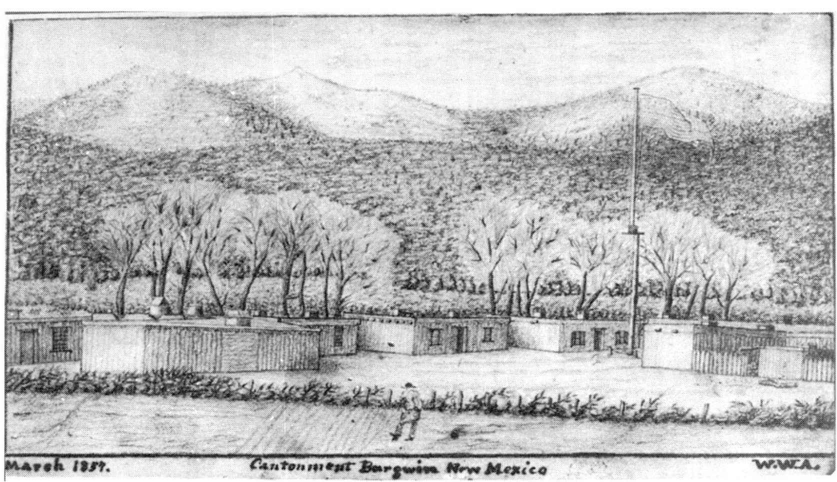

Located ten miles south of Taos, New Mexico, Cantonment Burgwin was poorly constructed of logs and was so dilapidated by the time Colonel Johnston arrived in 1859, many of the soldiers were living in quarters in nearby villages such as Talpa and Ranchos de Taos. (Illustration by Major William W. Anderson; photograph, neg. no. 8776, courtesy of the Museum of New Mexico, Santa Fe)

logs sat in the earth as in a stockade. They are now very much decayed, especially at the surface of the ground, too much so to be worth repairing. In some of the quarters this decay is perceptible to the sense of smelling.

The bakery, made of adobe, is much better than the other buildings. One baker can make in it about 200 rations of bread daily. The flour is excellent—a good post garden contains a variety of vegetables & enough for two companies.

The means of transportation are 9 wagons & 21 mules, besides 20 pack mules taken by the detachment which lately left the post. The condition of the public property is better than could be expected in such houses & indicates great care on the part of those having charge of it. In the last quarter the expenditures of the qr. m. amounted to $1745. The fact that hay is not produced in the neighborhood is an objection to this as a station for mounted troops.

The comm. has on hand provision enough to last till the end of September. The store house in which it is necessarily kept is absolutely ruinous. The quality of the provision received is very good, except the hams. The sum in the hands of the com. is $293.93. The hospital is as comfortable as the care of the comd. officer & surgeon can make it. The diseases of most of the patients are consequences of the vicinity of a New Mexican town.

Capt. Duncan's company fund amounts to $131.16.

The principal ordnance stores are two mountain howitzers & 96 cartridges for them.

I respectfully recommend the removal of this garrison to some point at which its presence may give protection or confidence to some portion of the inhabitants of the territory. The post was probably intended for the protection of the inhabitants of the valley of Taos from the Jacarilla Apaches, who frequent the mountains near it & was no doubt necessary when established, but there is now nothing in the numbers or character of the Indians to entitle them to the attention of our troops. The neighbourhood of a New Mexican town is in itself a strong objection to the position. Associating with the lowest & most vicious class in the country is as injurious to the discipline of our soldiers, as to their health & constitutions.

25 men are on extra duty, 8 sick, & 6 confined.

Most respectfully,

Your Obt. Servt.
J. E. Johnston
Lt. Col., 1st Cavalry

Endorsement: The Department commander will report why the requirements of General Orders No. 13, in regard to transportation have not been enforced.

J. B. Floyd
Secretary of War
War Dept
11 Jany 1860

ALBUQUERQUE DEPOT

Albuquerque, N.M.
August 18th 1859

Sir:

I have the honor to report that I inspected the troops & military depots at this place on the 16th and 17th.

The troops are a 1st & a 2d lt. (the latter sick) & 45 enlisted men of Capt. Trevitt's Co. (F), 3d Infy. Of these 9 are on extra and daily duty & 7 confined. It appears from the monthly returns that the company is full. The remainder being on detached service. The men are armed with the "Rifled Musket" (cal. 69). They are of good size & healthy & vigorous appearance. In the platoon movements of infantry they are not deficient, either in close order or as skirmishers. They exhibited, however, a decided want of skill in shooting. The bayonet exercise, as I have lately reported, is not in use in

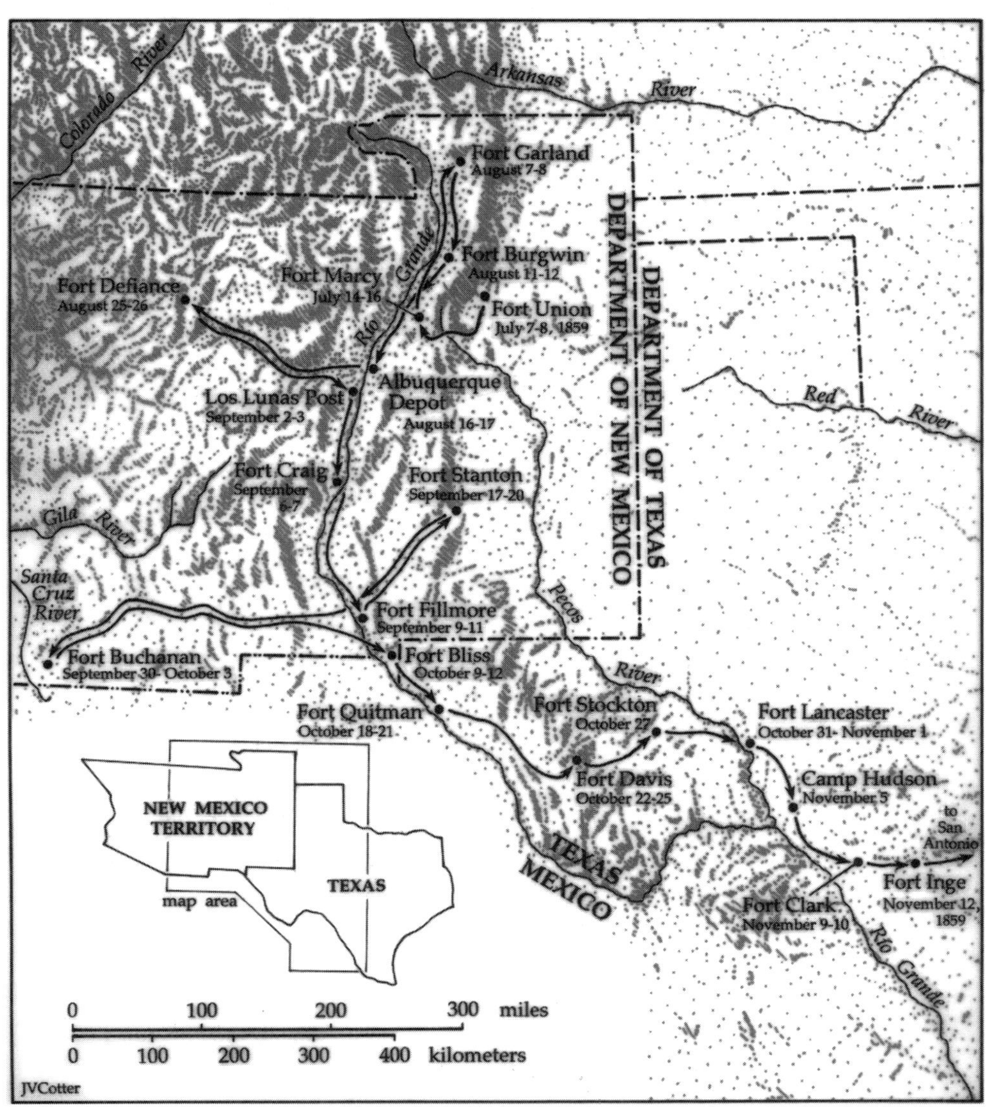

Johnston's 1859 Inspection

Albuquerque served as a major supply depot for the army during most of the 1850s. Johnston found a company of the Third Infantry stationed at the village in August 1859. This sketch shows the Plaza of Albuquerque. (Illustration from W. W. H. Davis, El Gringo*)*

any of our infantry regiments which I have seen. The clothing & accoutrements of the men are serviceable & comfortable. But they have lost their neatness of appearance during the detached service from which they & their commanding officer, Lt. Davis, have just returned. The large proportion of prisoners furnished additional evidence of the demoralizing effect upon our soldiers of being stationed in New Mexican towns. This company has the further disadvantage of being frequently divided for escort service, so that its commanding officer, the present one at least, can scarcely be held accountable for such deficiencies as exist in its discipline & instruction. The buildings rented for barracks, hospitals, store houses, bake house, guard house & prison are adequate & comfortable. The capacity of the bake house is such as to enable one baker to make about 120 rations of bread daily. The samples of flour shown to me are indifferent or bad. It is furnished by a contractor whose mill is in Santa Fe. The other articles of the ration are very good, good vegetables, & enough for the year, are supplied by the post gardener. There is also a company fund, now amounting to $113.10 & a respectable library. During the Summer mutton is issued instead of fresh beef, for the sake of economy. The number of men at the post being too small to consume an ox.

The records of the post & company are complete. The retained muster rolls show that payments have been regular. There is no sutler & no post fund.

The books & accounts of the Qr. M. of the post seem to be correct. The means of transportation at his disposal are 7 wagons & a cart, 20 mules, 2 oxen & 1 horse. The amount of expenditures in the last quarter was $642.75 & the sum now on hand $240.33. The monthly rent of the houses used by the garrison is $172.

The hospital serves also for the adjoining post at Los Lunas. Dr. De Leon is surgeon of both posts, as well as medical surgeon of the department. The dispensary is extremely neat, well arranged & well supplied & the wards well furnished & clean as possible & the patients well attended. Mattresses are not among the hospital stores of this department. Such straw beds as are used in barracks are substituted for them. Very comfortable woolen mattresses are made in New Mexico. They could be bought at prices as small or smaller than are paid for such as are used in our hospitals in the Atlantic States.

The store houses rented for the Medical Subsistence & Qr. M. Dept. are the best I have yet seen in New Mexico. The public property they contain is all well arranged & well cared for.

At present, the department is divided, for payment, into two districts usually into three. Maj. Fry pays all the troops north of Fort Fillmore except the garrison of Fort Stanton. The distances to be travelled make it impossible for him to pay all these troops every two months. Hitherto his district has included but five of the twelve posts of the department & even then he could pay every two months about three of the five. His accounts were found brought up to the day of inspection & show a balance of $67547.97, of which $51677.25 are deposited in New York and $5870.72 in his safe. As no cash has been sent into the department this year for the disbursing officers & the merchants have sent unusually large sums out of the territory it is apprehended that there may be difficulty in obtaining all the specie that may be required for military purposes.

The subsistence stores for the department are consigned to the commissary at Fort Union, except those for Forts Bliss & Fillmore, which are received from Indianola. From that point they are carried in new trains & at higher rates to Forts Garland, Burgwin & Marcy & to the depot at Albuquerque, whence, with the exception made above, they are carried in government wagons to all the other ports of the department. The stores on hand are well arranged & in good condition except the hams, many of which are spoiled. They are of the supply of last year of which 26,000 lbs. remain. Hitherto the depot comms., Lieut Wood, has issued provisions to the garrison. His expenditures in the 2d qr. were $1230.21. The sum on hand & exhibited, was $4562.60.

The books papers & accounts of the depot Qr. M., Bvt. Maj. Rucker, appear to be correct. The expenditures in the 1st quarter amounted to $21,631.58. The sum on hand at the time of inspection, $14,914.45 in specie in a vault & safe in the office.

The quarter master's stores, camp & garrison equipage & clothing for the department are consigned to the quarter master at Fort Union. By him they are sent to the depot at Albuquerque at higher rates & in new trains. From this point they are distributed to the several posts in U.S. wagons. For this purpose the depot quarter master has at present 65 wagons & 305 mules. The rent of houses, $287.33 per month. Hire of mechanics, teamsters, etc., $2900 per month & purchase of forage at $4 per fanega, for corn & $20 per ton for hay and fodder, must amount to above $100,000 per annum. By the present arrangement, the quarter master's stores for Forts Garland, Burgwin, Marcy, Union & Stanton, are carried 1579 miles instead of the merely necessary distance—516. When I inspected the depot, the qr. m's stores for Fort Union, just received from that place with the annual supply for the department, at the rate of about $2.70 per 100 lbs. were ready to be returned by the road over which they had come. This system has been long in operation. To avoid such useless expense, I suggest sending the annual supplies for the posts north of Santa Fe by the road up the Arkansas, thro' the Sangre de Christo range, to Fort Garland. Those for Forts Bliss, Fillmore & Buchanan, from Indianola & those for the other posts of the department, by the point on the Gallinas recommended in my letter of the 30th ulto. to be distributed from that point. Depots for reserve supplies to be also established there. Such an arrangement would require much smaller depots than those at Albuquerque & much smaller means of transportation & would greatly reduce the distances over which military stores are carried. The distance from Fort Leavenworth to Fort Garland by the route recommended, is less than that to Fort Union. The several distances from Forts Bliss, Fillmore & Buchanan to Indianola, are less by about 200 miles, than those from the same posts to Fort Leavenworth. If I am correctly informed the minimum price for transportation to Fort Union, fixed by the present contract, exceeds those paid by merchants by 15 or 20 per cent. Those from Fort Union exceed the rates of the country still more. It is probable, I think, that the contract for transportation within the territory could be advantageously made by the chief qr. m. of the department & that it might be economical to make several contracts, instead of one, for transportation to the department. I am told by reliable persons that during the season when cattle subsist on grass, more than half the year, there is but one price in New Mexico for transportation either across the plains or in the territory. A higher one is charged in winter. The minimum in the schedule of prices might therefore be for at least the half year ending in October. Grass is more abundant in the latter part of that period than in the earlier.

A garrison in Albuquerque seems to be unnecessary, either for preservation of public property or the protection of the inhabitants. The company stationed there might be much more useful elsewhere. Its discipline & morals would, no doubt, be improved by removal to the frontier.

Most respectfully,
Your obt. servant
J. E. Johnston
Lt. Col., 1st Cavalry

FORT DEFIANCE

Camp near the Puerco[7]
August 27th 1859

Sir:

I completed the inspection of Fort Defiance yesterday. Bvt. Maj. Shepherd's Co. B, Capt. Jones's C, Bvt. Major Brooks's G, & Capt. Clitz's E, 3d Inf., form the usual garrison. But Capt. Sykes, with his Co. K & 34 men of Bvt. Lt. Col. Chandler's I & Capt. Schroeder with 45 men of his company, are on temporary duty at the post. Major Simonson, who commands the troops in the Navajoe Country, is also in immediate command of the post for the time being. The strength of the garrison, present, is a Major, Asst. Surgeon, 3 Capts., 5 2d Lieuts. & 447 enlisted men of whom 61 are on extra & daily duty, 26 sick & 8 confined. The appearance of these troops under arms was very respectable. The arms accoutrements & clothing of the men good & in excellent order. Some of the officers think the material of the belts too weak. All think unfavorably of Maynard's primer which is very uncertain, even under favorable circumstances. The attachment interferes with the use of caps. They think, too, that the springs & screws are so brittle as to be very liable to break. The six companies maneuvered very well as a battalion under Capt. Sykes's command. Maj. Shepherd did not appear on account of a family affliction. The companies separately, also, both as infantry of the line & skirmishers, appeared very well, but best as the former. Their firing, however, was not satisfactory, like that of the other troops I have seen. The recruits at Governor's Island, I respectfully suggest, might be made tolerable marksmen. At least at short distances. This branch of the instruction of the troops necessary in this department seems to me very important, as skill with fire arms is more valuable in Indian warfare, than accuracy of movement.

The hospital & three of the company quarters are of pine logs, a good deal decayed, one of them even requires props to prevent its falling. The 4th is newer, of adobe & quite comfortable. The store rooms of the Qr. M. & Comm. are of stone & adobe & very good. The guard room & prison & workshops are of stone, & apparently durable. The Magazine is also substantial & sufficiently capacious. The stables are adequate to the wants of an infantry post.

The books & papers of the Commanding Officer, Quarter Master & Commissary & Assistant Surgeon, were complete to the day of inspection, except that the Asst. Surgeon keeps no "case book."

There are, for the use of the post, 2 wagons, an ambulance, 4 horses & 80 mules. The Quarter Master's subsistence stores are well arranged & kept with great care & are, consequently, in good condition. There is provision enough to last until the end of September. Alone 1500 lbs of hams have been condemned as unsound, in this month. The Qr. M. funds on hand amount to $1128.32. Those of the Subsistence Department, $137.89.

The hospital has capacity for 15 patients at most, but contains 17, 11 others are in a tent. They are as comfortable as it is practicable to make them in such lodgings. All the necessary medicines, & in sufficient quantities, are furnished, except anti-scorb[u]tics, of which an unusual amount is required from the prevalence of scurvy. There is so little water for irrigation that the post garden produces a very small supply of vegetables. The Surgeon considers a greater proportion than that contained in the ration absolutely necessary, in the present condition of the troops. I respectfully suggest such a modification of the regulations as to permit, in cases like the present, the issue of desiccated vegetables in addition to rice or beans.

Capt. Sykes's books & papers were left at his station, Los Lunas. Those of the 4 companies belonging to the post were complete & the company property as well stored as practicable. The amounts of the funds of the several companies were of B, $555.74; of C, $321.35; of G, $166.59; & of E, $326.81. It appears from the accounts of the company commanders, that these funds are used for the purchase of table furniture & condiments, subscriptions to periodicals, & purchase of books. Each company has a respectable library.

There are two field pieces with a sufficient supply of ammunition & 39,000 rifle musket cartridges, besides a small number in the possession of each company.

It seems to be apprehended that the troops assembled in & about Fort Defiance may be employed against the Navajoes. An attack upon this tribe would be very impolitic, & as much opposed to humanity & justice. These people have made more unassisted progress towards civilization than any Indian tribe that I have know[n]. They till the earth & keep herds of horses

In 1851, Lieutenant Colonel Edwin V. Sumner ordered Fort Defiance established at the mouth of Cañon Bonito in the heart of the Navajo country. The installation was the first post in what is today Arizona and the first in the department west of the Continental Divide. In 1853, Mansfield wrote that Fort Defiance was "the most beautiful and interesting post as a whole in New Mexico." (Illustration courtesy of the National Archives)

& large flocks of sheep & goats & the women spin & weave. The sufferers in such a war must be the possessors of property, who are never thieves. It is said, too, that the Mexicans hold numbers of their women & children in bondage. A serious war, which would destroy or deprive them of their grain & herds, would drive the whole tribe to theft & robbery, for [their] very existence. With very little assistance from the Indian department, it is thought by well informed persons, that these people would soon become the equals of our citizens who are their neighbours.

Most respectfully,
Your obt. servt.
Joseph E. Johnston
Lt. Col., 1st Cavalry

Endorsement: Attention will be called to the want of skill in the use of firearms; also to the neglect of the Assistant Surgeon at this and other posts in the Department in keeping no "case book." The number of extra duty men is excessive under ordinary circumstances and it is observed that the orders requiring that horses shall not be used in the quartermasters department has not been enforced. The chief commissary will report to the Commissary General upon the cause and remedy for so large a quantity of damaged hams in the Department. While the Navajoes must be held responsible for any depredations which they commit, the strictest caution will be observed to guard against undeserved attacks upon them and to protect them from unjust encroachments from whatever source, as far as the authority and influence of the military can properly be exerted. The Department commander will make it his duty to use his influence and every proper means to cause the restitution of captives taken from the Indians by Mexicans or others, and held without authority, whenever they can be discovered.

J. B. Floyd
Sec. of War
War Dept.
11 Jany 1860

POST AT LOS LUNAS

Los Lunas, N.M.
Sept. 4th 1859

Sir:

This place, a small village 22 miles below Albuquerque, is usually occupied by Cos. I & K, 3d Infy, Bvt. Col. Chandler's & Capt. Sykes's—but as I stated in my letter of the 27th ult., Capt. Sykes, a 2d Lt. & 98 enlisted men, are on detached service, leaving at the post a 1st Lt. & 65 enlisted men of the latter. 21 are on extra & daily duty, 11 sick & 7 confined.

The appearance of the men in the ranks, & their performance on company drill, including movements of skirmishers, were about equal to those of the companies of the same regiment at Fort Defiance. The condition of arms accoutrements & clothing equally good. The firing was the best I have seen, as yet. Lt. Whistler makes the objections to Maynard's primer & the manufacture of the rifle musket given in my report of the 27th ulto. The primer was used in the firing in my presence in which at least half missed fire, sometimes from defective machinery, at others by the fault of the primer itself. I reported that at Fort Garland lead was found in most of the muskets after 3 rounds had been fired. That opinion was formed too hastily. After 3 rounds at Los Lunas, the solutions were generally held in the barrels as at Fort Garland, which I attributed to lead stripped from the balls. On unbreaking the barrel in which this retention was strongest, I found nothing but the reduction of burnt powder.

The books & papers of the post & of Co. I, 3d Inf. are complete. The company fund, in the hands of Lt. Whistler, amounts to $650.90. There is also a small, but very good company library.

The Qr. M. & Comm. belongs to the detachment in the Navajoe Country & left his books & papers locked up. Lieut. Whistler has in his hands, received from that office, $133, belonging to the Qr. M. & $150.58 belonging to the Comm. Department. The company quarters, as well as the hospital, are too small & are not well ventilated. The houses have no other special defects. There are 8 wagons, 2 horses & 78 mules belonging to the post, 39 of the latter with Capt. Sykes's party. Two small store houses contain the Qr. M. & Comy's stores & protect them properly.

The hospital contains a dispensary, 1 room for patients & a very small one for kitchen. The supply of furniture is poor. It was received, however, late last winter, when the supplies in the dept. were nearly exhausted. All necessary articles can now be obtained. The Surgeon of the post is a civilian &, I think, well educated & intelligent & interested in his profession & duties.

Co. I has 2500 rifle musket cartridges. It has been furnished with ammunition for practice by breaking up old cartridges & making new of the materials. A pair of bullet molds being provided. Much of the old musket ammunition in the ord. depot at Fort Union might, I respectfully suggest, be beneficially used in this way. The bullet molds can be made at the depot.

This village is too small to furnish quarters & store rooms for two companies. The officer in command complains, like all others in the same situation, of the injurious effect upon his men, of contact with the lowest class of the population. A stronger objection to the post is that troops stationed here are too far from both frontiers to protect either.

Most respectfully,
Your obt. servt.
J. E. Johnston
Lt. Col., 1st Cavalry

Endorsement: The Department commander will report why the requirements of General Orders No. 13 in regard to transportation have not been enforced at this and some other posts. The number of extra duty men is excessive, under ordinary circumstances.

J. B. Floyd
Secretary of War
War Dept.
16 Jany 60

FORT CRAIG

Fort Craig
September 8th 1859

Sir:

I have the honor to report that I have just inspected this post, Bvt. Lt. Col. Porter's Co. F & Capt. McLane's I, R.M.R., compose the garrison, the strength of which, present, is a 1st & a 2d Lt, Asst. Surgeon & 110 enlisted men, 41 of the latter are on extra duty & daily duty, 6 sick & 7 in confinement.[8] They have 69 horses, 45 of which are reported unserviceable.

The arms, personal accoutrements & clothing of the men are in excellent order & the horse equipment very good. They have been taught all the movements in the school of the squadron, but appear best on foot, at quick paces on horseback they do not move with accuracy because many of the men do not manage their horses well. Nor are they exercised often enough for the instruction of the horses. If, however, as the officers of the regiment generally seem to suppose, they are not expected to fight on horse back, they perhaps ride & maneuver mounted well enough. The horses are indifferent. Most of them, indeed broken down. 15 of the 69, just received from the Qr. M's Dep't are altogether unfit for military service. Of the rest, 18 have served 8 years; 1, 7 years; 14, 5 years; 14, 4 years; 10, 3 years; and 2, 2 years, including 5 on detached service. The shooting with the rifle & revolver indicated the want of practice remarked at Fort Defiance.

This post was established in 1854 for two companies. The buildings & enclosures are of adobe. The walls of the former very good & the roofs very bad. The quarters are less comfortable than others made with much less labour. From the unusual breadth of the houses the joints are too long to retain their straightness under the necessary load of earth. The roofs of the stables & granary are still worse. The guard room & prison are better in this respect than any of the other buildings.

The "books, papers & files" of the post, companies, Qr. M., Comm. & Surgeon are complete & properly kept. There is no magazine. The only ordnance at the post being two mountain howitzers, without ammunition.

The company property is very well taken care [of]. As the company funds are ample, that of Co. F, $760 & that of Co. I, $282. The mess arrangements are very good. Each company bakery can produce 200 rations daily. Co. F has a good library.

The military offenses are generally petty breaches of discipline consequences of intemperance.

The means of transportation at the post are 5 serviceable wagons & 39 mules, the latter in very good order. The store house is secure except against

Fort Craig, New Mexico, stood at the northern end of the Jornada del Muerto (Journey of the Dead) in the middle Rio Grande Valley. Entirely enclosed, the installation was the most formidable work of military architecture in antebellum New Mexico Territory. (Photograph courtesy of the Rio Grande Historical Collection, New Mexico State University Library)

rain. It is so capacious, however, as to permit the property it contains to be arranged away from the leaks so that it is well preserved. The amount of money on hand is $808.18.

The commissary store house is like the Quarter Master's & the stores preserved in the same way. They are very good, except the hams, which the officers do not bag.

The hospital has two capacious wards & would be a good one if the roof were close. The surgery & store room are well arranged, the kitchen & wards clean & the patients well attended in all respects. The Surgeon, Dr. Perin, thinks that zinc chloridium & calcium iodidium should be ordered to the "supply tables" & that the quantities of pulveris alum & potassae iodidium should be doubled.

This post is on the west bank of the Rio Grande, 8 miles above the Jornada del Muerto & 25 below the thickly peopled portion of the valley. The road is on the east side of the river & there are no means at the post by which troops equipped for an expedition can cross it.

Most respectfully,
Your obt. servt.
J. E. Johnston
Lt. Col., 1st Cavalry

Company F has 4000 rifle & 6000 revolver cartridges & Company I, 12000 of the first & 6000 of the second.

Endorsement: The attention of the Department commander will be called to the number of extra and daily duty men, which seems excessive; also to the way of proficiency in horsemanship and the use of weapons. The mountain howitzers will be turned into the Ordnance depot, or, if required at the post, will be put in a condition to be useful. The quantity of ammunition in the possession of Company I is excessive.

J. B. Floyd
Secretary of War
War Dept
11 Jany 1860

FORT FILLMORE

Fort Fillmore, N.M.
September 12th 1859

Sir:

I reached this place from Fort Craig on the 9th inst. & have been engaged, since that day, in the inspection of the post. Bvt. Major Gordon's Co. H, 3d Inf., Bvt. Maj. Fitzgerald's D, 1st Dragoons & Bvt. Lt. Col. Roberts's C, R.M.R., compose the usual garrison. The company last named is now temporarily detached. There are present a Capt., 2d Lieut., Asst. Surgeon, Hospital Steward & 163 enlisted men. 31 of the latter are on extra & daily duty, 27 sick, & 7 confined.

The arms accoutrements & clothing of the infantry company are in good order, like those of the 3d Inf. already reported before. The men, however, who were seen both in close order & as skirmishers, are not well instructed. The firing was equal to that at Los Lunas. All the companies of this regiment have exhibited a want of skill which justifies me in regarding the differences observed as accidental. Maj. Gordon thinks unfavourably of Maynard's primer. His company has made some progress in the bayonet exercise & is the only one I have seen which has commenced it. Several of the men have not activity enough to be efficient as skirmishers.

The dragoon company is not well armed. All the men have sabres & Colt's Navy revolvers—a majority, the pistol carbine—some Sharps & a few, rifles of the cal. .54 of an inch. The clothing & accoutrements of the men are very good, but the saddles are much worn. The appearance of the backs of the horses proves that the shapes of these saddles are bad & Lt. Lord reports that all the officers of his regiment whom he knows, condemn them. The 75 men have 45 horses. About 45 of these men have joined the company this year. There are 5 old soldiers & 25 joined 2 years ago. The discipline of the company is better than the proficiency of the men in field exercises. The main deficiency is in horsemanship. 10 of the horses were in the Mexican War, 32 have served 8 years; 1, 4 years; & 2, 2 years. The use of the revolver on horse back has not been taught yet. The shooting with carbines, on foot, was equal to that of the infantry. The young officer now in command of the company, Lt. Lord, shows commendable zeal in its instruction.

Three of the men in confinement are undergoing sentences of general courts martial. Charges against the other four, who have been in confinement was two months, have been sent to department head quarters. It is here said to have been always difficult to bring prisoners to trial in this department. Most of the military offenses committed by the garrison are consequences of the neighbourhood of low drinking houses.

The quarters (for the companies), hospital, store houses, guard room & prison, are the best I have seen, altho' ragged in external appearance. The barrack rooms, however, are not quite large enough for full companies. The Magazine & bake house, altho' apparently substantially built, are not well roofed.

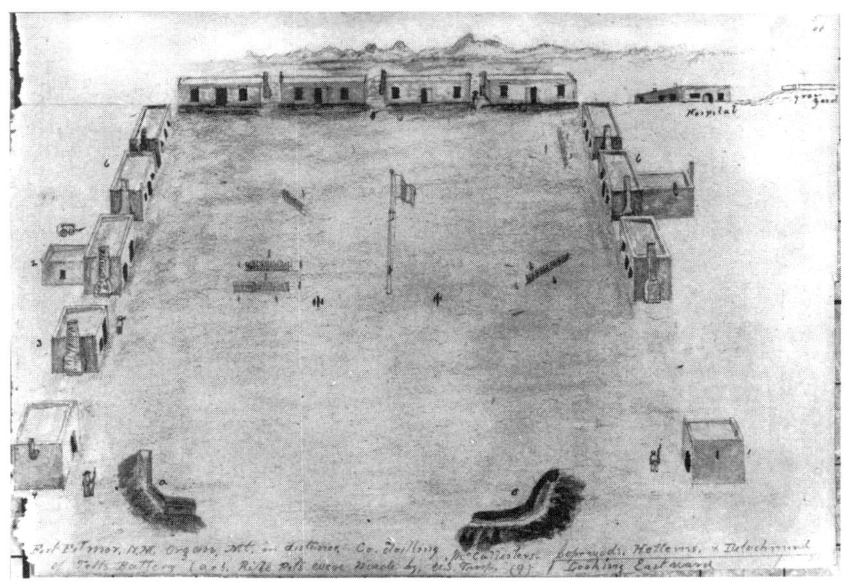

This sketch by Morgan Wolfe Merrick, a private in the Confederate Army, depicts Fort Fillmore, looking east. Drawn in July 1861, Merrick's illustration shows the rifle pits dug by Union forces shortly before they evacuated the post. (Illustration courtesy of the Daughters of the Republic of Texas Library, San Antonio)

The "books, papers & files" of the post, companies, Qr. M., Comm. & Surgeon are complete. The store rooms good & secure & the clothing & other property of both companies, kept with due care. The mess furniture & messing arrangements generally, are very good, as each company has a large fund. That of Co. H being $1499.25 & that of Co. D $969.73. The post bake house is capacious enough to furnish 400 rations of bread daily.

Major Gordon has $994 of regimental recruiting funds in his hands.

The hospital might serve as a model. The surgery, store room, wards & kitchen are all well arranged & extremely neat & the patients (now 12) find every possible care & attention. There have been 85 cases since the 1st of August. On being asked if the "supply table" contains all the medicines necessary here & in sufficient quantities, Dr. Cooper gave me the enclosed memorandum as he has served several years in this region, knows its diseases & is very capable of learning their treatment, I think that it may be useful to his department.[9]

The Quarter Master's stores are in excellent condition. He has 12 wagons, 1 serviceable ambulance & 101 mules, 23 of which are to be sent to Albuquerque. Forage is good & comparatively cheap. The amount of money on hand is $3288.05.

The subsistence stores are in good order. The supply, received last fall, is sufficient for a year. The balance of money on hand is $790.42. Lieut. Lord, the officer acting as Qr. M. & Comm., seems to be very attentive to his duties.

There are four mountain howitzers at the post, with about 100 rounds of ammunition. The only available ammunition for small arms, in the Magazine, is for Colt's Navy revolver, of which there are 19,000 cartridges.[10] There is a quantity of old musket cartridges which might supply materials for ammunition for target practice, if ball molds were provided. Each company has in its possession a small quantity of ammunition for the arms with which it is equipped. A chaplain has entered upon his duties in the past few weeks. There are 8 pupils, soldiers' children, in the post school.

The four senior sergeants are detailed as acting officers of the day, the others as non-commissioned officers of the guard.

Most respectfully,
Your obt. servt.
J. E. Johnston
Lt. Col., 1st Cavalry

Endorsement: The attention of the Department commander will be called to the deficiencies in the instruction of the troops and to the importance of bringing prisoners to trial as promptly as possible. If this cannot be done by General Courts, it is best to refer such cases as are not capital to the minor courts, habitual restraints and prompt punishments though mild being more effectual for discipline than heavy deferred penalties. The employment of more commissioned officers as officers of the day should be discontinued. A plan of the hospital building will be forwarded for the information of the Department.

J. B. Floyd
Secretary of War
War Dept.
11 Jany 1860
Fort Stanton

FORT STANTON

September 21st 1859

Sir:

From Fort Fillmore I came to this place, arriving on the morning of the 17th & have been employed since that time in inspecting the post. Maj. Ruff, Asst. Surgeon Ghiselin, a Hospital Steward, Cos. K, 8th Inf. & B & D, R.M.R., compose the garrison. The strength present, besides field & staff, is 1 Capt., 1 1st Lt., 1 2d Lt., & 155 enlisted men, 37 of whom are on extra duty, 7 sick (3 in hospital) & 5 confined.

The infantry company, commanded by Lt. Willard, is in all respects well equipped, well disciplined & well instructed. The arms accoutrements & clothing are in handsome order, the appearance of the company neat & soldierly & the men vigorous & healthy looking. They move with accuracy as infantry of the line & readiness & activity as skirmishers. Lt. Willard evidently bestows upon them much & judicious attention. Their firing before me was not equal to the record. Their commander reports that they have not practiced much, from want of ammunition. Good progress has been made in the bayonet exercise, since the order on the bayonet was received.

The arms accoutrements, clothing & horse equipage of the two companies of mounted riflemen are in excellent order & kept so habitually. They accompanied Col. Bonneville to the Canadian, which gave me an opportunity to observe them closely. The men, like those of the infantry company, are healthy looking & soldierly in appearance under arms. They march & manouvre well on foot, less so mounted, because many of them ride indifferently. At least as well, however, as those of the other mounted companies I have inspected. They use their rifles & revolvers rather better, perhaps. The horses are generally indifferent, 77 are reported serviceable, 25 unserviceable & 22 detached,

48 have just been received from Fort Leavenworth. Of the others, 17 have served 8 years; 19, 7 years; 2, 5 years; 13, 4 years; 10, 3 years; & 15, 2 years.

The quarters, hospital, guard room, prison & store houses are well & substantially built & of stone, except the Qr. M's storehouse, which is of adobe. It is the only post I have seen in the department which has an appearance of durability. As the materials were all near its cost, probably, was not above the average. It was intended for four companies. One set of quarters is capacious, but the other three are too small for full companies.

The "books, papers & files" of the post, companies, Qr. M., Comm. & Surgeon are complete & the accounts of disbursements, including post & company funds, apparently correct. The commanders of the post & companies seem to pay due attention to the health & comfort, as well as to the discipline of their men. Charges against four of the five prisoners were sent to Dept. Hd. Qrs. in March, but the decision upon them has not been received. The officer who preferred these charges, regarding the long confinement as a sufficient punishment, has asked to withdraw them.

The hospital is the best in the department & larger than is necessary in so healthy a climate. The surgery & store room are well arranged, the ward occupied very clean & the patients are comfortable as sick soldiers can be on straw beds.

There is a Magazine & no other ammunition than that in the possession of the companies, except a little for two mountain howitzers.

The Qr. M. store house is a large & very good one & the stores well arranged & in good condition. The neighbourhood can hereafter supply the post with corn & produces excellent hay. There are 6 wagons & 42 mules for post service & also a saw mill worked by water, capable of sawing about 30,000 feet of lumber monthly at no other expense than that of hauling the lumber & the extra duty pay of the two or three men required to manage it. The amount in the hands of the A.Q.M. is $2232.45.

The commissary's storehouse is large enough to contain a supply of provision for two years. The stores are in good condition & of good quality, except the hams. Beef is now furnished by contract. The bakery is large enough for the baking of 400 rations of bread daily. The A.Q.S. has in his hands $622.24.

This post, situated in the mountainous country frequented by the Mescaleros, has had much effect in controlling those Indians. It is one of the most valuable in New Mexico.

Most respectfully,
Your obt. servt.
J. E. Johnston
Lt. Col., 1st Cavalry

Endorsement: The attention of the Department commander will be called to the length of time the charges have been on file without action. The number of extra duty men is excessive.

J. B. Floyd
Sec. of War
War Dept.
11 Jany 1860

FORT BUCHANAN

Dragoon Spring[11]
October 4th, 1859

Sir:

I went from Fort Stanton to Fort Buchanan, reaching the latter post on the 29th ulto. & remaining until yesterday. The severe illness of Bvt. Lt. Col. Reeve & the absence of the Qr. M. & Comm. of the post, Lt. Cooke, rendered my inspection less satisfactory than it would have been otherwise.

The garrison present is Bvt. Lt. Col. Reeve's Co. B, 8th Infantry, & Capt. Ewell's G, 1st Dragoons.[12] The first, a Capt. (sick) & 56 enlisted men, including 6 on extra & daily duty & 22 sick. The second, a Capt. & 74 enlisted men including 22 on extra & daily duty, 17 sick & 4 confined, with 57 horses, 4 of which are reported "unserviceable."

The company of infantry is in an excellent state of discipline & instruction, the clothing, arms & accoutrements in good order. The men military looking, but without the healthy appearance usually belonging to American soldiers. In the bayonet exercise the men have been taught everything which, according to the system, should precede their practice with each other.

The Dragoon Company is better instructed than any other of the mounted troops I have seen in New Mexico. The men ride more like soldiers & the horses are better broken. It is evident that a regular course of instruction has been followed, instead of that of beginning with the school of the platoon, which I judge to have been the practice in this department. The horses are generally good & in excellent condition. 3 have served 9 years; 1, 7 years; 5, 6 years; 14, 5 years; 13, 4 years; 9, 3 years; 7, 2 years, 1, 1 year & the other has just been received. The men are well clothed & their personal accoutrements & horse equipments are good. There is, however, a great variety of fire arms, Sharp's, Hall's & the pistol carbine, the rifle (cal. .54) & musketoon—Colt's revolver of both sizes, & the old Dragoon pistols.[13] Capt. Ewell advocates Sharp's Carbine, in comparison with the musketoon, for he has had no opportunity to compare it with others of the same kind. The Capt. has made two requisitions for carbines annually for several years. His sabres are of the old pattern.

The quarters are very bad, a few of those for officers, of adobe. The rest & the store houses, of logs, or wooden slabs, set on end on the ground & the intervals closed with mud. Most of which, however, has fallen out. They are too open for winter & not sufficiently ventilated for summer. Fortunately very little labour, or, it is to be presumed, money, has been expended upon them.

The store houses are very bad & the stores, of course, much exposed. Great care is necessary to preserve them. In the Qr. M's Dept. there are 6 wagons & 34 mules. Corn, furnished by contract, costs $4.00 per 100 lbs., hay $19.00 per ton. According to the accounts in the office, the sum unexpended at the end of August was but $2.85. There are 4550 feet of slabs in store, brought when the post was established.

The accounts in the office of the A.Q.S. show that the sum of $3466.39 was in his hands at the end of August. In the absence of that officer the subsequent accounts could not be found. The provision on hand was brought from Albuquerque a year ago, except the flour which is made near El Paso. Of this there is a supply for near 6 months. It is not of good quality. The contract price was $12.00 per 100 lbs. A resident of Tucson told me that the market price there is now $8.00. Beef is furnished by contract at 12 cents per pound. The bakery can furnish about 500 rations of bread daily.

There is no magazine nor ammunition belonging to the post, except 200 cartridges for two 6 pdrs.

The infantry company has had no ammunition for practice until very lately when it received 20,000 cartridges. The Dragoons are well supplied also.

Both companies have large company funds & good gardens & of course, abundance of good food & the means of cooking it well, to which due attention is paid by their officers.

The hospital is a good building of its kind—of adobe, with flat roof & raised earthen floor. It is considered capable of accommodating 20 patients, but I should think that number too great in summer. The dispensary & store room contain all the supplies necessary & the wards are well furnished, except that straw beds are used instead of mattresses. The wards are clean & well aired & the appearance of the establishment indicates proper care and attention on the part of the surgeon & his subordinates. There were 172 cases in September, 420 in the last quarter, & 219 in the same quarter of 1858. The Surgeon, Dr. Irwin, attributes, in great degree, the unhealthiness of the post to a long strip of morass a few hundred yards distant, over which the prevailing winds pass to it.

I earnestly recommend the removal of this post to some point less unfavorable to the health of the troops. The Surgeon's quarterly reports furnish unanswerable arguments in favour of such a measure & neither the value of the buildings, nor of the position as a strategic point, a reason for continuing to occupy it. The Surgeon has reduced his sick report, temporarily, by sending twelve or fifteen of his patients to the Rio Grande, for change of air.

Most respectfully,
Your obt. servt.
J. E. Johnston
Lt. Col., 1st Cavalry

FORT BLISS

Fort Bliss
October 13th 1859

Sir:

I reached this post on the 8th instant, commencing its inspection on the 9th & concluded it yesterday.

The present garrison is an Asst. Surgeon, Hospital Steward, Capt. Elliott's Co. A, R.M.R. & a detachment of Capt. Pitcher's & 9th Infy., the former, a Captain, 1st Lt. & 69 enlisted men, 15 of whom are on extra daily duty, 6 sick & 7 confined.[14] The latter, a 1st Lt. & 36 enlisted men, of whom 9 are on extra & daily duty, 5 sick & 5 confined. Capt. Elliott has 62 horses, 6 of which are considered unfit for Military Service.

Capt. Elliott's company has been taught all the movements of the "school of the platoon" & makes them accurate on foot but the men generally are not good riders & 35 of the horses, received 10 days ago, are restless in the ranks. The captain bestows sufficient care & attention upon the instruction of his company, but commits the error which I think common in his regiment, that of passing over the "school of the trooper." The men practice regularly with their fire arms, with the revolver, still on foot. The arms, accoutrements, clothing & horse equipment are all in good order. The supply of ammunition is ample. Capt Elliott, like most of the officers of his regiment whole [sic] opinions I have heard, thinks the present rifle less accurate than that of cal. 54. The horses received are too low in flesh for service in the field, but the rest are generally in good condition, one has served 9 years; 1 8 years; 2 6 years; 1 5 years; 17 4 years; 3 2 years; & 1 1 year.

Capt. Pitcher's company left this post in Febry. last, as the escort of the Texas Boundary Commission. The men of the detachment now here were severely attacked by scurvy & sent back to the post some 3 months ago. They had joined the company as recruits but a short time before it left the post & before there had been opportunity to instruct them well. They have recovered from scurvy. Lt. Jackson, who has been in command of the detachment & for ten days is industriously engaged in its instruction. The arms, accoutrements & clothing are in good order & the men vigorous & healthy looking.

The "books, papers & files" of the post, Co. A, R.M.R., Qr. M., Comm. & surgeon are complete.

There have been no disbursements in the Qr. Ms. or Commissry Department since Lieut. Jackson took charge of them. Belonging to the former there are 32 mules, an ambulance (so called) & 5 wagons including a portable tank. Forage is furnished by contract, corn at $3.15 per fanega & hay at $28.00 per ton. The store rooms are secure & the public property they contain in good condition. The funds on hand amount to $1687.82.

The comsry store house serves its purpose very well & the stores it contains are well preserved. The flour is made in the neighborhood at Hart's Mill, upon which the southern parts of this department depend for breadstuff.[15] The bakery could, if necessary, produce 500 rations of bread daily. The amount of money on hand is $23,794.91—most of which is to pay for cattle soon expected from Texas.

The quarters are of adobe—comfortable & conveniently arranged. The rent paid for them is $225.00 monthly. The stables are suitable to the climate.

The guard house & prison are sufficient for a garrison of 3 or 4 companies. The breaches of discipline, usually punished by stoppage of pay & imprisonment are generally drunkenness & fits consequences which in an inhabited country, officers are seldom able to prevent.

The hospital can accommodate comfortably about 16 patients. The surgery, store rooms & wards are all in excellent order & the surgeon, apparently, very attentive to his duty. The number of cases in the last quarter was 95, in the corresponding one of last year, 111. Of the present cases at least one third are sickness produced by drunkenness or binges received in drunken brawls.

Maj. T. G. Rhett, paymaster, is stationed here.[16] His district comprises Forts Buchanan, Stanton, Fillmore, Bliss & Quitman. He showed me an acknowledgement by the paymaster general of the correctness of his accounts to the end of June. Since that time he has received, including the balance then on hand, $43,332.52, paid $36,484.40. He has in his possession $5400 & deposited in the Sub Treasury in New York $1148.13.

Most respectfully,
Your Obt. Svt.
J. E. Johnston
Lt. Col., 1st Cavalry

Fort Bliss had its origins in September 1848 as the "Post Opposite Paso del Norte" when Major Jefferson Van Horne led 257 soldiers of the Third Infantry west from San Antonio. Closed in September 1851, the post was reestablished near Magoffinsville in January 1854. (Illustration from W. H. H. Davis, El Gringo*)*

Endorsement: The number of extra duty men is excessive, unless for some extraordinary cause, which the Department commander will inquire in regard to.

J. B. Floyd
Sec. of War
War Dept.
11 Jany 1860

FORT FILLMORE

Co. C, R.M.R.
Fort Fillmore
October 17th 1859

Sir:

When I inspected this post Bvt. Lt. Col. Robert's Co. C, R.M.R., was detached. It returned yesterday & was inspected by me today.

The strength present is a 1st Lt., a 2d Lt., & 71 enlisted men, including 6 on extra duty, 5 sick & 1 confined with 57 serviceable and 9 unserviceable horses. The company has, since June, occupied a fixed camp in a high & healthy location. The arms accoutrements & clothing of the men are serviceable & in good order. New saddles & bridles of "McClellan's pattern" have just been received.[17] This saddle is generally preferred by those who have tried it, to that now in use. The bits, however, from defect of fabrication, frequently drop out of the horse's mouth. The men are vigorous & hardy looking, but are not good horsemen, nor are their horses well broken. Consequently the company does not move with accuracy. It has made some progress in the "Skirmish drill," which no other of the regiment has commenced. This system is a great improvement on the instruction for skirmishing contained in our "Cavalry Tactics."

The books & returns, including accounts of the company fund, are correct. The company fund amounts to $550.56. The company property is well preserved, tho' the store room is bad. It contains a sufficient supply of clothing & ammunition. The quarters are adequate.

In June last 1st Sergt. Wall knocked down & so severely beat a private (Appelzoller) for drunken insolence, as to break his jaw.[18] The fracture was so bad a one, that when Appelzoller was discharged, a few days ago, it was unhealed. On account of it, the Surgeon has refused to pass him for reenlistment. Neither Bvt. Major Gordon, the commanding officer nor Lt. Howland, commanding the camp, seems to have thought the case worth notice. It is very unfortunate for this company that its captain has long been absent from it.

Immediately after my inspection of this post, Co. D, 1st Dragoons, received a full supply of Sharp's carbines. The result of regular practice with this weapon are quite satisfactory. But as it is uncertain which of the several breech loading carbines reported upon by boards of officers is best for military service. It seems to me that two [*sic*] many of this construction have been purchased for our troops.

The iron bedsteads for this dept. were received at Fort Union after my inspection. I have been officially informed that they were sent complete. As the wooden parts can be made wherever there are soldier's quarters I respectfully suggest that there would be great economy in sending to a distance, only the iron frames. The cost of transporting these boards to the posts in New Mexico will be four or five times their price at those posts.

In my report of July 11th the expenditures in the Qr. M. Dept. since October 1st 1858 are stated to have been $482,130. Of this sum $27,788 were expended on Capt. Pope's artesian well, $5,600 on Lt. Steen's party which accompanied Mr. Beale.

Few of the horse shoes in this dept. are fit for cavalry horses. Many of them weigh 2 pounds. Models should be adopted & conformed to.

There are more than 700,000 cartridges for old calibers at Forts Union

& Fillmore. They might be used economically for practice, if ball molds & swedges were furnished to every company. These could be made in the ordnance depot at Fort Union.

The 26 companies in this department are dispersed in 12 posts This division of the troops prevents their proper instruction, reduces the force available for the field, & increases the expenditure of Qr. M. funds. 6 of these posts occupied by the companies, in my opinion, serve no useful purpose. Five of them, because in the midst of a dense population. The other, Fort Craig, because in the almost uninhabitable part of the valley of the Rio Grande & on the side of the river opposite to the road. The five are Santa Fe, Albuquerque, Los Lunas, Fort Burgwin & Fort Fillmore. The last is also too near Fort Bliss. These positions are injurous to the discipline, morals & health of our men, also. As the number of Indians east of the Rio Grande is greatly diminished, several of these companies might be sent into Arizona.

The troops in New Mexico are not proficient in military exercises because, 1st, they are in small bodies, 2d, their instruction is not the best consideration, & too many are employed at labour. See in my reports the numbers on extra duty. 3d, recruits are frequently sent into the field before there is opportunity to instruct them. After which, regarding themselves as veterans, they never lack, besides which their officers attend to the schools of the "soldiers' & "trooper." The remedy for the last would be the thoro' instruction of the recruits in those schools & the use of arms at the depots. When taken into the field without such instruction they are mere incumbrances.

Most respectfully
Your Obt. Servt.
J. E. Johnston
Lt. Col., 1st Cavalry

FORT QUITMAN

Fort Quitman, Texas
October 21st 1859

Sir:

I reached this post on the morning of the 18th inst. & finished its inspection to-day.

Fort Quitman is 6 miles above the point at which the road from El Paso to San Antonio leaves the Valley of the Rio Grande. It was intended for two companies but is occupied by one only. Bvt. Lt. Col. Bomford's H, 8th Infy., a Captain, 2d Lt. & 55 enlisted men present & 13 temporarily detached, with 4 men of Co. C casually at the post & an Asst. Surgeon & hospital steward. 27 of those present are on extra duty, 2 sick & 5 in confinement.

The arms & accoutrements of the company are good & in excellent order, the men well clothed & healthy looking. The company moves well & accurately in close order, but has not been exercised in skirmishing. Its instructor has been very much retained by the work of building the post, which is necessarily going on. As marksmen the men are equal to the generality of those mentioned in my previous reports.

The houses are of adobe with roofs of mortar, the guard house & prison are unfinished, the hospital barely begun. The quarters & office & storehouse of the Qr. M. & Comms. are quite good enough for this mild climate. The company quarters, however, are too small for full companies.

There is no magazine but a large supply of infantry ammunition at the post.

A house built for company quarters is used as a hospital. The surgery & store room are provided with everything necessary. The furniture is neat & the few sick well cared for. The position is a healthy one.

The Qr. M. store house is too small so that corn is kept under canvas. Hay seems to be thought almost unnecessary, because the pasturage is good during the winter. Stables seem to be thought unnecessary too, on account of the mildness of the climate. I think otherwise. There are 8 (constructed) wagons, 34 draught & 19 pack mules. The horse shoes, generally, are unfit for use.

The commissary store house is quite good enough & the provisions of excellent quality. It is furnished semi-annually from San Antonio except flour & beans, which are brought from New Mexico. Beef is furnished directly by the commissary. There are $1024.03 in the Qr. M. & $959.54 in the subsistence dept.

The bakery produces excellent bread & could furnish four times as much as the garrison requires.

"The books, papers & files" of the post, company, Qr. M., Comm. & Surgeon are complete & the accounts of disbursements seem to be correct.

The company & hospital funds are sufficient for the purchase of such vegetables as are necessary for health & diet.

This post like most of those in New Mexico, has several low drunkery houses in its immediate vicinity. The most frequent breaches of discipline, therefore, are drunkenness & its consequences.

Most respectfully,
Your obt. servt.
J. E. Johnston
Lt. Col. 1st Cavalry

Endorsement: The Department commander will enforce the requirements of General Orders No. 13, in regard to the allowance of transportation. Attention will be given to the instructions of the troops.

J. B. Floyd
Sec. of War
War Dept.
11 Jany 1860

FORT DAVIS

Fort Davis
October 25th, 1859

Sir:

I have the honor to report that, since the 22d inst., I have inspected this post. It was built for six companies, but is now occupied by one—Bvt. Maj. Selden's G, 8th Inf. & the Hd. Qrs. & band of that regiment. The strength present is a Lt. Col., Adjutant, Reg. Qr. M., Asst. Surgeon, 1st Lieut. & 101 enlisted men, including a Hospital Steward, Sergt. Maj., 9 Qr. M. Sgts. & 2 principal musicians. 23 enlisted men are on extra duty, 6 sick & 5 confined.

The appearance of the company under arms was very handsome. The men strong, healthy & well "set up." The arms, accoutrements & clothing in excellent order. Their movements accurate & ready both as infantry of the line & skirmishers. Their progress in the bayonet exercise handsome & from the record of three target practice, the improvement in that respect decided. I have great satisfaction in finding a commanding officer who appreciates the importance of military exercise. It is to be considered that these exercises are liable to constant interruption by the frequent detachments required for escorts. There is more evidence of attention to discipline & inspection at this than at any other post I have inspected.

The soldiers' quarters are substantial store buildings with good thatched roofs & stone floors. The officers' quarters are huts of the slightest kind.

The guard house & prison are contained in one of the stone buildings described above & are adequate. The usual punishments inflicted by reg. cts. m. are stoppage of pay & confinement. The most frequent military offence are drunkenness & the absence from duty caused by it.

Asst. Surgeon Sutherland is in charge of the hospital.[19] The house is unfit for the purpose, but great neatness gives it an appearance of comfort. The Surgery and Storeroom are well provided & everything is well arranged. He whatever depends upon attention. This hospital is second among those I have seen, only to that under the control of Dr. Cooper.

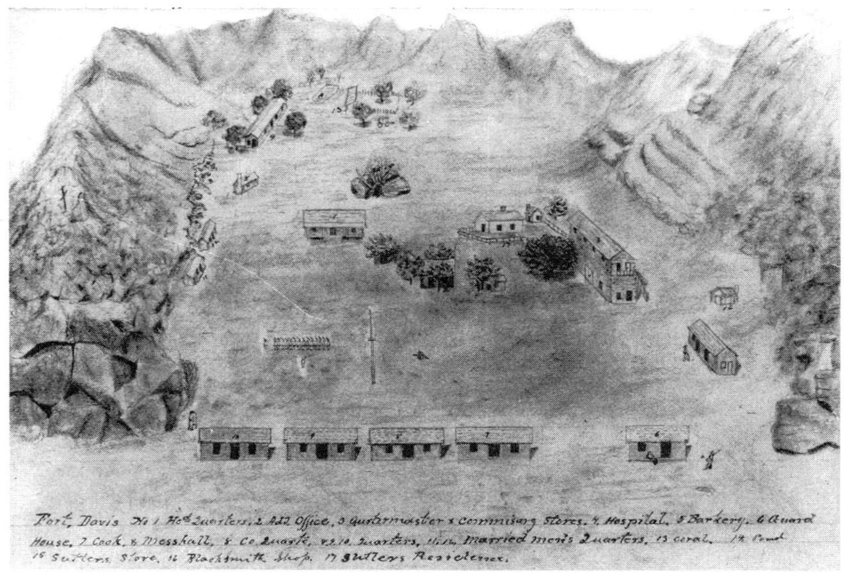

Morgan Wolfe Merrick, a young Confederate Texan, created this sketch of Fort Davis in 1861. (Illustration courtesy of the Daughters of the Republic of Texas Library, San Antonio)

The "books, papers & files" of the regiment, post, company, & hospital, are kept as prescribed & the accounts of disbursements correct.

A large well built store house contains the Qr. M. & Commissary Store rooms which are capacious & secure.

7 wagons, 46 draught & 14 pack mules, allowed to this post. There are 82–20 to be sent to San Antonio by the first opportunity. The expenditures in this department amount to about $2000 monthly. Hay, corn & fuel are purchased at reasonable prices. The sum on hand is $3153.46.

The subsistence stores are very good. Flour is brought from New Mexico—except a small quantity for officers which is sent from San Antonio. Its transportation costs nearly $8.00 per 100 lbs. The beeves, averaging about 450 lbs, cost $20.95 each & the extra duty pay of the men who keep them. The sum on hand is $2595.54.

The bakers (one baker) produces about 150 rations of excellent bread daily.

The company fund, $377 is applied principally to the purchase of vegetables for the mess table of the company.

There is a strong stone magazine containing alone 20,000 rifle musket cartridges & a large supply of ammunition for a 6 pdr. & two mountain howitzers.

The stable is a very good one, but much too small to contain all the mules.

An estimate of the funds necessary to repair & complete this post, has been asked for. I respectfully suggest the expediency of considering the question of changing the direction of the road which this post is designed to protect before making such expenditures at this point. The change in question, which I repeatedly proposed, while on duty in Texas, would make an improvement well worth all that belongs to the U.S. here.

Most respectfully,
Your Obt. Servt.
J. E. Johnston
Lt. Col., 1st Cavalry

Endorsement: The number of extra duty men is deemed excessive. The allowance of transportation is greater for the present garrison than that authorized in General Orders No. 13. The attention of the Department commander will be called to these points.

J. B. Floyd
Sec. of War
War Dept.
11 Jany 1860

CAMP STOCKTON

Pecos River
October 29th 1859

Sir:

I have the honor to report that I inspected Camp Stockton on the 27th instant. It is at Comanche Springs, about midway between Forts Davis & Lancaster & on the principal route of our marauding Indians into Mexico & occupied by Capt. Carpenter's Company H, 1st Infantry. A Captain, 1st Lt., 2d Lt. & 54 enlisted men present. 22 of the latter are on extra duty, 3 sick, & 2 in confinement. The company was established at this point in April & has been employed since then in building quarters for the winter in addition to the escort duty imposed by its position.

The arms, accoutrements & clothing of the company are in good order & they (the men) have all requisite physical ability, 20 of them are equipped like mounted riflemen, to pursue parties of hostile Indians. Their 20 horses are mostly indifferent & in poor condition & as the cold weather has already set in in these elevated regions & there are no stables, it is not probable that they will improve. This company has labored under several disadvantages during the Summer. Its Captain has been absent. It has been employed in building & like other troops stationed on the same road, has been required to furnish constant detachments for escort duty. Its discipline & instruction are below mediocrity. Its deficiency in the latter respect at least, I attribute to the long absence of Capt. Carpenter & as, since his return a few days ago, a lesson in the school of the company has daily preceded work upon houses. This deficiency will probably not be suffered to continue. The 2d Lieut (Sherburne) is either not familiar with tactics or careless on drill. The performance of the company as marksmen was equal to that of the other companies I have seen this summer. The bayonet exercise has not been begun.

Two thatched adobe houses for officers have been made fit for occupation. The company quarters are still without roofs. A sufficient bake house has been made. Neither storehouse nor hospital has been commenced. Unlike the establishment of Fort Davis, the young officers who directed the building here began with their own quarters.

The company "books, papers & files" are correct as well as the accounts of the Qr. Mr. & Comm. The company fund amounts to $321.23 & is applied chiefly to the purchase of vegetables for the company mess table. There is a sufficient supply of ammunition.

Dr. Olmsted, a civilian, is employed as Surgeon.[20] He reports the stock of medicines & surgical instruments inadequate & thinks the vegetable medicines unfit for all. A hospital tent contains the sick, the surgery & the storeroom. 112 cases occurred in the last quarter, the most serious of which were scurvy.

Three wagons & twenty mules are allowed for the camp. Corn costs $1.48 per bushel, hay $15.00 per ton, & wood $7.50 per cord. The sum in the hands of the Qr. M. is $3,003.05.

Provision is brought in monthly from Fort Lancaster, except salt meat, of which there is a supply for almost two years. Beef is furnished by contract at $0.10 per pound. The sum on hand is $124.95.

Most respectfully,
Your Obt. Servt.
J. E. Johnston
Lt. Col., 1st Cavalry

Sergeant Albert B. Peticolas of the Confederate Army of New Mexico rendered this illustration of Fort Lancaster, Texas, in 1862. (Illustration courtesy of the Arizona Historical Society, Tucson)

FORT LANCASTER

Rio San Pedro[21]
Nov. 4th 1859

Sir:

I had the pleasure to inspect Fort Lancaster, occupied by Capt. Granger's Co. K, 1st Inf., on the 31st ulto. & 1st instant. Present, a Captain, 1st Lt., 2d Lt., Asst. Surgeon & 51 enlisted men besides a Hospital Steward & Ord. Sergt. The 2d Lt is in arrest. 11 enlisted men are on extra duty, 2 sick & 7 on detached service (as escort). The appearance of the men under arms, the condition of their arms accoutrements & clothing & the state of discipline & instruction are highly creditable to Capt. Granger. Movements in close order were executed as well in double quick as in quick time. Those of skirmishers & the positions & motions of the bayonet exercise, have also been well taught. The shooting was the best that has been made in my presence.

The post was constructed for two companies & the quarters would serve for two in this climate. They are, generally thatched adobe houses. The little plank used in their construction was brought from San Antonio. There is now, of course, ample room to store public property securely. The guard room & prison are sufficient for this post. The latter is used less than is usual. The petty offenses which occur being properly punished by garrison court martial.

The "books, papers & files" of the post company & hospital are correct & neat, as well as the accounts of the disbursing officer. The company fund serves to be used as it accrues, for the purchase of books & periodicals for the company library & of vegetables & other additions to the supplies of provisions. The bakery is an excellent one—capable of producing 400 rations of bread daily.

The hospital is inadequate—being too small & unsafe. The position of the post renders it necessary to provide for more than the sick of the garrison. The location is very healthy, but eight cases occurred in the last quarter. The hospital is as neat & comfortable as the condition of the building permits & contains every thing necessary for the sick.

Four wagons & twenty eight mules are allowed to this post. Corn costs $1.55 per bushel, hay $19.00 per ton, & wood $7.50 per cord. Parties on the road draw largely upon the Qr. M. dept. here. The balance at the end of the last quarter & still remaining on hand is $465.

The Commissary of this post furnishes Camp Stockton. The supply of pork & bacon is sufficient for about two years. There is also in store a large quantity of flour. I could see the quality of thirty barrels the heads of which has been broken in transportation far into the interior. The sum on hand is $565.44.

There is no magazine, but the company storeroom contains a sufficient supply of ammunition.

Pvt. Heitcoker, K, 1st Inf., complains that extra pay as baker, to the amount of about $30 has been withheld from him. It appears that such a sum was due him in Sept. 1858 & that the council of administration refused to appropriate it, to punish, it is said, some insolence of his to the post treasurer. Cos. H & K, 1st Inf., then forming the garrison, have since been separated. It would be but just to require each of these companies to pay to Heitcoker the portion it received of the money due to him. A stoppage of pay by the council of administration was of course illegal—Capt. Granger not in command at the time.

Most respectfully
Your Obt. Servt.
J. E. Johnston
Lt. Col., 1st Cavalry

Endorsement: The allowance of transportation is greater than is authorized in General Orders No. 13. The number of extra duty men is greater than should be necessary habitually. The extra pay due Private Heitcoker will be paid from the company funds and the officers conceived in the stoppage will be advised that the duties of a council of administration, are administrative, not disciplinary or judicial.

J. B. Floyd
Secretary of War
War Dept.
11 Jany 1860

CAMP HUDSON

Camp Hudson
November 6th, 1859

Sir:

I inspected Camp Hudson yesterday. It is occupied by Bvt. Maj. Smith's Co. A, 8th Infry., & a detachment of Capt. Stoneman's E, 2d Cav. The strength present being a 2d Lt., Asst. Surgeon & 88 enlisted men including the Hospital Steward. 24 enlisted men are on extra duty, 10 sick & 3 in confinement. The arms accoutrements & clothing of the men are serviceable but their appearance is not particularly neat. Their discipline is interfered with by several drinking houses in the immediate neighborhood of the post & as they have just been paid for four months, the usual period in this portion of Texas, this effect is now at its maximum. The proficiency of the company in the movements in close order & in firing is not above mediocrity. They are going on respectably with the bayonet exercise, but their instruction as skirmishers is barely begun. The detachment of cavalry is without horses & it is to be presumed consists of the least effective men of their company, as they were left here by Capt. Stoneman when ordered into the field with his company. They are armed with Sharp's Carbines & some of the old heavy pattern. They seem to have had no practice with fire arms.

Altho' this post is called "camp" it differs in nothing from the "forts" of New Mexico & Texas. It has comfortable quarters for two companies, a hospital, substantial store houses, bake house & guard room. The stables, granary & prison are of the slightest kind.

The post, company, & hospital "books papers & files" are neat & correctly kept. The company fund amounts to $462 & is used to purchase condiments & vegetables for the company mess & to pay for newspapers. The company has good cartridges.

Sergeant Albert B. Peticolas left this visual record of Camp Hudson sketched in 1862. (Illustration no. 60301 courtesy of the Arizona Historical Society, Tucson)

The accounts & other papers of the Qr. M. & Comms. seem to be correct. The Qr. M. has 3 wagons & 19 mules for post service. Corn costs $0.94 per bushel, hay $29.93 per ton & wood $5.35 per cord. The sum on hand is $2,648.73. The rent of the ground occupied is $50 per month.

The articles of the ration are good of their kinds, except that an occasional barrel of flour requires sifting. After which excellent bread is made of it. Beef costs 8 cents per pound. The sum on hand is $474.76.

Most respectfully
Your Obt. Servt.
J. E. Johnston,
Lt. Col., 1st Cavalry

Endorsement: The number of extra duty men is excessive for ordinary purposes. Attention will be called to the want of instruction of the troops.

J. B. Floyd
Secretary of War
War Dept.
11 Jany 1861

FORT CLARK

Rio Seco, Texas[22]
Nov. 13th, 1859
Asst. Adjt. Genl.
Hd. Qrs. of the Army

Sir:

I inspected Fort Clark on the 9th & 10th of this month. It was occupied at the time of my arrival by Capt. Hill's Co. M, Bvt. Maj. French's K, Capt. Dawson's L & Capt. Jones's F, 1st Arty. Present, a Captain, 2 2d Lts. & 183 enlisted men including the Hospital Steward & Ordnance Sgt. 22 men were on extra duty, 21 sick, & 24 confined. A Captain, 1st Lt. & Asst. Surgeon temporarily absent. The two former on a Genl. Cr. M. & the latter to attend Lieut. Hazen, lately wounded in a skirmish.[23] Cos. L & M left the post on the 10th under orders to Fort Brown, after their arms & clothing & infantry exercises had been seen.

Bvt. Maj. French, with his battery, arrived at the post on the 26th of September, finding there Cos. L & M. As soon as he had prepared two six pdrs., two siege howitzers & four twenty four pdrs. for the purpose, the two companies were regularly instructed in the manuals of those classes of guns. Company F, on detached service until very lately, has just commenced the same course of instruction. The carriages of the above mentioned pieces are unkept for field service, in my opinion. Having suffered from exposure, perhaps neglect, before coming into the possession of the present commanding officer. I am informed that they were brought from one of the posts on the Rio Grande.

Maj. French's battery is in good order in all respects. The state of discipline & instruction of the men as gunners & drivers extremely good. The appearance of the men very soldierly, their arms clean & their clothing very neat. The horses (43) altho' they have not recovered all the flesh lost on the long march from the Mississippi are healthy looking & perfectly broken. The carriages are sound & the harness appears to be in good order, but as it has been in use for five years it can hardly be strong enough for the commencement of a campaign. The other companies are excellent infantry of the line. Co. M is also respectable in open order & in the bayonet exercise excels any that I have seen. Co. F is the only one of the three I had an opportunity to see at target practice in which it acquitted itself about as well as the majority of the infantry. The arms & clothing of these infantry companies were also in excellent order. Companies L & M were well provided for their march. There is no Lt. with the battery & but one officer, the 2d Lt, with Co. F.

The buildings erected by the Qr. M. Dept. are quarters for the commanding officer, a hospital, storehouse & magazine. The first two very unnecessarily expensive. All are of stone. There are no soldiers quarters, but seven small houses for officers were built at different times by companies & also a substantial bakehouse. The magazine is much too small for an artillery post. The troops are in tents & the ground is such as to prevent their being encamped together, this dispersion is of course very unfavorably to discipline. The more so from the neighbourhood of several drinking houses.

In respect to books, papers of all sorts & accounts of disbursements of public money & post & company funds, the regulations are observed.

The Qr. M. & Comms. was absent on a C.M. therefore I could not compare his accounts with the sums in his hands. The store houses are secure & the public property preserved with due care. The provision is very good except some barrels of hard bread, intended for scouting parties, which have been on hand too long.

The hospital is neat & comfortable & well supplied. The Surgeon as I say above, has been absent for several days. In the last quarter, 180 being the average number of men present, 157 cases occurred.

The sabre, I respectfully suggest, is not an effective weapon for men on foot. If small arms are required by artillerists the revolver seems to be far better. If, however, the sabre is retained it would be advantageous to substitute for the present course of instruction such a system as would prepare men to defend themselves with it.

Most respectfully,
Your Obt. Servt.
J. E. Johnston
Lt. Col., 1st Cavalry

FORT INGE

Castroville, Texas[24]
November 14th, 1859

Sir:

I have the honor to report that I inspected Fort Inge on the 12th instant. It is occupied by Capt. Maclay's Co. F, 8th Infy., a Capt., 2d Lt. & 53 enlisted men, with an Asst. Surgeon, Hospital Steward & Ordnance Sgt. 12 men are on extra duty, 6 sick & 1 in confinement. The 2d Lt., Hazen, was severely wounded a week ago, in the third successful pursuit of Indians in which he has exhibited activity perseverance & courage.

The state of things at the post shows decidedly, attention to his duty on the part of the commanding officer. The men have been taught all the company movements as well [as] those in close order & execute them well, both in quick & in double quick time. The bayonet exercise, however, has been begun but lately—on account of delay in obtaining the book. The arms & accoutrements are in excellent order & the clothing of the men very neat.

There are good quarters for one company, including officers. The storehouses are old buildings intended for other purposes but serve to preserve the property stores in them. The hospital would be a good one if a kitchen were added. The guard room & prison are sufficiently comfortable & secure & like the rest of the post in neat condition. The bakery is a very good one & provides excellent bread.

All the books papers & accounts required by the regulations are properly & neatly kept.

In the Qr. M's. Dept. there are 3 wagons, 20 mules & 11 horses. The latter for pursuit of plundering Indians. Lieut. Hazen was suffering so much from his wounds that I could not compare his accounts with the sums of public money in his hands. Corn costs $0.88 per bushel, hay $25.00 per ton & wood $2.44 per cord. The provisions are good but there is a little hard bread on hand, spoiled by age. It was intended for scouting parties. Beef costs 9 cents.

Started in March 1849, Fort Inge, Texas, sat on the east bank of the Leona River. In 1855, Frederick Law Olmsted found the whitewashed quarters at the post "pleasantly shaded by hackberries and elms." With the Stars and Stripes on its summit, Mount Inge can be seen in the right background in this 1867 sketch. (Courtesy of Ty Smith. Original in the National Archives)

The hospital contains all the necessary supplies & is kept in excellent order—as neat & with as much appearance of comfort as is possible with the means furnished.

The company fund amounts to $161.

The infantry officers I have seen think unfavorably of Maynard's primer & never use it in the field. The attachment impedes somewhat the placing caps on the cone. The rifle musket is thought by them to be an admirable weapon. The sights, however, are too coarse that at the muzzle should be of white metal—the other of blue or brown. The barrels should not be bright, their glittering prevents accurate aim & makes troops visible at great distances in sunshine & exposes sentinels by moon light.

I judge from what I have seen that the Comm., Dept. of Texas has been very well administered.

At most of the posts I have seen, too much of the time of the troops is contained in labour & too little devoted to military exercises but a small proportion of our officers seem to appreciate the importance of the latter. The best exceptions I have seen are Capt. Granger, 1st Inf., Capt. Sykes, 3d, Lt. Col. Seawell & Lt. Willard, 8th, Capt. Ewell, 1st Drags. & Lt. Jackson, R.M.R.

In mentioning the large supplies of salt meat at Camp Stockton & Fort Lancaster, I should have explained that they had been sent for a body of troops encamped near the former point & unconsumed when it was returned.

In the Medical Dept., I have every where seen evidence of zeal & efficiency. Its officers, in my opinion, compare favorably with those of any other branch of our service.

The regimental officers generally think that the service would be greatly benefited by regular & more frequent payments. In this opinion I fully concur. Weekly payments, by making soldier's life far more comfortable, would diminish desertion & increase reenlistment.

Most respectfully,
Your Obt. Servt.
J. E. Johnston
Lt. Col., 1st Cavalry

Endorsement: The attention of the Department commander will be called to the remarks upon the military exercises of the troops, and to the importance of regular payments every two months.

J. B. Floyd
Secretary of War
War Dept
11 Jany 1860

Joseph King Fenno Mansfield's Inspection of the Department of Texas

1860–1861

This portrait of Joseph K. F. Mansfield was taken shortly before his death on the battlefield of Antietam. (Photograph courtesy of the Library of Congress)

With a population of 7,307 in 1860, Galveston was the second largest city in Texas and a major transfer port for oceangoing vessels and coastal steamers. The cotton port was also a major supply depot for the army. By the time of Mansfield's September 1860 inspection, a railroad connected Galveston to Houston. (Illustration courtesy of the Library of Congress)

CORPS OF ENGINEERS AT GALVESTON

Indianola, Texas
26th Sept. 1860

Sir:

Conformably to the orders of the Gen-in-Chief to inspect the Dept. of Texas, I have now the honor to report that I reached Galveston on the 24th instant en route for Indianola at 7 A.M., and as the steamer was to remain there till 4 P.M., I proceeded to inspect the operations of Lt. W. H. Stevens of the Corps of Engineers, as follows:

Lt. W. H. Stevens has been stationed at Galveston since my inspection of him here in 1856. Since that time he has been employed in charge of the fortifications for the defense of Galveston and of the following forts: Pike, Macomb, Battery Bienvenue, Lower Dupree, Livingston, in Louisiana.[25] But recently orders have been received dated 4th Sept. for him to turn over all the works in Louisiana to Bvt. Maj. Beauregard of the Corps of Engineers, which he expects to do by the close of the month (The close of the quarter).[26] He has on account of these works, 503.17 dollars.

He has been for the same period Engineer of the Lighthouse District No. 9, which extends from the Rio Grande to the Mississippi, inclusive, and was inspector of lighthouses of the 9th District till April 1859, when Lt. Fry of the Navy relieved him.

In this period he has built and completed the following lighthouses & beacons, and closed his accounts therefor: A lighthouse in the 8th District between New Orleans and Mobile—and in the 9th District, a lighthouse at Sabine Pass, La., a lighthouse at Aransas Pass, Texas, a lighthouse at Timbalier, La., a lighthouse on screw-piles in ship shoal at sea between the mouth of the Mississippi and Galveston, a lighthouse on screw-piles on Southwest Reef at Atchafalaya Bay, La., a lighthouse on screw piles on Shell Key, La., two screw-pile lighthouses in Matagorda Bay, a lighthouse on screw-piles at Pass Christian, a lighthouse in Bolivar Point, Galveston, two beacon-lights at Pelican Spit, Galveston, a lighthouse at Corpus Christi, and raised the towers of lighthouses at Galveston and Pass Cavallo twenty five feet.[27]

He was engineer for building the customhouse in Galveston from July 1857 to July 1859.

He is member of the Board of Engineers for the defenses of Galveston & the Gulf Defenses, and has been member of the Board of Engineers for the examination of Fort McCray, Pensacola.[28]

The fortification for Galveston were commenced in this year under appropriations of 80,000 dolls in 1858 and 20,000 dolls in 1860. And to the close of June, there was expended 3652.53 dolls and a balance in his hands at that date of 1847.77 dolls. Since which he has received from the treasury, 13,000 dolls and expended to the close of August, 9628.73 dolls, and in September had expended at date, 2184.84 dolls. Thus leaving a balance in his hands of 3044.29 dolls, of which 350 dolls is in the April Treasury, and 2694.20 in cash in a safe.

All his accounts & returns appear to have been forwarded promptly. He has one office for all his duties & pays a rent of 250 dollars per annum—keeps one clerk, one overseer, & a few laborers & mechanics.

Lt. Stevens is a highly meritorious officer and has been steadily employed since my last report in constructing and raising 16 lighthouses and beacons, and in commencing the customhouse and the accumulating of materials for the fortifications of Galveston Bay.

This mode of putting down piles in quicksand without a pile driver, as practiced by him, is particularly interesting & creditable to him.

I am very Respectfully,
Your Obt. Svt.
John K. F. Mansfield
Col. & Inspt. Genl.
U.S.A.

INDIANOLA

Indianola, Texas
27th Sept 1860

Sir:

Conformably to my orders, I reached this post at 10 a. m. of the 25th instant. In the afternoon proceeded to inspect the depot here & have the honor to report to the General-in-Chief, as follows:

Quartermasters Department

At Indianola (Powder Horn) is the depot for receiving and forwarding all the supplies for the Department of Texas, with the exception of such as are sent to Brazos Saint Iago.[29] On my inspection of this depart. in 1856, it was placed at the old town of Indianola, some 4 miles westward from this point, and very inconvenient, compared with the present arrangement. It was then under the charge of Capt. W. K. Van Bokkelen, asst. quartermaster, who was relieved by Capt. R. E. Clary, asst. quartermaster, in March 1857, who was relieved by Lt. G. A. Williams, 1st Inft., in July 1857, who was relieved by Capt. A. W. Reynolds, asst. quartermaster, in March 1859, who was relieved by Lt. J. T. Shaaff, 2d Cavalry, in May 1859, who was relieved by Capt. A. W. Reynolds, asst. quartermaster, 1st Sept. 1859, who was relieved by Lt. J. P. Major, 1st March 1860, who is now in command here.

The removal of the depot to the general steamer landing, Powder Horn, was effected by Capt. Van Bokkelen before he left. The want of sufficient depth of water prevented the steamers landing at the old town. The public store houses are now very convenient to the wharf, and consist of one storehouse & yard attached, which is ample for mules, wagons, carts, & for which 100 dolls is paid per month, one commissary store for which 20 dolls is paid per month, one quartermaster's storehouse for forage for which 30 dolls is paid per month, one storehouse for which 25 dolls is paid per month, one office for which 20 dolls per month is paid, two storehouses for which 20 dolls per month is paid for each when used. Thus causing an annual rent of 2820 dolls. For the use of the wharf (which is very long here, reaching into deep water) in landing supplies, the customary charges are paid.

The supplies are necessarily stored & piled away in the yard till removed to the interior, which is done under contract made at San Antonio with G. T. Howard for the year 1860 by which he receives the articles here and transports them to the interior posts as certain specific prices, say from 1.10 dolls the 100 lbs. for 100 miles, to 2.70 dolls the 100 lbs. the 100 miles, according to the distance.[30] There is about 3,500,000 lbs. transported, hence yearly to the interior and mostly by ox teams, which move on an average 12 miles per day.

The port of Indianola on Matagorda Bay was established as a deep-water port during the Mexican War and served for thirty years as an army depot for frontier forts in western Texas. In 1856 and 1857 two shiploads of camels were landed at Indianola, which remained the second largest port in Texas until the catastrophic hurricane of September 1875 destroyed the community. (Illustration courtesy of the Library of Congress)

The quartermaster keeps here to meet emergencies, such as the transportation of the baggage of troops arriving, & c, two wagons and two mule teams of 6 mules each therefor one mule cart, two mule drays and 7 mules, in the aggregate 19 mules. He also employs a clerk at 85 dolls per month and a ration, a yard master & receiving clerk at 60 dolls & a ration, one watchman at 20 dolls & a ration, two teamsters at 20 dolls & a ration & 5 laborers at 20 dolls & a ration.

This force is ample & might on a demand for mules for public service, be reduced by one 6 mule team.

Most of the corn used in this department comes from New Orleans, and passes thru this depot & it costs delivered here, 1.25 dolls the bushel. Heretofore, large quantities of flour have passed thro' likewise, but it is presumed as contracts have been made to supply posts from mills in Texas, there will be but little more flow imported in future. There is but little quartermaster property pertaining to this post on hand, but a large amount here, ready for transportation to San Antonio. I condemned to be broken up two hind wheels, and 7 sets old running gear for transportation wagons as perfectly worthless in their present state. Fuel costs 8 dolls the cord & is brought from Corpus Christi. Capt. Reynolds turned over to Lt. Major the books and records of the depot in good order.

Lt. Major receives his funds thru Maj. D. Vinton, Chief Quartermaster at San Antonio, [and] has forwarded all his accounts and returns to the 31 August last, according to the regulations.

On the 31st August there was due the U. S., 114.56 dolls. Received since, 2000 dolls. Expended since, 426.41 dolls. Leaving a balance due U.S. of 1688.15 dolls. Of this amount, 1521.15, dolls is in the Assistant Treasury in New York, 4.12 dolls in the Assistant Treasury in New Orleans, and the balance of 162.38 dolls in cash [in] safe. He keeps the necessary invoice books, etc, to account for all the property passing thro' his hands & performs the duty very well & creditably to the service.

Subsistence Department

Lt. Major is also acting commissary of subsistence at this depot. He relieved Lt. J. T. Shaaf of the 2d Cavalry, 1st Feb. 1860, who relieved Lt. G. A. Williams, 1st Inft., on the 12th March 1859, who relieved Capt. R. E. Clary, asst. quartermaster, in June 1859, who relieved Lt. L. L. Langdon, 1st Art, in 1857, who relieved Capt. W. H. Van Bokkelen, asst. quartermaster.

Lt. Major receives his post supplies from New Orleans on special requisitions and his funds from Capt. W. B. Blair, chief of his department at San Antonio. He issues to the employees of the quartermaster's department and to such troops as require it, in passing thru this place. He pays 4 to 5 cts. the pound for fresh beef.

All his returns and papers are duly forwarded & he had in hand on the 31st August, 940.17 dolls, and has made no expenditure since. This money is in cash in a safe. He keeps one clerk at 75 dolls per month & a ration.

His supplies are all in good order except a lot that had accumulated on hand in consequence of recruits passing thru this place and turning over supplies. Accordingly, I have been obliged to condemn to be sold without delay the following articles as wholly unfit to be used, being weevily, sour, rotten & dirty, to wit: One barrel pork, 1133 pounds bacon, 18 barrels flour, 4 bushels beans, 165 pounds rice, 273 pounds hard bread, 15 pounds crushed sugar. Also to be thrown away, 22 gallons of vinegar.

Lt. Major conducts the business of this department well and creditably to the service.

I close this report with the expression of satisfaction as to the condition of the public property and interests of the service as directed by Lt. Major.

I am very Respectfully
Your Obt. Svt.
J. K. F. Mansfield
Col. & Inspt. Genl.
U.S.A.

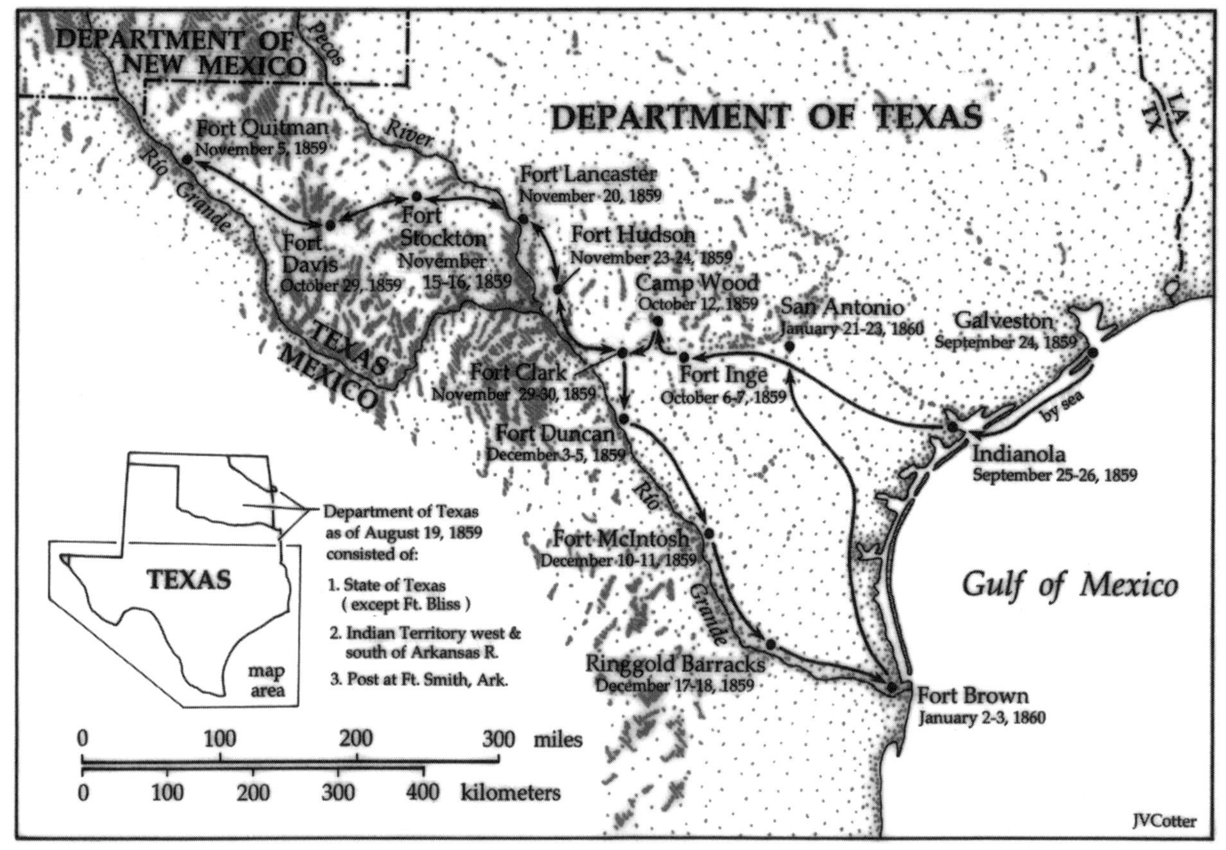

Mansfield's Inspection of the Department of Texas

FORT INGE

In Camp on the Upper
Nueces River 24 Miles
from Fort Inge, Texas
9th Oct. 1860

Sir:

I have the honor to report to the General-in-Chief that I arrived at San Antonio on the 30th ult. and deferred the inspection of the departments here, till my return from the inspection of the posts in the south and west, some time say in January next on account of the season & a more satisfactory report, after I had seen most of the posts, and left that place in the spring wagon drawn by four mules accompanied by an escort of ten privates & a sergeant of Company I, of the 1st Inft., Capt. King with three baggage wagons of 6 mules each, which transported, in addition to the baggage & forage, the escort above named & my servant. We reached Fort Inge on the morning of the 7th, and on the following day commenced and completed the inspection of that post as follows:

Fort Inge is an old post situated on the river Leona. It is 80 miles from San Antonio, about 3 miles to the southward of the village Uvalde on the same stream on the road between San Antonio and Fort Clark, 45 miles from Fort Clark, 45 miles from Camp Wood on the upper Nueces River & 70 miles from Fort Duncan. There are now no Indians about here, but in June & July last about 150 animals were driven off by the Indians from this neighborhood, & pursued by the troops into the region of the Devil's River and there lost. This post was occupied by the Mounted Rifles in 1853 when I passed thro' it en route from El Paso.[31] It was subsequently abandoned and afterwards occupied by the infantry, and finally by the present command. It is questionable whether this post is now of any importance so near the high road to El Paso, where the passing is now quite frequent, and where the Indians would be very careful not to expose themselves in this section of the country. If the country about here was of any value at all for the cultivation it would have been long since thickly settled by an agricultural community, but as it is, nothing but stock can be raised here, and not corn enough to feed the herders, so that there is an immense number of cattle to a very limited population, and of course the Indians can make a descent and drive off as many as they please, provided they escape the U.S. troops as above stated. So long therefore as the Indians exist and are in a state of starvation, just so long will this evil of their depredations continue more or less. The past summer, such was the drought that the whole country for June & July from this to the seaboard was so dry as to lose its green

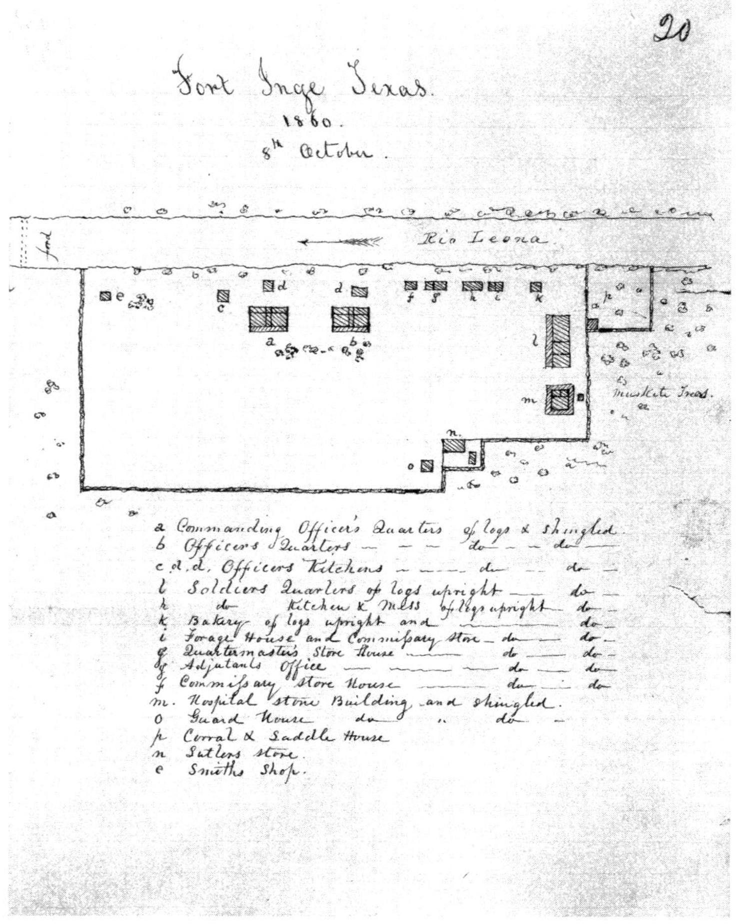

Sketch by Mansfield. (Illustration from LR, AGO, RG 94 courtesy of the National Archives)

color entirely & in some places the stock suffered severely. I need not add therefore in relation to this post that it has no garden, and I have thus written that the General-in-Chief may form an idea of the disadvantages the defence of this region of Western Texas lays under. All supplies therefore from this post except hay, wood, & water must come from abroad. A contract exists for the supply this year of flour made in this state, to the posts & the wheat for the mills in this quarter comes from Chihuahua in Mexico and the matter is yet an experiment. I doubt not, however, the posts to the northward in this state can be supplied by flour from the country about the Trinity River as I have in 1850 at Fort Belknap eaten the best of bread made of it.

Fort Inge is a rectangular enclosure, one long side of it resting on the river Leona, and the other three sides an ordinary stonewall fence. See plan hereunto appended. The quarters of the post are not sufficient to accommodate over one company, one building for the Capt. in command and one for all other officers at the post. There are log buildings, shingled, with stone chimneys, the space between timbers chinked in, no plastering nor ceiling, and floors loose boards that admit freely the water to pass thro' & the air to ascend. Each of these buildings has two rooms & two shed additions & a projecting shade roof in front & detached kitchens, one building for the soldiers wholly insufficient for a full company. It is of logs set on end on the ground & the spaces between chinked in & shingled over & a projecting roof in front for a shade. It has a stone chimney in its centre & is divided into two equal parts. The west half occupied by the present number of enlisted men with 28 bunks on a rough board floor and the east half subdivided to make an orderly sergeant's room, armory, & magazine, & a granary. There is no other building the soldiers can occupy. Their mess-hall and kitchen is a miserable hackale of logs on end & store chimney & shingled. The bakery is a worthless building of logs on end with a poor oven. The store houses of quartermaster & commissary & c, are also of the same class of logs on end chinked in & shingled but worse. The hospital is an exception to the buildings hitherto described. It is new and it being of stone with a good shingled roof and a piazza all round it being dispensary & one large ward-room. It has a detached company kitchen of logs on end & c. The guardhouse is also of stone & shingled & suitable with one prisoner's room & one cell & one guardroom. The smith's shop is a mere hackale and the corral for horses, wagons, & c, is unaccompanied by any shelter but contains a saddle house of logs on end like the other buildings. The sutler's store & house being his own are probably better than any other quarters or store houses.

This post is garrisoned by Company "C," 2d Cavalry, Capt. James Oakes commanding, who relieved Company G, 2d Cavalry, 10th February 1860, 1st Lieut. James B. Witherell present, Lt. Wm. B. Royale absent with 7 days leave since 2d June 1860, which was extended by the head of the department for 60 days & by Special Order No. 129, War Department, for 6 months.[32] This officer I understand has never served many months with his company since appointed. One sergeant, 20 privates, 3 corporals, 1 musician, aggregate 25 men, constitute the force here. Of these, 5 were on extra duty as follows: one cook & 1 attendant in hospital, 1 smith, 1 teamster, 1 baker, 1 quartermaster & commissary sergeant, 2 sick in hospital, 2 in arrest for sleeping on post since 15 August & 15 September—no court yet ordered—2 on detached service, one at Carlisle Barracks since 1st Dec. 1859, & 1 at Jefferson Barracks since 6th Jan 1860 in the Department of the West. This showing but 13 men for duty, 4 to 5 of which are required daily at the herding of the horses & mules and the balance for guard which is made up of one private & one non-commissioned officer & of this force, one is to be discharged on the 10th instant & one on the 10th December next.

Pertaining to this company, 60 horses, 5 of which inferior for the cavalry service, 71 Sharps carbines, 79 revolving belt pistols, 82 sabres, 78 bridles of different patterns, 54 saddles of different patterns, 500 Sharps ball cartridges, 500 revolving belt pistol cartridges, accouterments, & c, all serviceable. The company property was mostly boxed up for the want of new & store houses. There were but 9 privates, 3 non-commissioned officers, & 1 musician on inspection parade, two of these were recruits & the pantaloons were of both the old & new uniform. Thus there were not men enough to drill men to groom the horses. The company was reduced to this state by the expiration of the service of the men, who would not reenlist & it has not recently received recruits, one laundress only to this company.

Both Capt. Oakes & Lt. Witherell are highly meritorious & gallant officers & have distinguished themselves in the various Indian fights since they have been in this regiment. But I regret to report that Capt. Oakes cannot take the field nor mount a horse for duty now, as any extra ordinary exertion brings on a bleeding at the lungs, a complaint which his active & energetic scouts after the Indians has brought in him in connexion with his consequent suffering & exposure. He, however, can command a post and perform all other duty but that of recruiting & cavalry exercise. Discipline of his post is good.

Attached to this post are Assistant Surgeon R. L. Brodie, Hospital Steward Wilbern Grace, both unexceptionable.[33] The dispensary or wardroom records, & c, & c, in excellent order & according to the regulations. There is a hospital fund of between 5 & 6 dolls in the hands of the acting assistant commissary. Three sick in hospital & one of them from Company K, 2d Cavalry, here since 11th August last. There are 10 new bedsteads & all things ample for the sick & the post is called healthy. The time of the hospital steward expires on the 12th Dec. and he will not reenlist except for a position [in] another section of the country. An ordnance sergeant, John Pound, has been assigned to this post per general order from Washington, 28th Feb. 1860, but not yet joined. I do not see the necessity of an ordnance sergeant here. The only citizen here in the U.S. employ is a guide at 40 dolls & a ration & without troops this guide is useless.

The post & company records are properly kept. The men generally show a saving in the clothing list & the books. The following desertions: 18 in 1857, 30 in 1858, 16 in 1859. Those in 1857 deserted at Fort Clark & were mostly recruits. Those in 1858, took place at Fort Clark & Fort Cooper when under orders for Utah.

Capt. Oakes is recruiting officer & has 498 dolls cash on hand in the account in a paymasters check in Asst. Treasury at N.Y. He has a company fund of 36.48 dolls. There is no post fund, but an amount due the regimental fund of 5.40 dolls.

Quartermaster Department

The duty in this department has been performed by Lt. Witherell since 1st May 1860, when he relieved Capt. Oakes & his papers and accounts all properly forwarded, according to regulation. He had on hand in cash on 30th Sept due U.S. 2714.01 dolls & his accounts for the 3rd qtr. will be forwarded in a few days. Expended since, 200 dolls, leaving a balance on hand at date of 2554.01 dolls in cash in safe. He pays for hay 9 dolls the ton delivered, which the garrison cannot cut and has hitherto paid for wood 2.44 dolls the cord, but more is now purchased as a supply is on hand. He keeps 3 wagons, 43 mules & 4 horses. Here we see an excess of 21 mules & 4 horses beyond the regulations of the War Department General Order No. 13, June 17th 1859. I shall accordingly notify the commanding officer of this department, for at this post they certainly will not be wanting for at least one year for packs while in the field. The quartermasters store & clothing are as well stored as they can be in the miserable buildings at his disposal. One extra duty man does the clerking of his office.

Commissary Department

Lt. Witherell has also performed this duty since the 1st May & relieved Capt. Oakes. All the papers, & c, are properly forwarded to the close of September last, except his quarterly accounts & these will be sent off in a few days. There was due the U.S. on the 30th Sept., 282.80 dolls, and no expenditure since. This amount is in cash on hand. He pays for beef 7.08 cts. the pound net. All the supplies are good except a lot that had been on hand sometime & received from the infantry, rice, salt pork, flour, hardbread, pickles & hams. These were very bad and as they required overhauling, I recommended to Capt. Oakes to appoint a board of survey &

have them acted on definitively at once. The flour here used was brought from New Orleans & is good & the bread baked is fair. The same extra duty men as for the Quartermaster's Dept. does the writing of this.

Payments, & c, & c.

The troops are now paid here once in two months. No rent has been paid for the occupation of this site since the 1st January last. Under the old contract, 50 dolls per month had been paid one Daniel Murphey.[34] The title to the land seems doubtful from all I can gather here, and before rent is paid in [the] future, the ownership should be ascertained, 600 dolls per annum is a great price. The sutler of the post is Charles V. Frestoe, who keeps a suitable supply for the men & is taxed 10 cents each man for a regimental fund.[35]

With so small a force & mostly recruits there will be no military drills to test the instruction of the men. Recruits to fill up this company should be forwarded at once and [an] additional officer, a graduate, to drill them.

The large number of horses & mules & arms at his post are of no use without men to use them.

All which is Respectfully submitted
Jos. K. F. Mansfield
Col. & Inspt. Genl.
U.S.A.

CAMP WOOD

Camp on the Upper Nueces River
22 miles below Camp Wood
13th Oct. 1860.

Sir:

On the 9th instant, I left Fort Inge for Camp Wood at the head waters of the Nueces and arrived at that place on the 11th inst., & on the 12th, commenced the inspection of the same and have now the honor to report to the General-in-Chief as follows:

Camp Wood is situated on the east bank of the Nueces River, not far below the junction of three small streams forming the head of the Nueces. It was originally selected by Capt. G. W. Wallace of the 1st Inft. and named by him. The selection is very judicious. It is at the junction of many Indian trails leading down into southern Texas, & thence across the Rio Grande at Eagle Pass, & c, into Mexico. It is about 40 miles by trail from Fort Clark & about 90 miles by trail from Fort Chadbourne, & 60 miles by trail from

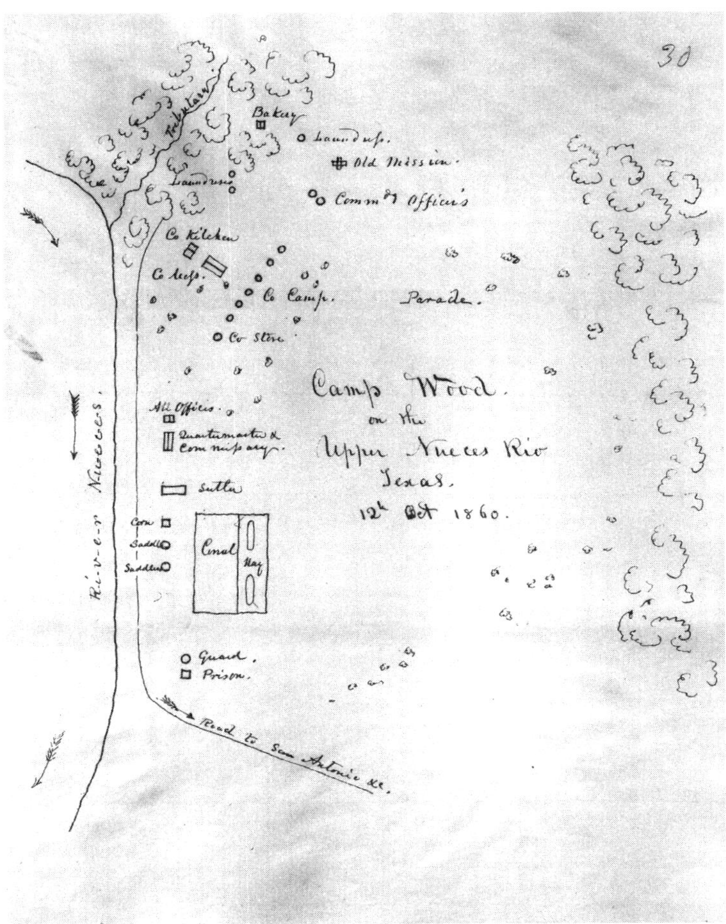

Sketch by Mansfield. (Illustration from LR, AGO, RG 94 courtesy of the National Archives)

Fort Mason. It is 45 miles from Fort Inge and 80 miles from Fort Clark by wagon road. Troops scouting east & west from this post will cross the trails of Indians moving out & into settlements and thus be enabled to capture them if possible. The whole of this upper Nueces abounds in turkey & bear and has been undoubtedly a favorite house of the wild man, who is now driven to take refuge in some other place. The site of the post is evidently the seat of an ancient Spanish mission.[36] There are the remains of a building & dam & irrigating ditch on a small tributary, which enabled them to raise vegetables. The site is high above the highest freshets and extremely picturesque, presenting to the eye an exquisite combination of mountain, hill, valley, & river.[37] The water is excellent, wood abundant of mesquite, cedar, oak, pecan, and the grass for grazing abundant & hay is cut within three miles. Add to this there is a fine prairie parade which is intermeshed with rich black loam over which cavalry can move & maneuver as well in wet weather as dry, & it is perfectly healthy here. The road to it, however, follows a large Indian trail & crosses the Nueces four times and the crossings are difficult for loaded wagons, & in high water impossible. A road undoubtedly can be laid out at little expense to keep on the east side of the river all the way. I therefore shall recommend such a road to the commanding officer of this department. There can be no garden here, without great labor to irrigate. But for the want of seasonable rains this valley would be studded with farms & the dead trees that are now interspersed among the living, would not be seen. In August last an avalanche of water descend this valley, which left its drift 40 feet above the present height of the water & many feet in parts of the road for miles as high as the tops of our wagons. Of course all provisions for the troops here are brought from San Antonio & the corn for the horses now comes from Mexico, 30 miles south of the Rio Grande. (See plan of the post herewith.)

After the infantry had been ordered away, the post was occupied by Company "K," 2d Cavalry, Lt. J. B. Hood at the time in command on the 21st January 1860, and has been held since. The command now is Company "K," 2d Cavalry, Capt. Chas. J. Whiting. Lt. J. B. Hood left on leave 4 September last, and since ordered to duty at West Point, Lt. J. P. Major, on detached service at Indianola since December 1859, as assistant quartermaster, 4 sergeants, 4 corporals, 1 musician, 1 farrier & blacksmith, 40 privates. Of these, 1 sergeant & 1 private absent on leave at San Antonio, 1 private absent sick in hospital at Fort Inge. The force at command therefore was 47 enlisted men who were accounted for at inspection as follows, 3 sergeants, 3 corporals, 1 bugler, 1 farrier, 1 orderly & 23 privates present, 4 sick, 3 confined, 3 privates & 1 corporal on guard, 2 company cooks, 2 express men. The company passed in review and were inspected & found in uniform, except 2 men with light blue pants. They were well armed with Sharps carbines & sabre & Colts navy size revolver, in good serviceable order. The revolvers, however, were not on parade for want of holsters which were expected soon. The saddles & bridles were good. The saddles being of the Texian tree & much liked. There were no valises & sword knots, & spurs, & canteens, & haversacks, & blankets knots were deficient, but a requisition had been made. The horses of the command, 68, were in good order, except 8 which I commended as unserviceable for cavalry, one having had a sore back for two years & the others broken down.

Capt. Whiting took this company thro' so much of the drill of the platoon as they could perform. The movements by fours & twos, & the right about, & the forming time to the front, & on the right and the wheel in circle. He declined to take them thro' the sword exercise, as there were many recruits among them, & they had not been drilled at it. The company dismounted, fired at the standard target 6' x 22" at 150 yards and 22 men made 7 hits with one round each, equal to 1 in 3, and with the revolver, one round each at 50 yards, 27 men made 47 hits out of 162, say 1 to 3½ .

The company books & records were in good order. There were 26 discharged in 1860, 11 desertions in 1857, 14 in 1858, & none in 1859. (A very favorable comparison with Company C at Fort Inge, in this particular.) There was a company fund of 68.58 dolls but no post nor regimental fund. There are 3 laundresses to the company, pertaining to the company were 85 Sharps carbines, 78 Colts pistols, 85 cavalry swords, 85 saddles & bridles, 10,000 Sharps ball cartridges, 10,500 Colts pistol ball cartridges. The company were in Sibley tents, elevated about 4½ feet above the ground on posts set endwise.[38] The company stores were also in Sibley tents like elevated & the men were comfortably accommodated. Capt. Whiting's tent was the same. The company mess hall [was] simply a canvas shade [with] a ridge pole & kitchen the same with a stone chimney. Bakery & laundresses in like manner. Bread good & oven of stone. The guard house was a Sibley tent elevated in the same way & a stone prison house in rear with two cells. The guard was 4 strong & 1 non-commissioned officer & one sentinel only over the corral & animals. The corral was about being completed of oak posts on end all around & a hay yard in which a large supply of hay was being stacked for the winter. The quartermaster's and commissary's store & the adjutants, & c, offices were of upright logs & canvas roofs. The corn house the same & the saddle house & saddler's shop, Sibley tents mounted on upright logs like the others. There were three prisoners under guard, one undergoing sentence, and two for sleeping on post, 1st Sept. & 17 August, and charges preferred, but no court ordered yet.

The hospital was an hospital tent, which contained the dispensary, sick in wooden bunks & was well provided with the necessaries. It was in charge of a regularly appointed hospital steward, W. C. Foster, who was competent.

Capt. Whiting has performed the duties of asst. quartermaster since 1st September last. All his papers & returns to the close of September had been forwarded. His account current showed a balance due the U.S. as follows: received of Lt. Hood, 6437.87 dolls. Expended since, 3094.68 dolls leaving a balance of 3343.46 dolls. The actual payment, however, was not so much by 2106.25 dolls, which he informed me was still due Mr. Stratton, a contractor. He had paid him 837.68 dolls in an amount due him of 2943.93 dolls and was waiting to hear from the Assistant Treasurer in N.Y. to whom he had remitted a draft for 6000 dolls from Maj. David H. Vinton, Chief Quartermaster at San Antonio, being a part of the amount reported received from Lt. Hood, above, before he could give him a check for the balance. This is contrary to the regulations and I called his attention to the regulations & it will probably not occur again. No further notice need be taken in this matter as I feel confident it was done with no improper notice & will be all right so soon as he hears for the assistant treasurer. Capt. Whiting has no taste for accounts & papers, but is strictly honorable & honest in all of them. He pays 15 dolls the ton for hay & 2.16 dolls the bushel for corn, delivered at 56 lbs to the bushel. Corn is brought from Naver in Mexico via Eagle Pass.[39] He keeps 3 wagons, 18 team mules, & 26 pack mules. The pack mules are indispensable to a scout. There are no citizens in the quartermaster's employ except Richard Hopkins, a guide at 40 dolls per month & a ration per day. An extra duty man does the duty of Quartermaster Sergeant & another of clerk.

Capt. Whiting is also acting assistant commissary since the 1st September last & all his returns & accounts have been forwarded to the 30th September. At that date there was due the U.S., 307.77 dolls, which is in cash in a trunk in his quarters. He pays for fresh beef, 9½ cts. the lb. net. All other supplies are brought from San Antonio. The same extra duty men as for the quartermaster's dept. do the duty of commissary sergeant & clerk.

Capt. Whiting is also recruiting officer & has on hand in that account in cash, 207 dolls. The troops were last paid to the 31st August by Maj. Daniel McClure paymaster, thro' the sutler as deputy.

Daniel C. Richardson has been sutler since 14th Feb. & keeps a good supply of goods. A scout takes place from this post once a month, and as it crosses the trails leading north & south, pack mules are the only means of transporting supplies.

I have to remark in conclusion, the discipline is good, but this company wants drilling, and the regulations forbid a post being left without two officers, very properly and it is impossible for one officer to perform all duties of this post & drill the men & command the scouts.

It is also a bad system for paymasters to appoint sutlers as substitutes to pay off the men. There are many reasons why it should not be done & most prominent is the indebtedness of the men to the sutler.

Complaint was made that the material of the new uniform, dark blue pants, is not so durable as the old light blue pants of the old uniform. I shall probably hear more of this at other posts.

All which is Respectfully Submitted
Jos. K. F. Mansfield
Col. & Inspt. Genl.
U.S.A.

FORT DAVIS

In Camp at Dead-Mans-hole[40]
en routeto Fort Quitman, Texas
31st Oct. 1860.

Sir:

My last report was the inspection of Camp Wood on the upper Nueces, which post I left on the 9th Oct. I have since travelled steadily along, calling at Forts Clark, Hudson, Lancaster, & Stockton, and passing on to Fort Davis, which place I reached on the 28th Oct., and as my mules required shoeing & rest, I commenced the following day the 29th & inspected that post and have to report to the General-in-Chief as follows:

Fort Davis has been established several years. It is located at the Limpia, so called, say 455 miles from San Antonio & in a canon very pleasantly situated and is a very important post to hold in connexion with the overland mail & emigrants, as a resting place, unmolested by Indians. In short it should not be abandoned & should be a two company post on account of the necessity for escorts & being on one of the great cross trails of the Indians into Mexico over the Presidio del Norte. I inspected the post in 1856 when there were 6 companies, 8th Inft., here stationed, under the command of Col. W. Seawell.[41] It has since been inspected by Acting Inspector General Jos. E. Johnson on 22d Oct 1859. It is 80 miles from Fort Stockton & 121 miles from Fort Quitman.

This post is temporarily under the command of Lieut. J. J. Van Horn of Company "G," 8th Inft. attached to Company "H," 8th Inft. commanded by Brevet Lt. Col. J. V. Bomford, who assumed command of this post, 1st July 1860, but has been absent since 18th September at Fort Bliss on a court martial & has taken with him a detachment of his command.

The whole force now appointed at this post consists of Company "H." Bvt. Col. Bomford absent as above, 1st Lt. Wm. McE. Dye detached as regimental quartermaster at Head Quarters San Antonio, 2d Lt. John G.

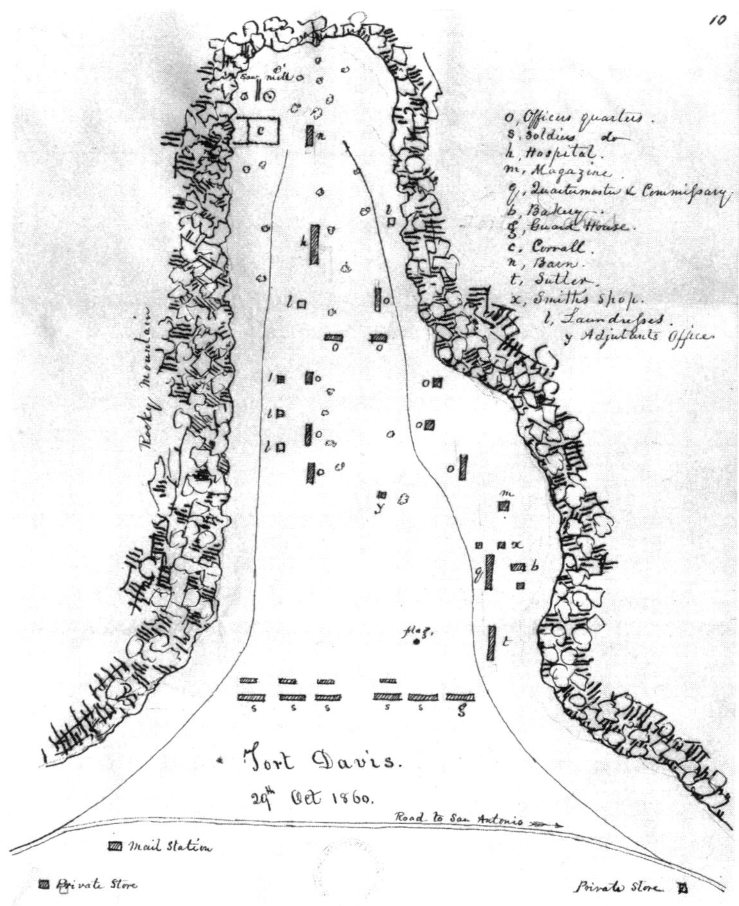

Sketch by Mansfield. (Illustration from LR, AGO, RG 94 courtesy of the National Archives)

Taylor left at Fort Quitman in command of two sergeants, one corporal & 19 privates (one of which is confined), waiting to be relieved, one corporal, 1 musician, 7 privates, with Lt. Col. Bomford as above, two corporals, 1 musician, 19 privates present for duty of which 1 corporal & 9 privates were on extra daily duty, 3 privates confined, leaving but one corporal, 1 musician & 6 privates for military duty proper. One private at Fort Columbus since 10th July 1860, & 2 privates at San Antonio on detached service, one private absent confined at San Antonio since 27th August 1860. One private on furlough since 1st May last, one on furlough since 28th August last, & one on furlough since 6 Oct. last. Thus showing of Company "H," 3 officers & 37 men absent, and 22 men present in the aggregate 59 enlisted men. To this company is attached 1 officer, Lt. Van Horn, & 1 sergeant & 7 privates of Company "G," which was broken up & of these, one is absent on detached service & 2 on extra daily duty, & 1 in arrest, leaving 1 sergeant & 3 men for military duty proper. Thus the available force is 1 officer & 29 men.

On inspection parade there were but 10 men inclusion of 1 sergeant, 2 corporals & 1 musician. The residue of the force was accounted for as follows: 1 corporal & 3 men on guard, 6 confined, 4 herders with the beef cattle, 2 teamsters detached, 1 smith & 2 in hospital. There are 4 laundresses to this company.

There was also temporarily here, two in hospital & one on extra duty. On this staff Asst. Surgeon DeWitt C. Peters & Hospital Steward Carl E. Borgguest.

The aggregate present therefore was 1 officer, 1 asst. surgeon & 33 enlisted men. A force so small combined with sick and prisoners & other demands of the service as to compel the men to go on guard every other day. On this account it would have been better if Col. Bomford had taken the Overland Mail instead of an escort to Fort Bliss. The force is too small to maintain discipline. On one occasion recently, the corporal & almost the entire guard were drunk & in such cases, where is the force to execute & enforce orders? Lieut. Van Horn is a highly meritorious officer & performs the duty well, but there are two whiskey shops within 500 yards of the post, one east and the other west, & men that will get drunk can get drunk. In a few days it is expected Lt. Taylor will arrive from Fort Quitman with that detachment, which will greatly strength[en] the command.

I was unable to see the armament & equipment of Company "H" as Col. Bomford had taken off his return with him and there was no one to give an account of it. The few men on inspection were in full uniform and armed with the rifled musket. No drills of course were attempted. The company books were in order but the company fund book, Col. Bomford had also taken them. There were 4 men discharged in 1859 and 33 in 1860, & 16 recruits joined last March. There were 4 desertions in 1857, 6 in 1858, 9 in 1859, and 11 in 1860. The orderly sergeant (attached) of Company G was present & I condemned sundry articles of camp & garrison equipage, & c, worn out, for which Lt. Van Horn was accountable. He had also a "G" Company fund of 204.25 dolls in cash.

The post ordinance I am unable to speak of with certainty as the post ordnance return had been taken off by Col. Bomford. There were, however, on the parade two mountain howitzers & one 6 pounder field piece, all bronze, with caissons complete & in good order, covered by tarpaulins.

There was in the magazine a large supply of ammunition made up and some arms boxed up with sets of harness for the artillery & apparently in good order. The magazine was of stone & shingled roof, but I regard it as very unsafe although it stands alone & some 50 yards from any other building. If the roof were to take fire, no body would go near it. The roof should be raised & an adoby covering be interposed to guard against fire.

The guard consisted of one corporal, 3 privates. They occupy one of the stone buildings for company quarters, within which has been built a prison room & 3 cells. One sentinel only is kept over the quartermaster & commissary store & magazine. For a post of this magnitude in this locality, I regard it insufficient. There were 6 prisoners, 2 undergoing sentence, 1 temporarily confined, 2 drunk on guard & charges made out, & 1 for trading public mules. James Conway, sentenced to hard labor for 12 months, complained to me that his time had expired 18th September last & wished his discharge. I stated the law would hold him till his sentence had expired but that I would mention the case to the General-in-Chief. This man was the corporal of the guard at the time the men of "G" company took from the guard a citizen & hung him. Will the General-in-Chief examine into this case?

The hospital is a worthless building of posts set on end, and chinked in, & rotten, & thatched roof, & rough floors, & braced outside, but will soon fall down or be blown down. Another should be provided immediately. I would recommend that one of the stone soldier's quarters be taken down (see plan of the post hereunto attached) and the material used in erecting a suitable building for a hospital. This will leave 4 others ample for two companies, & their kitchen & one for the guard as it now is. The hospital has been under the charge of Asst. Surgeon DeWitt C. Peters (a very excellent officer) since the 17th May last & he has a good hospital steward & is well supplied in every way, except as above. I regard the building & all the parts attached to it as less, & kitchen, & c, & c, as worthless & dangerous. The records, & c, are in excellent order & the post healthy. There are 22 iron bedsteads & one nurse, one cook & one matron, & a fund of only 62 cents. The temperature in June, July, & August at 2 P.M. averaged from 68° to 98°. For the seven months from March to September, 214 days, there were 32 slight showers. This post is about 4000 feet above the sea & its temperature accordingly in connexion with its latitude.

The post bakery is of stone & a good stone oven, but thatched roof. There is outside of it an extra oven. The baker, however, has never served a regular trade at the business & this may account in some measure for the indifferent bread.

The adjutant's office is a small building made of slates on end & store chimney & thatched roof.

The officers' quarters are all of logs on end & chinked-in with thatched roofs & rough floors. In number they are ample & to spare. The great number of them marked in the plan (see plan herewith) was caused by a large force of 6 companies having been stationed here. They are valueless except for temporary purposes. The soldiers quarters are of stone with thatched roofs but no glass windows & stone & dirt floors. The roofs should be shingled and glass windows put in to make them comfortable. There are 5 of these buildings, four of them have kitchen attached, that are mere hackalls & about falling down & should be taken down & burnt for fire wood. For a two company post it would be best to make each alternate building a kitchen & mess & the 5th one should be taken down & the store used in erecting a hospital.

The quartermaster's department has been under the charge of Lt. Van Horn since 1st July 1860. He relieved Lt. W. McE. Dye. His quarterly & monthly papers to the 30th Sept. have all been forwarded. At that date there was due the U.S., 2023.94 dolls, & expended since, 75 dolls. The balance, 1948.94 dolls, is covered by a check on and of Maj. David H. Vinton on the Assist. Treasurer at San Antonio for 2000 dolls. The quartermaster supplies are in the 2d story of a good & new stone building, shingled roof, in which is his office and all in excellent order. Some supplies, & c, & c, are in one of the vacant soldiers' quarters. He keeps an extra duty man as clerk & one as quartermaster sergeant, 1 as smith, 3 as teamsters, 2 herders & one citizen guide at 80 dolls per month & a ration per day. There are 43 mules on his return, 26 of which were in San Antonio with Lt. Col. Seawell not yet receipted for, leaving 17 for garrison purposes. In addition he has 22 pack mules & 1 donkey. These he has received orders to send to San Antonio on the 1st opportunity. He also has 7 wagons on his return, 4 of which he has received no receipt for from Lt. Col. Seawell who took them to San Antonio, 1 horse cart. He pays for wood, 4½ dolls the cord, for hay, 23.49 dolls the ton, for corn, 3.47 dolls the fanega of 154 lbs. There prices are reasonable. His funds he receives from Major Vinton, chief quartermaster at San Antonio. At present, two teamsters & wagons are absent with Brevet Lt. Col. Bomford. A good & safe corral and stable for mules & horses at the upper end of the canon and a mule power saw mill at present out of order. A temporary saddler's shop & a stone smith's shop with adobe roof. He pays 300 dolls per annum to the owners of the land on which this post is built.

Lt. Van Horn has been acting assistant commissary from the 1st July last & relieved Lt. Wm. McE. Dye. All his quarterly and monthly papers in this account to the close of September have been forwarded. On the 30th September there was due the U.S. 3911.27 dolls, & no expenditures since. This amount was in Maj. D. H. Vintons check on the Assistant Treasurer, N.Y., for 2000 dollars, & Capt. W. B. Blair's check on Asst. Treasury, San Antonio, for 330 dolls, and Lt. W. McE. Dye's check on Assistant Treasury, N.Y. for 1242.68 dolls, and the balance in cash in a safe. He buys beef cattle in the herd at 4.44 dolls the 100 lbs on the hoof, the net cost about 5 cts, has on hand 226 beeves. The supplies are good, well stored, & in excellent order. The flour is quite dark and not such as should be furnished. It is made of Mexican wheat. He keeps as clerk the same extra duty man as the clerk of the quartermaster department and four extra duty men as herders. Flour costs about 9½ cts the lb. delivered. All other supplies except beef come from San Antonio, & he receives his funds from Capt. W. B. Blair, chief of the commissary department at San Antonio. All supplies are stored in the 1st story of a stone building which is used in the 2d story for quartermaster supplies & for an office of both departments. This duty is well performed by Lt. Van Horn.

There was a tolerable garden the past season, effected after much labor in digging well holes to obtain water by buckets for the plants, in a location in the creek bottom about a mile distant. The two other locations in former years having proved failures.

Alexander Young is the sutler of this post and keeps it well supplied with all the requisitions for the troops & gives satisfaction.[42]

Water for the supply of the garrison is brought about [i] mile (from the creek) and keeps one 4 mule team constantly at work.

All which is Respectfully Submitted
Jos. K. F. Mansfield
Col. & Inspt. Gen'l.
U.S.A.

FORT QUITMAN

In Camp on the Rio Grande, Texas
5 miles below Fort Quitman
7 Nov. 1860

Sir:

The last post I inspected was Fort Davis. On the 3rd inst. I reached Fort Quitman, and on Monday the 5th, commenced my inspection of that post & have to submit to the General-in-Chief as follows:

Fort Quitman is situated on the Rio Grande about 85 miles below El Paso and five miles above where the road from the east first strikes the river & 116 miles from Fort Davis, and is about 3700 feet above the sea. It was established about September 1858 by Capt. A. T. Lee, Company "C," 8th Inft., by the orders of the commanding officer of this department. It is planned as to the arrangements of the buildings, & c, for a two company post (see plan hereunto annexed), but one company is ample for this position on the frontier. The principal buildings are of adobes & of adobe roofs, & glass windows, but earthen floors, and most of them leak when it rains hard, and are ample for a one company post as they stand in all respects, with but trifling exception hereafter to be mentioned. The wood in this vicinity is cottonwood, which grows all along the banks of the river bottom as far as the eye can see. But the wood used at the garrison to burn are the roots of the mesquite which are dug out of the ground, there being no other kinds of wood here.[43] It is a remarkable fact in relation to this bush, that the roots are quite large, when the top is but a small bunch. The mesquite in certain parts of Texas grows large & is an excellent fire wood.

There is no grazing of consequence in this immediate vicinity and not enough for the commissary beef cattle.

It is to be regretted this post was not established where the road first strikes the Rio Grande from the east as that point is the first water west of Eagle Spring, 33 miles distant & here the emigrant & traveller first wants protection in rushing to the water. The Indians could cut off such parties now, in spite of Fort Quitman, 5 miles off. There is more wood and grazing, and in my opinion a safer & better seat for the fort against freshets at the point mentioned. The road from where it first strikes the Rio Grande to Fort Quitman is along the bottomlands & sandy & heavy to travel over and I am told it rains oftener here and above the fort, than at the seat of the fort. This may be owning to the proximity of a mountain to Fort Quitman. Now that the post is here, I think a reconnaissance for a road direct from the mouth of the canon (some 6 miles from the river) to Fort Quitman should be made, & if practicable, the road be opened by the garrison. This would save perhaps 5 miles in the route to El Paso. Will the General-in-Chief order such a reconnaissance made by the officers of the post?

I recommended in 1853 the establishment of a post at the point where the road from the east first strikes the Rio Grande. The mail station has since been placed there, some 2 or 3 men only to keep it.

Capt. A. T. Lee & company were relieved in the command of this post on the 18th June 1859 by Bvt Lt. Col. J. V. Bomford commanding Company

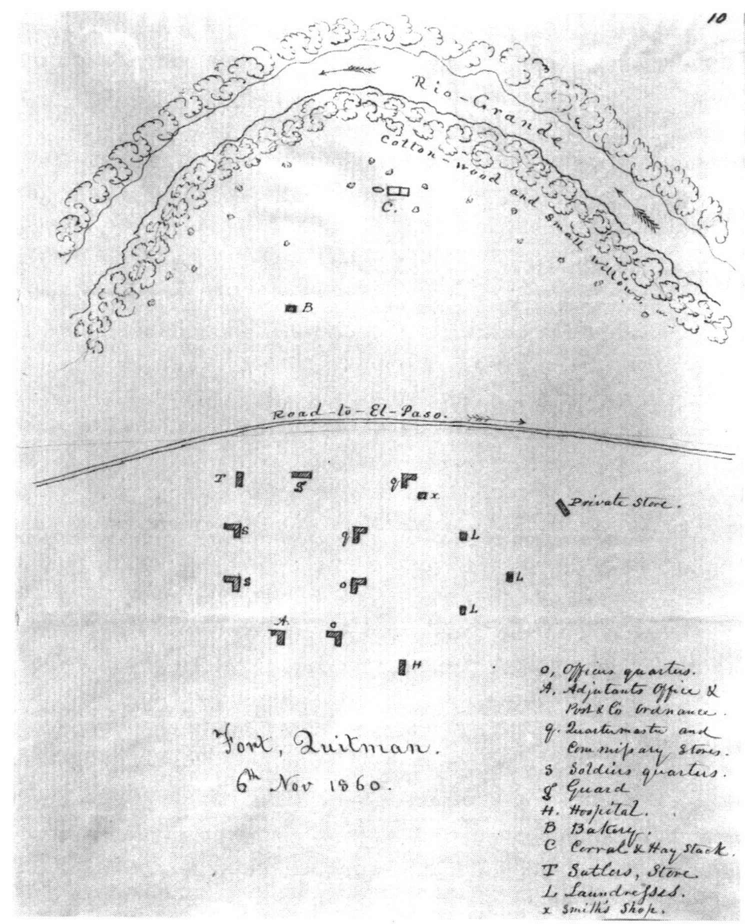

Sketch by Mansfield. (Illustration from LR, AGO, RG 94 courtesy of the National Archives)

"H," 8th Inft. Lt. Col. Bomford left a detachment of his company under the command of Lt. J. G. Taylor, when he was ordered to garrison Fort Davis, and Lt. Taylor was finally relieved by Lt. E. D. Blake on the 27 Oct. 1860, and I found Lt. Blake with Company "F," 8 Inft., in command & Lt. Taylor & detachment had left.

Capt. Robt. P. Maclay of Company "F" was absent with leave, 2d Lt. W. B. Hazen absent with leave, 4 sergeants, 3 corporals, 1 musician, 45 privates. To which add 7 privates of Company "G" attached, & we have one officer & 63 enlisted men in the aggregate to which must be added the hospital steward. Of these enlisted men, 9 were in confinement, 1 absent sick at Fort Duncan, 2 sick in quarters, 1 on detached service at Fort Bliss, 1 absent sick at Fort Davis, 1 herder, 2 cooks, 1 baker, 1 sergeant & 6 men on guard, leaving 38 enlisted men who appeared on inspection parade. These men were completely armed & equipped for the field, with new knapsacks, canteens, haversacks, and their arms in excellent order, with the fatigue uniform & caps. Having just arrived from a march from Fort McIntosh, they could not appear in full uniform. Lieut. Blake took them thro' the manual which was well performed. They however could not go thro' the manual of the bayonet exercise, not having been drilled at it. They went thro' the movements of the light infantry drill well & as skirmishers tolerably. At the target, 6' x 22" & at 100 yards, 25 men, one round each, made 15 hits, & at 200 yards, 6 hits, about 60 & 24 percent hits, which was better than I expected. There were recruits among them & they all required drilling.

The company property was well cared for & the books & records in order. There were 19 desertions in 1859 & 13 in 1860. The records of desertions in 1857 & 1858, I presumed were not fully written up from the appearance of the book. 33 recruits joined in 1860 & 29 men were discharged in 1860. Pertaining to the company were 5 old muskets, 83 rifled muskets, 2500 musket rifle ball cartridges, & 2000 blank cartridges, 72 knapsacks, 58 haversacks, 58 canteens. There were 4 laundresses to the company and there was a company fund of 93.42 dolls in the hands of Lt. Blake.

I commend to be turned into the Ordnance Department as unserviceable 6 tompiers, 6 screwdrivers, 1 musicians sword belt & flag, and to be turned in to the quartermasters dept., 33 tent knapsacks as unserviceable. Altho' new the material was so rotten as to be ragged & worthless. Relative to these tent knapsacks, as they were an experiment, it is a pity the material was not good. They were provided with stout straps, & c. Also to be dropped, 55 canteens, 40 haversacks, 14 knapsacks, 3 numbers, 1 letter, 1 cap bugle, 11 eagles, 20 spades, as worn out.

The company was quartered in a good adobe building, but it had no bunks & there were no means of making them, as there was not lumber enough to make coffins. The mess & kitchen was an L in the same building, but no benches for the men to sit down. The non-commissioned offices had a mess by themselves in an adjacent building. There should be lumber furnished & these deficiencies supplied at once. It is remarkable that two years have elapsed since the post was commenced & no bunks nor benches yet. Much depends on the energy of the commander. Lt. Blake will probably soon supply these deficiencies. He complains that he has repeatedly written for blank discharges for his men but has not received them.

This company last paid by Paymaster McClure to the 31 August at Fort McIntosh, but this post is paid by a paymaster of the Department of New Mexico.

The post records are in order in the adjutant's office, which is a good adobe building & adobe roof & earth floor. This is also the company's office and the same building is the armory of the company & post and contains the ammunition, with 6 Colts revolvers, 8000 musket ball cartridges, 1082 Colts pistol cartridges, belonging to the post.

The clerk is a daily duty man & there has been no post fund since 31st August last. Lt. Blake has a post recruiting fund of 30 dolls & a company recruiting fund of 453 dolls. These are covered by a treasury warrant on N.Y. for 500 dolls.

The hospital is also an adobe building and under one roof is the dispensary, store room, steward's room, ward & kitchen & mess. This in excellent order in every respect, under the direction of a regular hospital steward, James Mason. There was no assistant surgeon here as Asst. Surgeon R. O. Abbott has been absent sick since 30th June 1859 & will be till the 1 December 1860. One cook an extra duty man & a matron. There was no sick. All the records were very neatly kept by the steward. There were 11 iron bedsteads & medicines, & c, ample, & there was a small hospital fund of 25.63 dolls in the hands of the acting commissary of subsistence. The register shows 2 small showers in January last, 4 in Feb, 0 in March, 2 in April, 1 in May, 3 in June, 9 in July, 4 in August, 6 in Sept. 2 in October, & in September, 2 large showers. The temperature in May at 2 P.M. ranged from 71° to 90,° in June from 82° to 95,° in July from 82° to 94,° in August from 71° to 93.° There is freezing weather in winter occasionally.

The guard house is an adobe building, & ample except the prison rooms & 6 cells. They are made of adobes & are of trifling consideration. The guard is 1 sergeant & 6 privates, & 1 sentinel placed at the guard house, & one at the corral, which is say 500 yards off & nearer the river. It would not be difficult to kill the sentinel with an arrow and drive the mules over the river. There were 8 prisoners, two undergoing sentence, 1 for desertion & 5 minor offenses.

The duty of assistant commissary of subsistence has been performed by Lt. Blake since the 1st inst, when he relieved Lt. Taylor. As yet of course he has made no returns. His supplies are good & ample with the exception of 739 lbs. [of] hard bread which was so destroyed by the weevils that I condemned it to be fed to the beef cattle or thrown away & there was a large quantity somewhat damaged by weevils & his flour is not what it should be. He has a very large supply of hard bread, rice & bacon on hand, and 40 beef cattle which were poor for want of good grass, and I recommended they be fed, and beef hereafter be procured by contract ready butchered. Beef costs about 4¾ cents the lb. net. The supplies were stored in adobe buildings & in good order & state of preservation. He received from Lt. Taylor, 607.42 dolls of which 504.85 dolls was in Assistant Treasury in New Orleans, & 92.57 dolls in cash. An extra duty man does his clerking & issuing in connexion with the quartermaster's department, & he employs, two extra duty men as herders.

The post bakery is a mean little hackale attached to a poor oven made of adobes. There was not room enough for the baker to lay down in it. Lt. Blake ordered an old Sibley tent to be pitched for the baker. The bread is ordinary.

The duty of assistant quartermaster has been performed by Lt. Blake since the 1st inst. He relieved Lt. Taylor. He has the same clerk & sergeant as in the commissary department and occupies the same two buildings but separate apartments. All the property is well stored & cared for. His supplies are ample except a deficiency of mules shoes. He pays 6.75 dolls the cord for wood (mesquite roots), 20 dolls the ton for hay of which he has about 15 tons on hand, & 7 dolls the fanega or 145 lbs for corn, which is high. There are 3 teamsters & one smith extra duty men & a guide at 30 dolls per month and a ration per day, has 21 mules & 3 wagons. The corral is badly fenced of bushes & the hay is stacked & there is a small adobe smith's shop sufficient for the command. He received of Lt. Taylor 2364.42 dolls in cash which is in a safe in his quarters.

There is no garden at this post & no prospect of one for want of seasonable rains and there is no facility for irrigation. All supplies except fresh beef, hay, corn & flour come from the Atlantic states, and funds are received thro' the chiefs of departments at San Antonio. Alexander Young is the sutler & keeps a suitable supply for the men & officers, and also keeps the Overland Mail post office & the mails pass up & down twice a week.

The discipline is good. There seems to be no owner for the land on which the posts is built, and some hackales are a little too close to the garrison.

There are no Indians in this vicinity, but they sometimes travel over this region & will commit depredations when opportunity presents.

All which is Respectfully Submitted
Jos. K. F. Mansfield
Col. & Inspt. Gen'l.
U.S.A.

FORT STOCKTON

Escondido Creek[44] 24 miles east of Fort Stockton 17th Nov 1860

Sir:

My last report was the inspection of Fort Quitman, dated 7th Nov inst. On the morning of the 15th, I reached Fort Stockton and in the afternoon commenced the inspection of that post, and have now to submit to the General-in-Chief the following:

Fort Stockton was established by order of the commanding officer of this department, dated 13th January 1859, & the buildings commenced about March of that year by Lt. J. P. Sherburne of Company "H," 1st Inft. Capt. S. D. Carpenter. It was located at Comanche Springs, very judiciously. For it is here the Overland Mail via Fort Chadbourne and the mail from San Antonio meet, and this too has been one of the great resorts of the Indians to commit murders & depredations on travellers and in Mexico. The springs here are numerous, clear & beautiful, and are the sources of Comanche Creek, which runs off in the direction of Fort Chadbourne for some miles & finally sinks. It is also judiciously seated on a plateau about 40 feet above the springs and commands the ground within a mile, & is but a few rods from the water (see plan hereunto appended). It is 87 miles from Fort Lancaster & 80 miles from Fort Davis. Capt. Carpenter assumed command of his company 23rd October 1859, after two of the buildings had been mostly completed. The buildings are all of adobes, with the exception of the Guard House, which is of stone, and all thatched roofs. It is one of the best built and arranged company posts I have seen in the service & made essentially out of the mud, water, & grass on the spot, and is highly creditable to Captain Carpenter & his company. I understand it to be the 3rd or 4th post this company has been chiefly instrumental in erecting & now it is under orders to proceed to Camp Cooper, as soon as relieved by a company of the 8th Inft. from Ringgold Barracks. Capt. Carpenter has been untiring in his efforts for a garden & has finally succeeded in one located on the creek & so arranged as not to require irrigation, by ditching & diking to connect with the creek. He raised some melons, corn, squash, pumpkins, & c, for his men. He has also a beef cattle corral very judiciously made, by ditching & diking across a bend in the creek so as to require no fencing.

The garrison now here is Company "H," 1st Inft., Capt. S. D. Carpenter, 1st Lt. Walter Jones, 2d Lt. J. P. Sherburne on leave of absence from 3rd May 1860, for 60 days, afterwards extended four months, and on detached service since 12th Oct. 1860 by special orders from head quarters of the Army, 4 sergeants, 4 corporals, 2 musicians, 59 privates, in the aggregate 69 enlisted men. Of them, one is on furlough for 2½ months from 15th Sept. last & one for four months from Oct. 15 (last). Leaving 2 officers & 67 men available. To these add a deserter, and 2 men waiting the arrival of the company from Ringgold Barracks, casually at the post, and the staff Assistant Surgeon E. P. Langworthy & Hospital Steward, Patrick Duffy, for the whole command present as follows, 3 officers & 71 enlisted men.

On inspection parade there were 4 sergeants, 3 corporals, 2 musicians, 44 privates, the captain, & lieut. & assistant surgeon, in the aggregate 3 officers & 53 men. The residue were accounted for as follows: 1 corporal & 7 men on guard, 5 prisoners, 1 sick in hospital, 1 cook in hospital, 2 cooks in quarters, & 1 hospital steward.

The company were in full uniform, with knapsacks, canteens, haversacks complete, & their arms and accoutrements in excellent order. They passed in review at quick & double quick time. Went thro' the manual of arms, & the manual of the whole bayonet exercise well, and drilled at the light infantry, and at skirmishes well, and at the target of 6' x 22," 48 men, one round each, at 100 yards, made 30 hits, say 62½ percent; at 200 yards made 20 hits, say 40 percent, at 300 yards made 7 hits, say 14½ percent. There were but 7 snaps of the tape primer out of 144 and the balls held up well. This shows a vast improvement on my previous experience at the target, and that the gun, ball & powder were well proportioned to each other and the men well instructed.

The soldiers were quartered in two buildings and were comfortably provided with double bunks on an earthen floor, the best for this locality, and a mess room and kitchen sufficient and in good order. The non-commissioned officers had a separate mess table. There were 4 laundresses & a hospital matron to the command, well & neatly lodged in little separate buildings by themselves, with their children which indicated contentment in their positions. They were the loves of the soldiers.

The company books were all in order and written up, 20 discharges in 1860, 7 desertions in 1857, 1 in 1858, 2 in 1859, 4 in 1860. It is rarely a company has so few desertions. I think it a test in some measure of a judicious discipline. There was a company fund of 675.63 dollars in cash in the hands of the captain. The company ordnance & c, was in a room, a part of one of the soldier's quarters & well cared for. Pertaining to the company were 69 serviceable & 9 unserviceable rifled muskets, 1 Sharps rifle, 5 Colts pistols, 6900 rifle musket ball cartridges, 440 Sharps ball cartridges, 3800 Colts pistol cartridges, 500 Harpers Ferry rifle ball cartridges, 2700 blank cartridges, & camp & garrison equipage & c, & c, ample, & in good condition, excepting

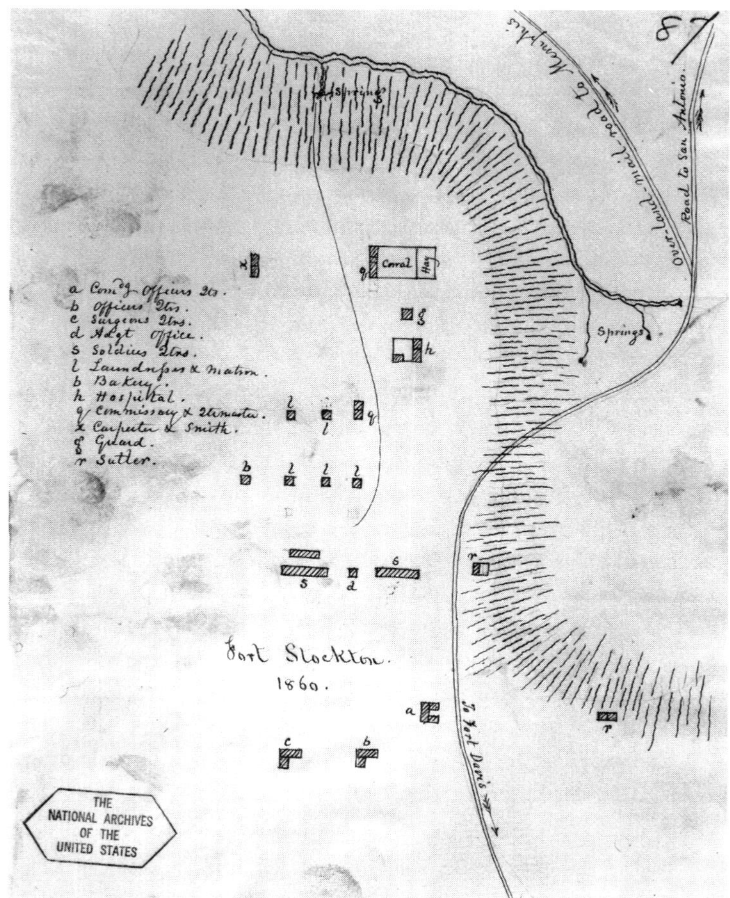

Sketch by Mansfield. (Illustration from LR, AGO, RG 94 courtesy of the National Archives)

some small articles & the above 9 rifled muskets, which I condemned to be turned in to the ordnance, & c.

The guard house was small of stone with a prisoners room. The guard was composed of 1 corporal, 1 lance corporal and 6 privates, & two sentinels posted, one at the corral, & one at the quartermasters & commissary's stores. During the day, 3 of them are sent out with the herders. Three prisoners were in charge for desertion & 2 for other offenses.

The hospital is an adobe building not originally constructed for this purpose. It was small, only 3 iron bedsteads in the ward room, a small room for the steward & dispensary, & a small kitchen, detached, with a store room. It is, however, neat and in good order and the steward a regular appointment. Asst. Surgeon Langworthy has had the whole under his daily supervision since the 8th Nov 1859 when he relieved Dr. J. H. Olmsted, a citizen. There was one sick, one cook, one matron. The post is healthy. The medicines were ample & there were 10 iron bedsteads on hand & all the books & records were properly kept. The temperature in June at 2 P.M. ranged from 75° to 103,° in July from 80° to 103,° and August from 70° to 100.° From Feb. to Nov. 16, in 277 days there was 23 slight showers of rain & one heavy shower. This post is about 3500 feet above the sea. There was no hospital fund.

The bakery was a good adobe building thatched-roof, & a good oven, & there was a first rate baker, & good flour, & bread excellent.

Lt. W. Jones has been acting assistant quartermaster since 1st March last. He performs the duty well, and all his quarterly returns & accounts have been forwarded to date, & his monthly statements, & c, to the close of October, have been forwarded. There was due the U.S. on the 30th Sept. 4431.14 dolls. Expended in October 2650 dolls. and no expenditure this month. Leaving a balance due the U.S. at date 1781.14 dolls. Of this 1000 dollars is in Maj. D. H. Vinton's check on Assistant Treasury, New Orleans, 586.14 dolls and 195 dolls in cash in a safe in his quarters. His office is the adjutant's office & he has parts of two store houses occupied for quartermaster's stores, which are of adobes & thatched and which are otherwise occupied as [a] commissary store. He has a smith & carpenter's shop & a corral for animals & for hay. He keeps 21 mules & 3 wagons and employs an extra duty man, 1 carpenter, & 1 smith, 1 herder, 3 teamsters, and he pays 20 dolls per month for the site of the post, 17.25 dolls the ton for hay, of which he has about 40 tons, 13 dolls the cord for wood of which he has about 200 cords on hand. Wood is the mesquite root & difficult to obtain. He has about 200 bushels [of] corn on hand which is high & fluctuating in price.

Lt. Jones has receipted for a mountain howitzer & carriage with its caissons, but the spokes of the wheels are loose, and it wants repair & painting, & it should be sent to the ordnance arsenal at San Antonio. It is simply useless against Indians. He also has in charge 5 extra teams, & wagons, & drivers (citizens), sent some time since to transport Capt. Carpenter's company to Camp Cooper. He has also receipted for 16 horses belonging to the post for a mounted command. This command is a doubtful expedient, and conflicts very much with the duty of an infantry soldier, & not at all necessary for escorts. I would recommend these horses be withdrawn as they require grooming. & c. It often happens that an infantry escort has to accompany a train, & c, to the next post. But it is performed in this way. The escort with its supplies are put into a 6 mule wagon & its duty is simply to protect the trains & parties, & not to scout in search of Indians. Nor is an infantry soldier armed appropriately for scouting on horseback.

Lieut. Jones is also acting commissary of subsistence & performs that duty well. His quarterly papers are all forwarded. His monthly papers also to the 31st October. There was due the U.S., 30 Sept last, 415.60 dolls, and received in October, 259.48 dolls, and expended 27.75 dolls. Also expended this month, 87.50 dolls, leaving a balance due the U.S. at date of 559.87 dolls, which is in cash in a safe in his quarters. He employs one extra duty man as clerk & commissary sergeant who is the same man as in the quartermaster's department. Beef has cost as high as 10 cts. the lb. net for the last quarter. Now it costs on the hoof 4.20 dolls the 100 lbs. Those on hand were bought are 619 lbs the average & turn out about 590 lbs net and in same instances over-run by grazing & fattening. He keeps 4 herders & has a large number of beef cattle on hand. The grazing about here is good. His supplies are all good & well stored in two buildings of adobes partly occupied by quartermaster's supplies. Five ox carts & teams with commissary supplies arrived on the day of my inspection. The bill of lading was dated 25 Sept. at San Antonio. Thus taking 40 days to reach here, a distance of 383 miles at the rate of 9 miles per day, where as the contract calls for 12 miles, I think per day on the average, and it should have been but 34 days. This slow transportation detains escorts on the road & sometimes supplies are damaged.

Lieut. Jones is also post treasurer & has 114.45 dolls in cash in safe at date. He is also regimental recruiting officer and has on hand 162 dolls in cash in a safe.

J. D. Holliday is the sutler & has a sufficient supply of goods and keep the Overland Mail post office & the mails from the east, & is also the mail agent here.[45] The post is conveniently situated to receive dispatches from both head quarters of the department & Washington City by mail and, if necessary, to forward them to other posts.

This post was last inspected by Acting Inspector General Jos. E. Johnson, 26th Oct 1859. Of course this same company was inspected by him. It was last paid by Paymaster McClure to the 31 October last.

The post records are all in good order in a suitable adjutant's office of adobes & thatched roof, and the command in a good state of discipline.

This post was made a double ration post by the General Orders No. 9 of the War Department to commence from the 1st January 1860. Where as most other posts have been made double ration posts from their establishment and occupation, I think there must have been an accidental difference on the part of the Hon. Secretary of War, & I would ask the General-in-Chief to call his attention to it. There is no post that requires double rations more than this, for here the mail-routes from Memphis and San Antonio meet. The hospitality of the commander is on that account alone often taxed.

The officers quarters are good & ample.

Capt. Carpenter commands with ability and zeal and does justice to the service & the country. His name is entered on the Army Register of 1860 as not being a graduate of the Military Academy, but this is a mistake & should be corrected in the next register.

All which is Respectfully submitted
Jos. K. F. Mansfield
Col & Inspt Genl
U.S.A.

Endorsement: A copy will be furnished to the Department commander. The ordnance stores in the possession of the company will be made to conform to its proper armament. See General Orders No. 23, 1859, War Department. The mountain howitzer will be sent to the Ordnance depot for repair. The Departmental commander can judge whether it is required at the post. The horses will be returned to the Quartermasters' department; the use of them for mount[ed] infantry deemed unnecessary and inexpedient. The loss of time by the contractor in the transportation of supplies is a matter for correction by the Department by the Department commander.

[John B. Floyd]
Secretary of War
War dept.
29 Dec. '60

FORT LANCASTER

Howard Spring, Texas[46]
32 miles east of Fort Lancaster
21st Nov 1860

Sir:

My last report was the inspection of Fort Stockton dated 17th inst. On the 19th, I arrived at Fort Lancaster and on the 20th inspected that post & have now the honor to submit to the General-in-Chief the following result:

Fort Lancaster has been established several years. It is on the road to El Paso, on Live Oak Creek, near its junction with the Pecos & four miles from the crossing of that river. It is 97 miles from Fort Hudson, and 87 miles from Fort Stockton. It was inspected by me in 1856. There was then two companies here & the quarters and accommodations quite inferior. The soldiers then occupied the Turnley Cottages for quarters.[47] Since that time they have proved a failure, as I then anticipated, and their place has been filled by good adobe buildings, with wooden floors & about half of them shingled & the residue thatched roofs (see plan of the post herewith) and all the command are comfortably lodged.

Capt. R. S. Granger of the 1st Inft. is in command with his Company "K," 1st Lt. James B. Green[e], 2d Lt. A. M. Haskell on leave of absence for 60 days, per Dept. Order No. 119, 23rd Dec. 1859, extended by Special Order, Adjt. Gen. No. 57, March 15th 1860, for 4 months, extended to the 1st Oct. 1860, S. O., A. G. 124, 30th June 1860, ordered on detached service per Special Order No. 111, Head Quarters, Army, 21 Sept. 1860. To accompany recruits about to be sent to the Department of Texas. Absent since 10 June 1860, 10 months & 10 days, 4 sergeants, 3 corporals, 2 musicians, 57 privates, in the aggregate, 2 officers, 66 enlisted men at command. Of these, 1 sergeant & 7 men detached on an escort of California animals to Fort Hudson, 1 on furlough, 1 absent sick at the insane asylum at Washington. Thus having for duty 56 enlisted men of the company. Of these, 4 were on guard, 1 baker, 2 teamsters, 4 prisoners, 3 cooks, 1 hospital attendant & 1 orderly & 40 men on parade. These men were on inspection in uniform, except that some had dark & some light blue pantaloons and were well equipped for the field, in excellent order in every respect. They passed in review in quick & double quick time well. Went thro' the light inft. drill well and at skirmishes & thro' the manual of the bayonet exercise well. And at the target 6' x 22" at 100 yards, 32 men, one round each, made 20 hits; at 200 yards made 18 hits; at 300 yards 9 hits. Equal at 100 yds to 62½ percent, 200 yds. 56½ percent, 300 yds 28 percent, the best ball practice I have seen.

Their quarters were two buildings of adobes, one shingled, & the other thatched, with wooden floors & two fire places in each, and comfortable, and neat with double bunks and mess & kitchen in a good detached building, of adobes, with earthen floors & thatched roof.

The company books were in order. The discharges in 1860 were 19, and desertions, 1 in 1857, 2 in 1858, 4 in 1859, and 5 in 1860. The few desertions are in my opinion, in some degree, an index of good & judicious discipline. The company armory is an apartment joining the 1st sergeant's room in the soldier's quarters, and the arms, camp, & garrison equipment & c, well cared for. There were 76 rifled muskets, 2 Harpers Ferry rifles, 2

Colts pistols, 2500 blank cartridges, 7400 musket ball cartridges, 700 Colts pistol ball cartridges, 74 canteens, 60 knapsacks, 71 haversacks. There were 4 laundresses very neatly & comfortably accommodated in small buildings by themselves. A company fund of 128.64 dolls in the hands of Capt. Granger. I condemned some few articles of camp & garrison in equipage as worn out.

The guard house was of stone & thatched [and] a prisoners' room. The guard was one lance corporal and four men. One sentinel at the guard house and corral and one at the east side of the garrison quarters. There were 4 prisoners, one undergoing sentence, and 3 waiting trial for desertion. Charges forwarded since September last.

The staff consisted of Assistant Surgeon Jos. R. Smith, Hospital Steward W. W. Webster, Ordnance's Sergeant Edward F. Brenner.[48]

The hospital is a very poor adobe building, braced up on one end. But as this post was originally built for two companies, there is a set of soldier's quarters that could readily be used as a hospital now vacant. There is one cook, one nurse, & one matron on attendance, & only one wounded man, a Mexican citizen, accidentally shot in the left breast, in hospital. The dispensary & store room are one & in good order, wardroom only large enough for three beds. Supplies ample. I condemned sundry store & medicines & e, as worthless and worn out. There was a small kitchen attached. Books and records all in order, a hospital fund of 20.93 dolls. From Nov. to March, 275 days, there were only 28 slight showers of rain and the temperature in June ranged, at 2 P.M., from 88° to 110,° in July from 96° to 109,° and August, 73° to 102.°

There is no necessity for an ordnance sergeant here as there is no post ordnance. He, however, acts as postmaster. The records were in order. There has been no post fund since 31st August last.

1st Lt. J. B. Green[e] has performed the duty of assistant quartermaster since 1st March 1859, when he relieved 2d Lt. Haskell. The supplies are ample and well stored in an adobe building and thatched roof. He has 1800 bushels [of] corn on hand, which cost 2.45 dolls the bushel, very high, 100 tons [of] hay which cost 11.26 dolls the ton, quite reasonable, and he had a winter supply of wood which cost 7.43 dolls the cord, wood is hard to get. He keeps one clerk, 3 teamsters, 1 smith, 1 carpenter as extra duty men. The last two are temporary. His books & papers & records are all in order & his quarterly & monthly returns & statements & accounts forwarded to date. There was due the U.S. on the 30th Sept. last, 1235.84 dolls, and no expenditure since. Of this amount, 39.67 dolls is in the Assistant Treasury, N. York & 1016.41 in the Asst. Treasury, N. Orleans, and the balance is

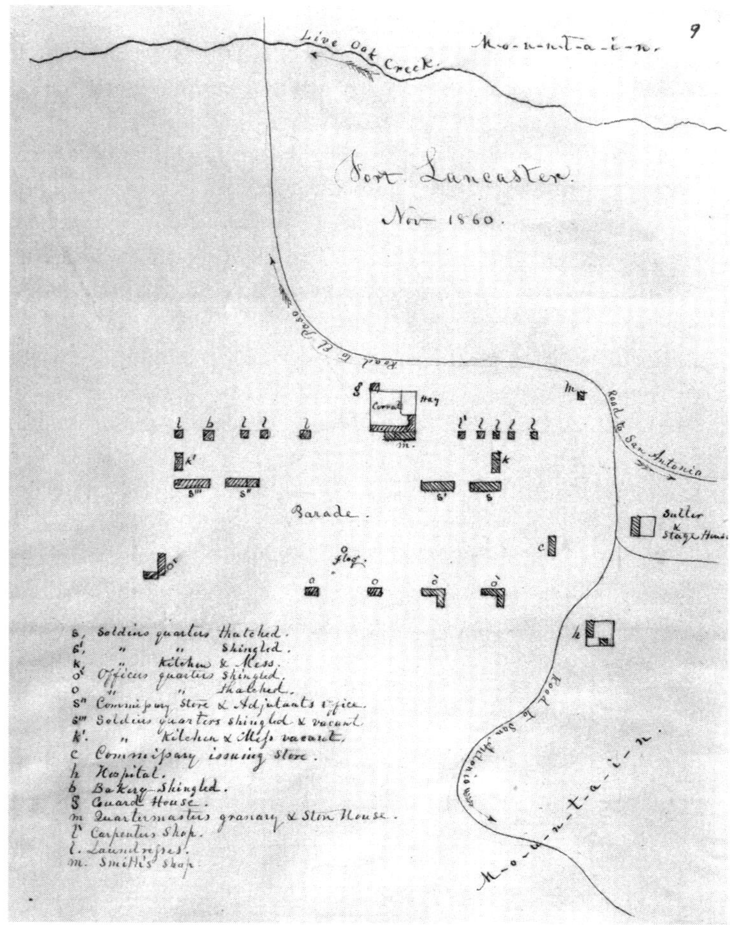

Sketch by Mansfield. (Illustration from LR, AGO, RG 94 courtesy of the National Archives)

cash in a safe in his quarters. He has 22 mules, 3 wagons, a good stone smith's shop shingled & a good carpenter's shop, a good granary & store room under one roof, and a good corral & hay yard attached & all in excellent order.

Lt. Green has also been in charge of the commissary duties since 1st March 1859, when he relieved Lt. Haskell. His supplies are good, flour particularly excellent. There is some damaged rice by weevils on hand, which Capt. Grander can condemn. His supplies are kept in two buildings & in excellent order. The books and records are all in order. His quarterly &

monthly returns & abstracts & accounts have all been forwarded to date. There was due the U.S., 30th Sept., 156.08 dolls, received since, 389.72 dolls, aggregate 545.73 dolls. Expended since, 161.33 dolls. Due at date, 384.40 dolls. This amount is in cash in a safe. The clerk & commissary sergeant is the ordnance sergeant of the post. Eight & i cents is paid for fresh beef the pound net & flour costs 8⅕ cts.

Lt. Green is also company recruiting officer and has on hand at date, 267 dolls in cash in a safe.

The bakehouse is a good adobe building, shingled, and with a good brick oven, and an excellent baker. The bread of the first quality.

This post was last inspected by Acting Inspector General Jos. E. Johnston, 3rd Nov. 1859, and last paid by paymaster McClure to the 31st Oct. last. It is a highly important position in the midst of Indian depredations. About 6 weeks since two men were murdered by them about 10 miles off, on the Pecos, and a few days since 4 Indians ran off 7 mules of the stage company, which has a station here. Numerous trains pass here & very often they need assistance in repairs or supplies, which the commanding officer is obliged to afford & sometimes escorts. One inft. company, however, is ample here.

The sutler, D. E. Lessier, keeps a good supply of necessaries. Capt. Granger commands with ability and satisfactorily and is untiring in his efforts in the performance of his duties. He has repeatedly made efforts for a garden and the passed season by great labor, has succeeded well in supplying his men with melons and summer vegetables to a considerable extent. But all the plants have to be watered by hand.

The discipline of the post is good.

All which is Respectfully Submitted,
Jos. K. F. Mansfield
Col. & Inspct Genl
U.S. Army

FORT HUDSON

In Camp at California Springs[49]
26th Nov. 1860

Sir:

The last inspection report I made in this department was that of Fort Lancaster. I arrived at Fort Hudson on Friday the 23rd inst. in the afternoon & on the next day, the 24th, inspected that post & have now the honor to submit to the General-in-Chief the following:

Fort Hudson is located on the Devil's River at the second crossing of the same, by the road from Fort Clark to El Paso. It is on an elevated plateau about 75 feet above the river and is bounded on the north by the river valley, on the east and southwest by the river valley & a deep ravine, and on the west & north east by mountains. There is abundant wood & good water, but little grazing. On the north side of the river directly opposite the post is the mail station. Formerly this was one of the homes of the Indian, but now it has become the marauding ground for the wild man, and he commits his murders & depredations whenever opportunity presents. The Indians can move where they please on the extended mesas which border the river & make their descents at will. The position of this post is probably the very best point to occupy on this river. It is 78 miles from Fort Clark & 97 miles from Fort Lancaster. It was established on the 4th Oct. 1857, conformably to Special Orders No. 99 of the 4th August 1857, from Head Quarters of the Department, and by Capt. J. N. Caldwell with Companies "A" & "D," 1st Inft. and Company "G," 8th Inft. The 22nd May 1858, Bvt. Maj. L. Smith with Company A, 8 Inft., assumed command & relieved Companies A & D, 1st Inft., agreeably to Department Orders No. 39 of 30 April 1858. On 22nd August 1858, Capt. A. G. Brackett, 2d Cavalry, relieved Bvt. Maj. L. Smith, who went to Fort Inge with his company. By Special Department Orders No. 38, May 31st 1859, Bvt. Maj. L. Smith's company ordered to Fort Hudson and it relieved Company F, 1st Art., on 11th June 1859, and has remained here since.

Bvt. Maj. L. Smith is now in command of his Co. "A," 8th Inft., 2d Lt. Z. R. Bliss left on leave of absence, 6 Sept. & now "en route" with recruits, 1st Lt. T. M. Jones on detached service since 19th Oct. 1858, acting adjutant [of the] regiment at Head Quarters at San Antonio, 4 sergeants, 4 corporals, 1 musician, 32 privates, in the aggregate, 41 privates. Of these one corporal detached to office duty at head quarters of the regiment, one private detached with Asst. Surgeon Lynde since 25th Oct., to return on the 31st inst. To this force must be added four men of Company "G" attached of which one is on detached service at Fort Clark and the staff assistant, Surgeon R. D. Lynde, & a hospital steward James Clavin. This making an aggregate available force at date of one officer & 42 enlisted men besides the staff. Of these, 2 sergeants, 3 corporals, 24 privates & 2 musicians [were] on parade, 1 sergeant & 6 privates on guard, one in hospital, 1 sergeant sick, 1 cook in quarters, one baker.

The company passed in review at quick & double quick time very well & on inspection were in full uniform with light blue pants & with arms, knapsacks, canteens, haversacks in good order. They went thro' the light infantry drill well & at skirmishes very well & were divided into three squads at

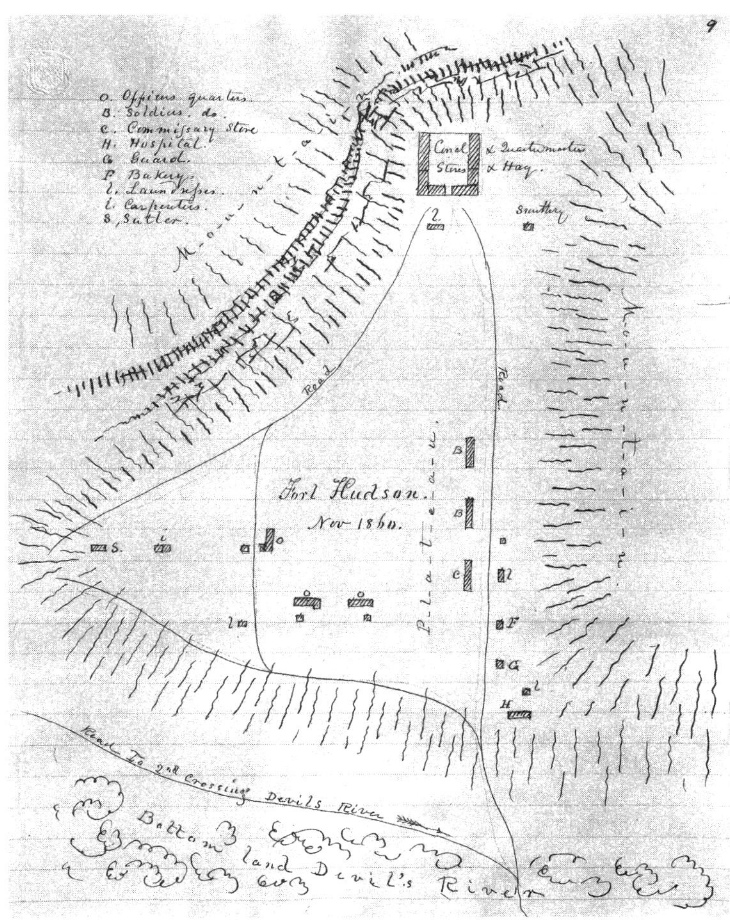

Sketch by Mansfield. (Illustration from LR, AGO, RG 94 courtesy of the National Archives)

the manual of the bayonet exercise, under non-commissioned officers, & two of the squads were very well instructed on the whole of the manual, but the third was not as well advanced. At the largest, 6' x 22," 26 men one round each at 100 yards, made 12 hits, about 46 percent, at 200 yards, made 6 hits, about 23 percent. This firing shows great progress in target shooting in our service. This company could have made a better exhibit under more favorable circumstances [for] on this occasion the wind blew to considerable effect and the day was cold. They immediately fired again at 100 yards, & made half as many more hits. But with a view to compare companies I have adopted one round of each of the distances above named as a standard.

The soldiers' quarters (see plan herewith) were built of mud concrete with earthen floors & shingled roofs. They were neat with inferior double bunks made by the men. The quarters were originally designed for a two company post. There is a centre chimney & two fire places in each. One of the buildings is now converted into a messroom & kitchen & the room is ample for one company. Each building is deficient in sashes for two windows, much wanted, the opening being closed with canvas. The soldiers having made themselves bunks, of course there is no uniformity in them. The orderly room & armory is in one end of the quarters in which are kept the company books & it is occupied by the first sergeant. The books are neat & property in a good state of preservation. The records show 39 discharges in 1860, 6 desertions in 1857, 5 in 1858, 16 in 1859, 9 in 1860. Pertaining to the company, 63 rifled muskets, 10 flint lock muskets for bayonet exercise, 4500 musket ball cartridges, 73 canteens, 50 haversacks, 82 knapsacks, two laundresses well quartered in little buildings by themselves, a company fund of 456.52 dolls in the hands of Bvt. Major Smith.

One of the musicians on parade was a drummer boy only 11 years old, enlisted by authority, is entirely too young & will not drum well for several years. He fills the place of a good musician. He is the son of a sergeant.

The guard house is of stone & mud with a division in it forming a very poor prison room & it has a thatched roof. The guard is one sergeant & 6 privates & a sentinel at the guard house and one at the corral at night. There was one prisoner & he belonged to "G" Company, broken up, and is attached to "C" Company, 8th Inft., daily expect to arrive "en route" westward.

The hospital has been under the charge of Assist. Surgeon R. D. Lynde (now absent on leave since 25th Oct. to return 30th inst.), since 12th Feb. 1858. There is a regular steward, James Clavin, a dispensary & store room, a large ward and 16 iron bedsteads, a hospital matron & a cook, but no sick & no hospital fund. The building is of mud concrete and shingled roof & there [is] attached to it a small shed for a kitchen. The whole is sufficient for the present. The post is healthy & the records well kept & in order. From March to November 24th, inclusive, 275 days, there were about 30 slight showers & one heavy rain in August last. The temperature in June ranged from 96° to 105,° July from 95° to 107,° in August 75° to 104.°

The bake house is of mud concrete & shingled roof, a good stone oven, & good baker, & good bread, & each should be.

Bvt. Maj. L. Smith has performed the duty of assistant quartermaster since 16 April last, when he relieved Lt. Bliss. The supplies are ample but stored in inferior temporary buildings on the corral, but they are not very valuable, except the corn of which there were about 14,000 lbs. on hand. The supply of hay quite limited say ½ ton, but a contract is made for hay which has to be brought 40 miles from San Felipe at 24.50 dolls the ton delivered. This hay, however, is very inferior, only fit for bedding. Hay cannot be got nearer & there is no grazing here of consequence. A contract has been made for wood at 4.62 dolls the cord. There is wood enough on the river but it belongs to private parties & the wood on the property occupied by the post has been mostly used. Fifty dolls per month has hitherto been paid for rent with the privilege of wood. The wood is now most all cut & there is no grazing. The rent of the land at 600 per annum is high for it is perfectly worthless except as a military position.

There is a smith's shop of mud concrete & shingled roof, a carpenter's shop, a mere shed, & a good corral, with shed shelters on 3 sides for mules, & c. There are 3 wagons & 17 mules. He keeps a quartermaster's sergeant, 3 teamsters, 1 herder & 1 carpenter as extra duty men.

All his quarterly & monthly returns & abstracts to date have been duly forwarded. On 30th Sept. there was due the United States, 3472.29 dolls. Expended in October, 502.27 dolls. Expended in November, 689.50 dolls. Leaving at date, 2271.50 dolls due the U. States.

To meet this amount & other amounts due the U.S., he has in the Assistant Treasury at New Orleans, 2679.21 dolls, and in the Assistant Treasury at New York, 2352.50 dolls. The quartermaster's office is in the building occupied by the Commissary Department.

Bvt. Maj. L. Smith has also been acting commissary of subsistence since 16th April 1860, when he relieved Lt. Z. Bliss. The commissary supplies are all well stored & in order in a good mud concrete building & shingled & in excellent order. All his papers & records are in order & forwarded at date. There was due the U. States, 30th September, 895.79 dolls. Received in October, 57.71 dolls. Expended since, 100.55 dolls. Leaving a balance due the U.S. at date, 852.95 dolls, which is in the Assist. Treasury as stated for quartermasters department. He pays for beef 7 cents, & for flour 7 cents the lb., & for beans 3.50 dolls the bushel. The commissary sergeant is the same man as the quartermaster sergeant.

Bvt. Maj. Smith is also company recruiting officer & has on hand 105 dolls at date, covered as above.

Bvt. Maj. Smith commands the post well, is a good drill officer & the command in a good state of discipline.

There is no garden at this post & cannot be for want of seasonable rains.

The post was last paid by Paymaster McClure to the 31st October, and last inspected by Acting Inspector General Jos. E. Johnson in November 1859.

Capt. G. Stoneman of the 2d Cavalry with his company has been reported on the returns of this post. But as he has been scouting all the season in the lower Rio Grande and no part of his company, & c, is here. I have not noticed him as belonging to the post at all. In that this is no station for cavalry, as there is no grazing, and all the supplies of hay & corn are brought a great distance & if trains of supplies are well escorted by the infantry command from post to post, as is the orders, the company is not at all required here on account of the Indians.

All which is Respectfully Submitted,
Jos. K. F. Mansfield
Col. & Inspector Gen'l.
U.S.A.

FORT CLARK

In Camp at Water Hole "en route"
for Fort Duncan, 22 miles
south of Fort Clark, Texas
1st Dec. 1860.

Sir:

My last inspection report of this department was of Fort Hudson. On the 28th November, I arrived at Fort Clark and on the 29th & 30th, was engaged in the inspection of that post and have now the honor to submit to the General-in-Chief the following result:[50]

Fort Clark has been established for several years, I think since about 1850 or 1851. It was here in 1855, as I passed out of New Mexico, and [it] was in that year inspected by Asst. Adjt. Gen. Bvt. Lt. Col. Freeman. It was inspected by me in 1856 and was inspected by Acting Inspector General Jos. E. Johnson on 9th Nov 1859.

It is well located on the Las Moras, just where the roads from San Antonio and Fort Duncan meet, say about 14 miles from the Rio Grande. It is 123 miles from San Antonio, 45 miles [from] Fort Duncan, about that same from Fort Inge, and 75 miles from Fort Hudson on Devil's River. It is a military position that cannot well be abandoned on a frontier like this. Yet it has improved less in accommodations for the military command than any post I have hitherto see. While other posts have been built & rebuilt, this post has hardly progressed at all. This may be the fault of the commanding officers & the result of the frequent changes of the garrison. I think it's not unlikely both.

It is now, however, under the command of Col. B. L. E. Bonneville and the head quarters of his regiment, the 3rd Inft. This regiment is distributed in orders as follows: Company "B," Capt. & Bvt. Maj. O. L. Shepherd, at this post expected daily from New Mexico; Company "D," Capt. H. B. Schroeder, at this post, present; Company "H," Capt. and Bvt. Maj. W. H. Gordon, at this post, present; Company "K," Capt. G. Sykes, at this post, present; Company "G," Capt. & Brevet Major W. T. H. Brooks, at this post expected daily from New Mexico; Company "A," Capt. R. V. Bonneau, at Ringgold Barracks; Company "I," Captain Brevet Lt. Col. D. T. Chandler, at Fort McIntosh; Company "E," Capt. H. B. Clitz, at Ringgold Barracks, en route from New Mexico and expected daily; Company "C," Capt. W. B. Johns at Ringgold Barracks, expected from New Mexico, daily; Company "F," Capt. J. Trevitt, at Fort McIntosh.

The staff of the regiment & post is as follows: Assistant Surgeon W. J. H. White, Adjutant Lt. W. H. Wood, a sergeant major, a quartermaster sergeant, an ordnance sergeant, an hospital steward, two principal musicians & seven privates in the band. In the aggregate, 3 commissioned officers & 13 enlisted men. The regimental quartermaster Lt. L. W. O'Bannon on 8 months leave, Special Order no. 63, War Dept., April 1860, and left the command, 1st May 1860. In his stead, Lt. M. L. Davis of Company "F," temporarily attached to the post and acting regimental quartermaster since 1st August 1860 & commissary of the post at date.

The records of the regiment and post are kept in the adjutant's office, which is a building of logs on end & shingled roof & a stone chimney. This answers well & compares favorably with other temporary buildings. The books and records of the regiment are in excellent order. There is a regimental fund of 174.43 dolls in the hands of the adjutant. The adjutant is the regimental recruiting officer and has in his hands 313.75 dolls in cash.

The post records are also in excellent order.

Col. Bonneville arrived here 29 July 1860, and relieved Brevet Major W. H. French with Light Company "K," 1st Art, with three companies of the 3rd Inft, "H," "D," "F," "F" Company left on the 5th [of] Sept. for Fort McIntosh and Company "K" joined on the 16th October. Assistant Surgeon White was here on the arrival of Col. Bonneville & Assistant Surgeon W. W. Anderson joined with the Colonel, but left on leave 11th August for 30 days for head quarters of the department & absent without leave since 11th Sept. 1860. I must remark, however, in relation to Assistant Surgeon Anderson that he is here reported absent without leave because the order changing his station has not been received at this post. I left him in San Antonio the 4th October under orders for Fort Chadbourne. The ordnance

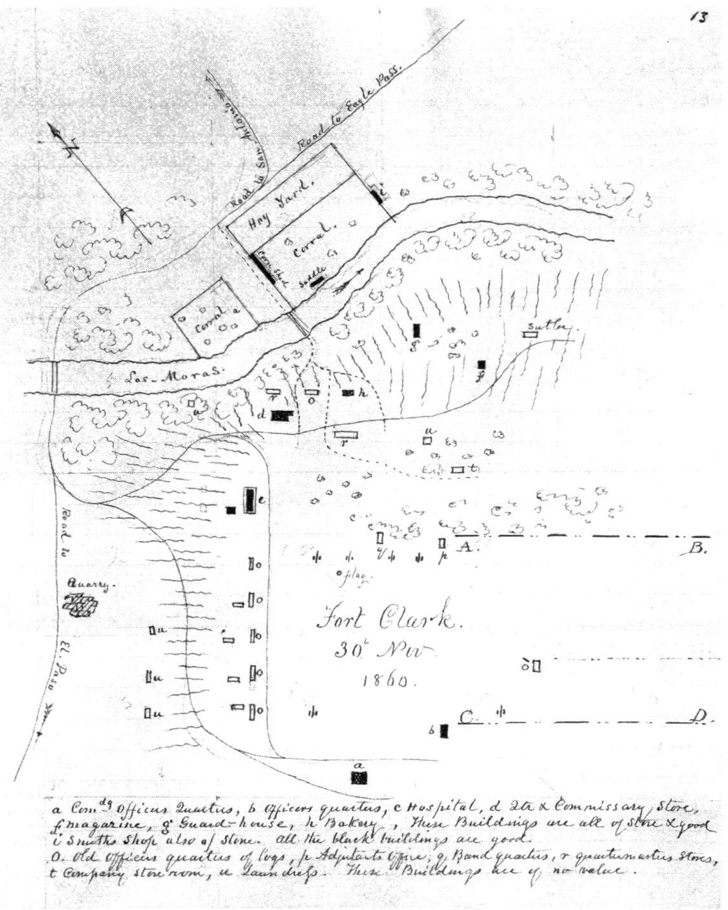

Sketch by Mansfield. (Illustration from LR, AGO, RG 94 courtesy of the National Archives)

sergeant, Thos. Reordor has had charge of all the ordnance at this post since 1854 and as he is [a] very trusty and intelligent man, has also the duty of commissary sergeant to perform which he does well.

There is a small magazine at this post & at present it is full of powder in kegs & otherwise in fixed ammunition. It is built of stone and has an earthen cover surmounted & a shingled roof & a sheet iron covered door. It is tolerably safe but too small. Some ordnance property is deposited in an old temporary quartermasters store house of logs on end and open joints, and some in the quartermaster's store building. Two large rectangular piles of 8 inch shells in front of the magazine well la[c]quered. On the parade are the following: 4 siege 24-pounder guns mounted complete with limbers, one 6-pounder howitzer & caissons complete, one 6-pounder brass gun & caisson complete, one iron sling cart, two 8 inch howitzer mounted complete. These carriages all wanted painting and the vents aprons. They had recently been la[c]quered. The large guns all wanted [tar]paulins to keep off the weather & sun. I recommended the sergeant to apply for the deficiencies at once. He had also ten Harpers Ferry rifles, 9 cavalry sabres, 1 Colts revolver, 4 Colts Navy revolvers, 3 cavalry carbines. There was also the following powder & fixed ammunition, to wit: 6364 lbs. cannon powder, 12 lbs. rifle powder, 1000 holster pistol cartridges, flint & lock, 5820 Colts pistol ball cartridges, 7060 rifle ball cartridges, 300 cavalry carbine cartridge, 14190 musket ball cartridges, 600 blank carbine cartridges, 1000 blank Colts pistol cartridges, 156 twelve pounder cartridges, 40070 rifle musket caps, 152 strapped 6 pounder shots, 27 spherical case shots, 28 six pounder canister, 96 twelve pounder strapped shells, 70 spherical case 12 pounder shots, 14 canister 12 pounder shots.

It is presumed that most of this ammunition will be eventually wanted in practice of the artillery at Fort Duncan, as well as the heavy guns. They can be of no use here and the carriages will eventually rot down. At present they will stand some service.

On inspection parade, Col. Bonneville was too feeble to appear. He was just recovering from a long, and protracted, sickness which seized him soon after his arrival from New Mexico via the Pecos River, which he followed all the way & says it is the shortest and best route to Santa Fe. The command present consisted of Companies D, H, & K and the staff. The whole passed in review in quick & double quick time imperfectly. The staff were in their appropriate uniforms. The companies on parade were without knapsacks, canteens & haversacks. These will be noticed hereafter.

Company "D": Capt. H. B. Schroeder on 8 months leave of absence, S.O. 63, War Dept., 2d April 1860. Left the company 1st May 1860. 1st Lt. A. Jackson in command, 2d Lt. W. H. Bell present but temporarily in command of Co. "H" (Bvt. Maj. W. H. Gordon sick), 4 sergeants, 4 corporals, 24 privates, 1 musician on parade, 8 confined, 1 detached to San Antonio. In the aggregate, 41 men present at the post. Those on parade were in full uniform, neat & arms in good order. It drilled at the light infantry under Lt. Jackson and went thro' most of the company movements & at skirmishes has been in a considerable degree instructed. It could not go thro' the manual of the bayonet exercise not having been instructed in it at all. At the target, 6' x 22," at 100 yards, 24 men made 9 hits, say 36 percent; at 200 yards, made 3 hits say 12 percent; at 300 yds., made 6 hits, say 25 percent, only one round at each distance. The discipline of the company was good and its officers competent, but its instruction in all its exercises incomplete. This is owing to the fact that this company has been for a long time in the Navaho Nation and in New Mexico scouting & in marching say for the last 12 months, and until its arrival here, probably had not been much instructed, as at others stations this side of El Paso. It has much to learn. The drills at this post have been commenced & I doubt not this company will soon be in good training. These remarks are applicable to the other two companies here & I will also remark that every company should occasionally be withdrawn from the field to recruit and be instructed, especially as recruits cannot be instructed in the field.

It was quartered in a worthless temporary building of logs set in the ground & thatched with earth floor, no fire place nor glass windows. The orderly sergeant in a tent & the company kitchen a tent and no mess room.

The books and records of the company were in order and written up, a company fund of 49.92 dolls in the hands of Lt. Jackson. It had 81 rifle muskets, 400 rifle musket balls cartridges, & 2000 musket blank cartridges, 72 knapsacks, 49 haversacks, 129 canteens. They were all in a worn condition from a long march. The company ordnance & property was in a temporary log building and thatched roof by itself.

The discharges in 1858 were 7; in 1859, 5; in 1860, 39. There were 6 desertions in 1858, 3 in 1859, 14 in 1860. 3 laundresses were attached to this company & were occupying hackalls.

Co. "H," Capt. & Bvt. Maj. W. H. Gordon sick, 1st Lt. W. H. Wood adjutant regiment & post, 2d Lt. R. V. Bonneau on leave of absence for two months, S.O. 82, Sept. 19th 1860, extended two months, S.O. 120, Head Quarters Army, Oct. 13th 1860. Left the company [October] 29th 1860, 2 sergeants, 3 corporals, 25 privates on parade at inspection, 5 prisoners, 2 sergeants & 1 private on furlough, 3 on detached service, 1 corporal on extra duty in corral, 1 private on guard, 1 in hospital & 2 nursing Bvt. Maj. Gordon. In the aggregate, 43 privates at command & no officer for duty. The company was commanded by Lt. Bell of Co. D above. There was no musician to the company, and the same remark is applicable to this company as to discipline & instruction as for Co. D, except the men had not progressed quite as far at the drills.

Those on parade were in full uniform with light blue pantaloons, neat & their arms in good order. At the target 6' x 22," 24 men one round each made at 100 yards 13 hits, say 54 percent; at 200 yds, 5 hits say, 25 percent;

at 300 yards, 4 hits say, 16 percent.

This company was quartered in an extension of the building occupied by Company D, a worthless structure. There was no mess room and no kitchen but a tent. The orderly sergeant & company ordnance & property was in a hackall of logs thatched roof by itself.

The books & records of the company were in order & written up. There was a company fund of 741.20 dolls in the hands of Bvt. Maj. Gordon, 75 rifled muskets, 7000 rifle ball cartridges, 4500 blank musket cartridges, 300 Colts pistol ball cartridges, 4 knapsacks, 20 haversacks & no canteens. One laundress attached to this company occupying a hackall. There were 9 desertions 1858, 6 in 1859, 4 in 1860. The discharges were 1 in 1858, 6 in 1859, 40 in 1860.

Co. "K," Capt. G. Sykes, 1st Lt. L. W. O'Bannon, Regimental Quartermaster, on leave, 2d Lt. Henry W. Freedley, 3 sergeants, 2 corporals, 21 privates, 1 musician on inspection parade, 4 detached to San Antonio, 5 prisoners, 3 sick, 1 cook, 1 absent with leave, 1 absent confined, 1 corporal & one private on guard. In the aggregate, 2 officers & 43 men available.

The men on parade were neat & in uniform & their arms & equipment in good order. The same remarks as to discipline & instruction as in Co. D & H will apply to this. This company was not in quarters but in 3 hackalls & 3 Sibley tents & no mess room, & kitchen, a tent. The 1st sergeant in a hackall with company stores. The arms & ammunition were mostly stored in the old quartermaster's temporary store house.

The books and records were in order. There were 3 desertions in 1858, 6 in 1859, 9 in 1860. There was a company fund in the hands of Capt. Sykes of 402.16 dolls. There were 78 rifled muskets, 4800 ball cartridges, 900 blank cartridges, 88 knapsacks, 49 canteens, 84 haversacks. 3 laundresses accommodated in tents & hackalls.

At the target, 6' x 22," 24 men, one round each, at 100 yards, made 12 hits or 50 percent; at 200 yds, 5 hits or 21 percent; at 300 yds., 3 hits or 12 percent.

Thus it appears at the target practice these three companies are greatly inferior to the 3 companies at Hudson, Lancaster & Stockton, and yet their shooting is much better than many companies I reported on in the Pacific Department. They require rest and time for instruction. In their drills, particularly, as recruits will soon be added to their numbers. The officers are as a body competent & meritorious, and will eventually bring out a good result.

Capt. Sykes, who commanded on inspection, carried the three companies thro' a small part of the battalion drill as light inf't. but it was incomplete.

The guard was 1 sergeant, 1 corporal, & 9 privates. One sentinel at the guard house, and one at the corral. The guard house was a stone building shingled and a prison room within. There were 18 prisoners, 9 of them had been tried by a general court & 3 by a garrison court, 5 were for drunkenness on guard, 1 for stabbing a non-commissioned officer, 3 for desertion & the residue minor offenses.

The bakery was a good stone building & shingled & with a good brick oven and the bread good. Two bakers were employed.

The hospital is a good stone building & shingled & a piazza all round it with wooden floors & c. Attached to it is a good kitchen and mess with stone floor and a dead house. Assistant Surgeon W. T. H. White has the control of the hospital. He has a regular steward, August Barge, a good dispensary & well supplied, a store room, two large wards, 30 iron bedsteads & c. The records were all properly kept and the sick better provided for than any other department of the service. There was a hospital fund of 9 dolls. 2 attendants, 1 matron & only one sick in hospital. The post is healthy.

The temperature in June ranged at 2 P.M. from 85° to 103,° in July from 95° to 105,° and in August from 79° to 102.° March to November, inclusive in 1860, 275 days there were 29 showers all slight except one heavy rain in August.

The band was accommodated in an inferior temporary building with thatched roof, office of the commissary store.

The sergeant major's quarters a poor hackall, thatched. The ordnance sergeant slept in the quartermasters department is under the direction of Lt. M. L. Davis, temporarily here. He relieved Lt. H. W. Clossen of the first artillery on the 1st August last. I must here refer to the plan of the post herewith accompanying. This department has an excellent 2-story stone building and shingled, which is used in the 1st-story, and a projecting shed also of stone, by the commissary department. In the 2nd-story are the officers of both departments and the quartermaster's supplies. There is another quartermaster's store, a temporary building of logs on end and shingled but this is open between the logs & not a suitable store for many articles of artillery harness, ammunition, & c, that are necessarily put into it. There is also another building more inferior still called the corn house. This has had the corn removed from it as unsuitable. These are all the quartermaster's store houses west of the stream. On the east of the stream there are two large corrals, bounded in part by the water, so that the arrivals may drink at will, and also a hay yard. In the south corral is a corn shed, and a saddle shed, & yard master's room, & shed shelters for animals on two sides. The other corral is also provided with sheds. The hay is brought 25 miles and delivered at 8.84 dolls the ton, quite reasonable. There is about 200 tons on hand & [a] good Fairbanks scales to weigh it. Here I will remark that every post where hay is bought, should be provided with [a] Fairbanks scales, for when the posts are removed or broken up the scales can be taken up. It will prevent cheating in the weight and estimates of loads. The quartermaster general should consider this matter. Corn is brought from Mexico and it costs here 1.93 dolls the bushel & there is 600 bushels on hand. On the outside of the south corral is a good stone smith shop & shingled and spacious and every way ample. A picket guard is constantly kept at these corrals.

The quartermaster sergeant of the regiment is his clerk and all his papers, returns and statements have been forwarded to date. He keeps as extra duty man, a yard master, a carpenter, a smith, & 8 teamsters. He pays 50 dolls per month for the site rent of the post, keeps 60 mules, 9 wagons, & 4 carts.

There was due the U.S., 30 Sept., 3261.39 dolls. Expended in October, 825.31 dolls. Expended in November, 25 dolls, due U.S. at date, 2411.08 dolls. Of this amount there is in the Assistant Treasury N. Orleans, 1404.47 dolls and in the Assistant Treasury N. York, 845. 85 dolls and in cash, 111.76 dolls.

The property of the department appears well cared for, and the duty is well performed by Lt. Davis.

Lt. Davis is also the acting commissary of subsistence and relieved Lt. Closson on the 1st August last. His supplies are all good and stored as above in the quartermaster's stone building. He uses the shed port as an issuing room. As before stated, the ordnance sergt. is the acting commissary sergeant and keeps the books and records & c. He has 175 lbs. hard bread on hand. Too much for this post & some should be removed, if found good. The beans are from New Mexico & cost 3.50 dolls the bushel, beef costs 3⅓ cts. the lb. delivered net, flour 6 cts. & of Texas manufacture. All his returns & statements & accounts have been duly forwarded at date. There was due the U.S. on 30th Sept., 713.03 dolls, received 3174.21, expended in October, 1004.16, and in November, 1465.12 dolls. Leaving a balance due the U.S. at date of 1417.96 dolls. This account is in a safe in his office. Lt. Davis also performs the duty well. All the supplies [and] funds for both commissary & quartermaster come thro' their respective chiefs of departments at San Antonio.

The quartermaster occupies on the east side of the Las Moras for his corrals & c. Yet on that side of the river there is another owner of the land as Landerstand and a village of trading stores has been put up there to the number of 5 or 6 & some hackalls & the stage station is there & it is called Brackettsville.[51]

The postmaster at Fort Clark is the ordnance sergeant & a mail leaves once a week for San Antonio & for El Paso & for Eagle Pass (Fort Duncan).

There is not, however, a settlement on the road to Eagle Pass for 38 miles.

A garden has from time to time been made on the Las Moras below the post & has been more or less productive. It depends entirely on the commanding officer for success I presume.

I have referred to the slow progress at this post in improvement. I will now call attention to the plan herewith & I have to remark that since 1856 two stone buildings have been erected, A & B, for officers. These are good buildings. But there is not a soldier properly quartered. The buildings marked o were most originally intended for the soldiers, and it was the intention to place the officers opposite, on the line of B. The officers, however, took them & now they are rotten & of little value for every purpose, sealed with cotton cloth. The building O is an old rickety building of logs on end, always occupied by the assistant surgeon. This is of no value. It is to my mind clear that the rank & file have been too long neglected in providing quarters for them when the officers are comparatively comfortable. I would recommend a change in the plan of this post. I would build soldiers quarters about along the prolongation of the band & adjutant's officer on A, B, fronting to the westward and extend them at will southeastly for the ground will admit of this & eventually when officers quarters are built, I would erect them on a parallel line fronting eastwardly, say from B with line C, D, and in due time, remove the present officers quarters. These quarters should all be built of stone, one-story high, from the quarry at hand, and they would cost but little, if done by extra duty men & the windows & doors imported from San Antonio.

There will be 5 companies here soon & no quarters for the soldiers at all. I have therefore to recommend that an appropriation be made for the soldiers quarters of Fort Clark this session of Congress of 15,000 dolls.

All which is Respectfully submitted
Jos. K. F. Mansfield
Col. & Inspc't. Gen'l.
U.S. Army

FORT DUNCAN

In Camp at the Esse's, 36 miles
south of Fort Duncan Texas,[52]
6th Dec. 1860

Sir:

My last inspection report was that of Fort Clark. I arrived at Fort Duncan on the 2d inst. & on the 3rd, 4th, & 5th, was engaged in the inspection of that post and have to submit to the General-in-Chief the following:

Fort Duncan is located on the Rio Grande at Eagle Pass and directly opposite Piedras Negras, a village in Mexico. Eagle Pass is a trading village & there is a ferry to cross the river and a custom-house officer. There seems to be a good understanding between the citizens of both sides. The Mexicans bring over corn, onions, sweet potatoes, and oranges, to the great accommodation of the garrison, as there is no garrison garden here, and the corn finds a ready market for our horses and mules, and it is transported to Fort Clark, and the wheat to the Texas flouring mills. It is 45 miles from Fort Clark & 118 miles from Fort McIntosh. There is a post office kept here by the sutler of the post, Lodivick Colguhorn. And there is quite a trading village, near the ferry adjourning the post. The accompanying plan of the post shows there are quite a number of buildings, sheds, & c, & c, very necessary to a command like this & that about 800 dolls more would put into quarters the 3rd company here now in tents. As a whole this position for the present school of the light battery practice & c, agreeably to Orders No. 10, War Dept, 9th May 1859, is probably the best in southwestern Texas. Agreeably to that order the mounted troops can be readily supplied, as the corn for horses must come across the river from Mexico, and the grazing is good & hay as cheap as at any other place probably in this region, and good mesquite wood can be had readily.

It is rumored here among the officers that another and entirely new position is to be occupied by this artillery station within two miles of Fort Inge and below it on the river Leona. That position they represent to me as unsuitable for this school in many respects, and as being much more expensive as to supplies than this. It is certainly about 60 miles further by land for the transportation of corn from Eagle Pass. Before the undertaking of an entire new post, the cost of the same should be considered. It is now in this department difficult to get a small amount expended on the old posts (which are highly important to this frontier) just as it was in 1856, when even a pound of nails was prohibited. In short, all expenditures for repairs, & c, have been prohibited by orders from headquarters of the depart. when the soldiers have worked gratuitously in many instances to make quarters for themselves, and private funds & company funds applied there to & where they are not now sheltered from the excessive heat of the sun. In my opinion it is time our soldiers were relieved from this business of building posts & then abandoning them and that their time should be employed of their military instructions. A particular & crucial examination of the locality and plan of Fort Duncan will show that it is almost complete for the accommodation of three companies & that too in a great measure at private cost of

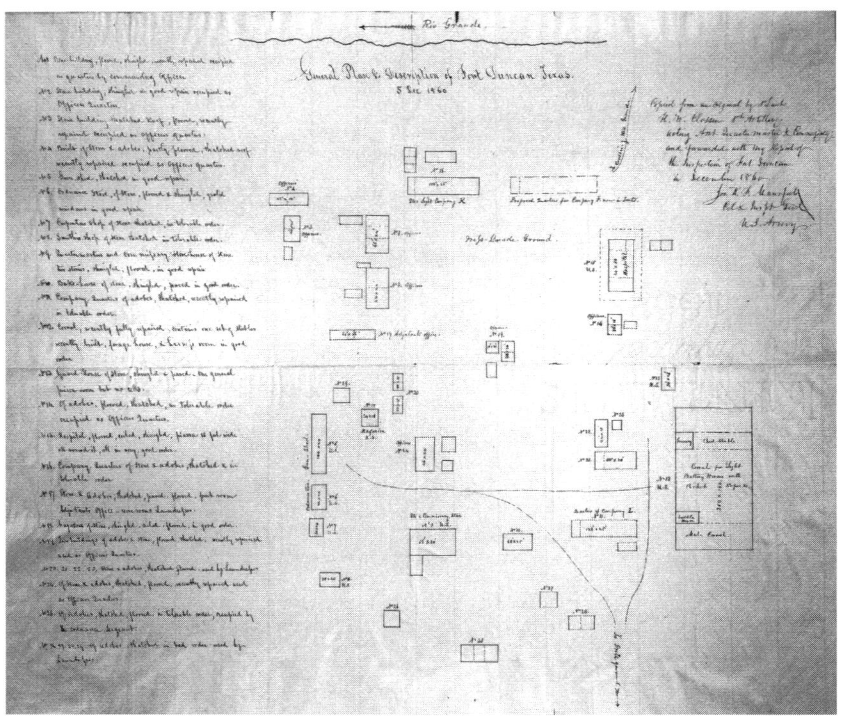

Sketch by Mansfield. (Illustration from LR, AGO, RG 94 courtesy of the National Archives)

soldiers & officers. The water is always good & the drill ground & place of target practice for both small arms & field battery & siege battery is complete as the shot are stopped in their course by the mountains.

The great objection to this post is the excessive heat and the want of seasonable rains. This is peculiar to this latitude and the frontier of Texas and cannot be avoided.

I found in command of this post Bvt. Maj. W. H. French with his Light Battery "K" and Companies "L" & "F" of the 1st Art. with a staff composed of Assistant Surgeon C. Southerland, ordnance sergeant, Thos. Drury and two ordnance enlisted men, one a saddler & the other a smith.

The two companies & the light battery passed in review at quick & double quick time very well.

Light Company K on inspection, Bvt. Maj. W. H. French in command, 1st Lt. S. F Chalfin sick in quarters since 10th November, 1st Lt. J. E.

Slaughter sick in quarters since 15 inst., 2d Lt. F. L. Childs, 4 sergeants, 4 corporals, 16 drivers, 21 privates, 1 guidon, 2 buglers, aggregate on parade 2 officers, 58 men, 4 sick, 2 confined, 1 in hospital, 2 cooks, 1 baker, 1 absent st Fort Monroe, aggregate 4 officers & 69 men. There were 40 horses on parade & 1 in stable, 3 six-pounder guns & 1 howitzer 12-pounder on parade. The carriages, caissons, guns, harness in excellent order & the company in the old light artillery uniform recently restored & made a fine appearance.

The following day they were taken through the drill of the battery by Maj. French and fired with blank cartridges which was handsomely done, and they fired at the target with round, spherical-case, shells & canister & the pieces armed by the non-commissioned officers, & the firing was efficient, well done, & very satisfactory. On the 3rd day at morning parade, they were taken through the manual of the sabre, by Lt. Childs & afterwards by the 1st sergeant of the company & showed they were well instructed in this arm. There was attached to this battery a travelling forge & battery wagon both in good serviceable order. There was a good gun-shed & a good shed in the corral for the horses. They were regularly groomed at the stable cells both morning and evening and in good condition, but-required their full allowance of grain instead of the half allowance recently ordered by the department commander. It is impossible for battery & cavalry horses and for mules to work with this reduction. (Here I must earnestly call the attention of the commanding general to this order reducing the allowance of forage to one half, say to 6 lbs. corn for a horse & 4½ lbs. for a mule & half allowance of hay.) I would recommend if the state of the finances require a reduction, that it be modified to 10 lbs. corn for a horse & 7 lbs. for a mule per day with a full allowance of hay when practicable. My own mule teams on the road are failing & I shall have to purchase grain for them out of my own private means or they will be left on the road. There is a store granary & a harness and saddle house of adobes with thatched roofs attached to the corral & very convenient. The roof of the harness house needed repair. A picket guard of one sergeant & 3 privates was put over the corral & horses & a sentinel kept on post at night & the yard policed by it during the day.

This company was quartered in a stone building with thatched roof, glass windows, earth floors, with two chimneys & two fireplaces, and detached from the same & one another, a kitchen & mess room of stone, & thatched roofs. In these buildings were the orderly & company store room, saddle shop, & c. They seemed to be ample & comfortable comparatively. There were 4 laundresses accommodated where they could find a room.

The books were in good order. There were 9 desertions in 1859, 9 in 1858, 25 in 1859, 8 in 1860, and 12 discharged in 1859 & 10 in 1860. The large number of desertions in 1859 was the year of the march of the company from Fort McHenry to Fort Clark. This company left Fort McHenry the 9th June 1859 via rail road, steamer, & marching; arrival at Fort Clark, Texas, 26th Sept. 1859. On 19th November, following a section of the battery, with forge, 33 men & 29 horses detached to Fort Merrill with Lt. A. C. Gillem, 1st Art. comd'g & returned to the post of Fort Clark, 7th Dec. 1859, having marched 390 miles. A detachment of 25 men & horses of this battery returned from a scout after Indians, 14th Dec 1859. A section of the battery, 25 men & 18 horses, detached 27th Dec. under Lt. A. C. Gillem for Brownsville. 18th June a section of this battery under Lt. E. L. Hartz, 8th Inft., returned having marched 400 miles. 27 men under Maj. French scouted from 14th to 20th from Las Moras to Devil's River. On the 18th, 19th, & 20th May 1860, this company scouted in pursuit of 200 Indians & made 94 miles in 36 hours from 2d to 6th June. Maj. French & Lt. Slaughter & 33 men scouted after Indians, and from the 7th to 14th June, Maj. French & Lt. Childs & 41 men scouted after Indians.

This company left Fort Clark, 30th July "en route" per Dept. Orders of 16 July, to take post at Fort Duncan & arrived there the 1st August. Thus it appears that this company, which was to take the direction of the artillery instruction at Fort Clark agreeably to Orders No. 10, War Dept., 1859, heretofore mentioned, has performed heavy duty in the field in addition to the commencement of a school of instruction. The order on this point has been complied with as far as circumstances would admit. The non-commissioned officers of the 3 companies have had instruction by recitation three times a week, but there has been no rotation in instruction of the officers by battery, as the officers of the other two companies present had been in a light battery, & probably will better instructed than the subalterns of the battery. There are no facilities for laboratory instruction here.

Pertaining to this battery were 50 Sharps rifles, 25 Colts revolvers, 54 sabres, 14 spherical case 6-pounder shot, 107 spherical case 12-pounder howitzer, 120 shells for 12 pr. howitzer, 64 canister for 6 pounder, 255 round 6-pr. shot, 30 canister 12-pr. howitzer, 2000 Sharps rifled ball cartridges, 800 blank 6-pr. cartridges, 1000 Colts ball cartridges, 32 knapsacks, 5 haversacks, 9 canteens, a fund of 12.65 dolls. The ammunition is stored in the magazine of the post, which is of stone & shingled & well secured. There is no post ordnance. There were 2 artificers. Thirteen recruits arrived & were added to this company the evening after I had closed my inspection.

Co. "L" on inspection, Capt. S. K. Dawson on leave for two months, S.O. 7 Head Quarters, Dept., 30th Ap. 1860, extended 6 months G.O. 124, War Dept., 26th June 1860. Left company 2d May 1860, 1st Lt. W. Silvey. adjutant of the regiment, left the company 22d April 1854, 1st Lt. J. W. Robinson in command of the company, Lt. R. H. Jackson on detached service at Fort Columbus with recruits for Dept. of Texas, S.O. 104, Head Quarters Army, 11th Sept. 1860, 3 sergeants, 3 corporals, 1 musician, 1 artificer, 31 privates, in the aggregate 1 officer & 39 men on inspection parade, 3 detached at Fort Brown confined, 1 sick, 4 confined, 1 sergt., 1 corpl., 5 men on guard, 1 excused, 2 cooking, 1 in hospital, aggregate 4 officers & 58 enlisted men.

The men on parade were in full uniform, neat, & arms, & c, in good serviceable order, but with a few haversacks deficient. This company went thro' the manual of the bayonet exercise handsomely & drilled well at the light inft. and at skirmishes and at the target, 6' x 22," 40 men one round each at 100 yards made 14 hits say 35 percent; 200 yards made 6 hits say 15 percent; 300 yards made 4 hits say 10 percent. The target firing was not good, owning in part to some 8 or 9 of the men not having practiced at the target at all.

The company arrived here 14th October 1860, from Fort Brown. It occupied quarters of adobes and thatched, built by "C" Co., 1st Art., out of their company fund and by subscription of the men, earthen floor, window glass broken and protected with cotton cloth, worthless bunks, a kitchen in rear of adobes, and thatched but no mess room, company property in a shed added to one end of the quarters. The quarters were clean & the men tolerably comfortable. There are 4 laundresses lodged in adobe huts & thatched roofs.

The books of the company were neat & in order, but the old descriptive book not completely written up, as no desertions and discharges are entered since 1852. There were 2 desertions entered in 1859 & 26 in 1860. Discharged in 1859 & 1860, six. There is a company fund at date of 413.71 dolls in Lieut. Robinsons hands as follows: in checks on Assistant Treasury New Orleans 356.80 dolls & the balance in cash. There are 75 rifled muskets, 5000 rifled ball cartridges, 46 knapsacks, 44 canteens, 23 haversacks.

The company had but one musician & one artificer, 2d Lt. R. H. Jackson, and twenty five recruits arrived and were added to this company the evening after my inspection closed.

Co. F on inspection, Capt. Samuel Jones absent on detached service, S.O. 156, War Dept., 3rd Nov 1858, and left company 21st May 1858. 1st Lt. W. Jenkins on detached service, Military Academy, S.O. 135, War Dept., 29th July 1859, left company 3rd March 1859, 1st Lt. H. W. Closson commanding company, 2 Lieut. D. Ramsay, 3 sergeants, 4 corporals, 1 musician, 1 artificer,

31 privates, in the aggregate 2 officers & 40 enlisted men on parade.[53] 5 privates on guard, 1 orderly, 5 prisoners, 1 sergt, 1 musician, 1 artificer & 5 men sick, 2 in hospital, 1 baker, 1 teamster, 2 cooks, 2 absent without leave. In the aggregate, 4 officers & 67 enlisted men. The men on parade were in full uniform with light blue pantaloons, neat, & arms and accoutrements in good serviceable order. Some few haversacks deficient, but in good condition to take the field. They went thro' the manual of the bayonet exercise handsomely & drilled well at the light inft. & at skirmishes, At the target, 6' x 22," 39 men one round each, at 100 yards, had 17 hits, say 43½ percent; at 200 yards made 7 hits, say 18 percent; 300 yards made 5 hits, say 13 percent. This company fired and drilled at the bayonet manual a little better then Company L.

This company left Fort Clark for this post 1st March 1860. It then had but one officer, Lt. Closson, who was doing the duty of quartermaster & commissary at that post till the 1st August. This company is in tents, 6 Sibley tents, 4 wall tents, 1 bell tent. The kitchen, a tent & no mess room. The company property is in a tent, 4 laundresses to the company accommodated in the various little buildings about the post.

The books were all in order & neat, no company fund. There were 17 discharges in 1859, 21 in 1860, 3 desertions in 1857, 6 in 1858, 4 in 1859, 4 in 1860. There were 80 rifled muskets, 5000 rifled ball cartridges, 500 blank 6-pr. cartridges, 50 knapsacks, 80 canteens, 80 haversacks. Three recruits arrived & were added to this company the evening after I had done my inspection.

In addition to the forementioned drills, there was a short battalion drill of Cos. "L" & "F" commanded by Lt. Robinson, but it was incomplete.

The guard house is built of stone & adobes & shingled, a prisoners room & a guard room. The guard is a sergeant, a corporal & 12 privates, a sentinel at the guardhouse, one at the artillery pack, 1 between the hospital & sutlers store, one across the parade. There were 14 prisoners, 6 waiting sentence, 3 undergoing sentence, 5 for minor offenses. The guard is mounted after breakfast & the morning parade & an officer of the day on duty.

The hospital is a good stone building & shingled with a piazza all around it, two chimneys & 4 fireplaces, good is dispensary, and store room, two large wards, a good kitchen & mess detached. It is ample in every respect, but wants painting very much, and its appearance on this account is discreditable to the government. The medical dept. is under the control of assistant surgeon C. Southerland, who relieved Dr. Olmsted, citizen, on the 6th June last. There is an acting steward, a matron, 2 attendants, 1 cook. The books & records are all in order and nothing serious wanting. The post is healthy. The temperature in June at 2 P.M. ranged from 90° to 112,° in July from 89° to 106,° and in August from 82° to 105.° The rain here from June to November, inclusive, 179 days was 19 slight showers, except one heavy rain in August. There are 20 iron bedsteads & a hospital fund of 1.03 dolls.

The adjutant's office is a stone building thatched with a stone floor. The records are all properly kept. The morning report book is a temporary one made at private expense. The book for that purpose sent by the quartermaster is too small, being simply an unruled bound foolscap, agreeably to paragraph 84 of the Army regulations. I must call the attention of the General-in-Chief to this regulation book. In my opinion its size is wholly inadequate. It will not admit a consolidation of the reports of companies & staff, & c, each day, and if it will not; then it cannot exhibit the strength of the garrison each morning and as a reference for troops & detachments does not answer the object I presume intended by a morning report book of a post.

The guard report contains the firing of the old guard at the target, which at this post is 900 yards, and only the hits in the bulls eye are counted. In the month of August last, the bulls eye was hit 9 times, which if we suppose 12 men to fire, would be about 2½ percent.

The drills at the post vary from once to twice a day. The light battery generally 3 times a week. This command is not called on for escorts here, as it would be, if stationed at Fort Clark; hence this is the best location for it & time of the men can be devoted to instruction thro' their officers.

Lt. H. W. Closson has performed the duty of assistant quartermaster since 20th March 1860, the reoccupation of this post & all his papers & records are well & properly kept, and forwarded to date. He has a carpenter's shop & a smith's shop of stone & thatched, a good mule corral adjoining the light battery corral, a granary. Corn is purchased at 1.83 dolls the bushel, hay at 15 dolls the ton, hauled 20 to 30 miles, wood at 3.50 dolls the cord, hauled 7 to 8 miles, pays 130 dolls rent per month for the post, keeps 6 wagons & 38 mules & 6 teamsters, a quartermaster sergeant, a yard master in charge of forage, a herder, smith, carpenter, as extra duty men when required.

The quartermaster's office is of stone & shingled, & camp & garrison equipage stored in it. There was due the U.S., 30th Sept., 79.80 dolls, due on 31st Oct., 4.70 dolls, received in November 2500 dolls, expended since 2378.24 dolls, due U.S. at date 126.41 dolls. This amount is in the Assistant Treasury, New York. This duty is extremely well performed by Lt. Closson. He is systematic energetic & competent.

Lt. Closson has also been acting commissary since the reoccupation of this post on the 20th March last, & all his books & papers & returns & statements well kept, & forwarded, to date. On 30th Sept., there was due the U.S. 206.35 dolls. Received in Oct., 159.04 dolls. Expended in October 316.55 dolls. Due U.S. on 31st Oct., 48.84 dolls. Received in November 116. 47 dolls. Expended in Nov. 196.44 dolls. Thus leaving a balance due to Lt. Closson at date of 31.13 dolls. He pays for flour 7½ cts. the lb., delivered. It is made in Texas of Mexican wheat. Before good bread is made of it, the experienced baker here says he has to mix ⅓ of imported flour with it. The same extra duty man fills the office of commissary & quartermaster sergeant.

A good stone two story building shingled roof is the commissary & quartermaster's store & all the supplies are well cared for. The bake house is a good building of stone & shingled, the oven fair, & bread good.

Lt. Closson is also post recruiting officer & has on hand at date 154.20 dolls, 50 dolls of it in Assistant Treasury, N.O. & 104.20 in cash.

The sutler, L. Colquhoun, keep a good supply of goods, but the soldiers's have access to other stores in the village.[54]

There seems to be harmony at the post, 4 of the officers have their families here, and the U.S. custom-house officer, W. Wallace, lives within the chain of sentinels, in a building of his own. The officers are comparatively, comfortably quartered and live in buildings erected by fatigue parties & at private cost. The soldiers quarters were built at the expense of companies. The only building erected at the expense of the government, are the hospital, magazine, quartermaster & commissary stores, guardhouse, gunsheds & stable sheds. The estimate for a set of adobe quarters for Company "F," now in tents, is but 800 dolls, and double this amount, say 1600, should be appropriated at the present session of Congress for the soldiers quarters and repairs of soldiers quarters here & 400 dolls for fences of office quarters & repairs.

On the arrival of this light battery at Fort Clark, 26th Sept. 1859, there was at that post Cos. L, M, & F, 1st Art. L & M Companies were ordered to Fort Brown, 12th Nov 1859, F Co. left Fort Clark for Duncan, 1st March 1860, and the Light Battery, Co. K, was the only command at Fort Clark, till the 29th July 1860, when it was relieved by Col. Bonneville's command & it left for Fort Duncan.

This post was last paid to the 31st October by paymaster McClure.

Accompanying this report is a plan of this post made by 1st Lt. W. H. Clossen, acting assistant quartermaster, to which I invite particular attention.

At this post only one officer employs an enlisted man as a servant & I think it would be better for the service if none were employed in that capacity in the army.

All which is Respectfully Submitted
Jos. K. F. Mansfield
Col. & Insp't. Gen'l.
U.S. Army

FORT McINTOSH

In camp at "Noria de los Federales"
34 miles east of Fort McIntosh[55]
13th Dec. 1860

Sir:

My last inspection of report was that of Fort Duncan. On the 9th instant, I arrived at Fort McIntosh, and on the 10th and 11th inspected that post & now have to submit the following report of the same to the General-in-Chief:

Fort McIntosh is located on the Rio Grande, about ¾ of a mile above the town of Laredo, which has a population of about 1200 souls, mostly of the Mexican race, and say 116 miles from Fort Duncan & 120 miles from Ringgold Barracks. The town of Laredo has improved some since I passed thro' it in 1856, but the post having been abandoned, is now in a forlorn condition as to quarters for both officers & men & for store houses. After the troops left it, altho' on private land, it was robbed of doors, windows, boards & c, & c, and some of the roofs taken off & buildings pulled down. There has been no time nor opportunity nor means to repair these damages & the orders of the dept. commander forbid expenses. So it stands in a very unsatisfactory condition much inferior to its condition in 1856, which I then regarded as bad in these particulars.

As to the importance of this post to the frontier, I can say that if the town contained an American population of 1200 souls, there would not be the least necessary for the post here, as they would be respected by all such marauding fellows as Cortinez & his gang.[56] As it is, this Mexican race is no security to an American citizen among them. But this is our frontier & the opposite bank of the river belongs to another nation & another race, who do not like us & perhaps with good reason, and it is proper for a great country & people like our own to keep up a system of frontier posts, & this is a good and necessary position for one, & should be now maintained, particularly as we have already built a field fort here. The fort, however, was

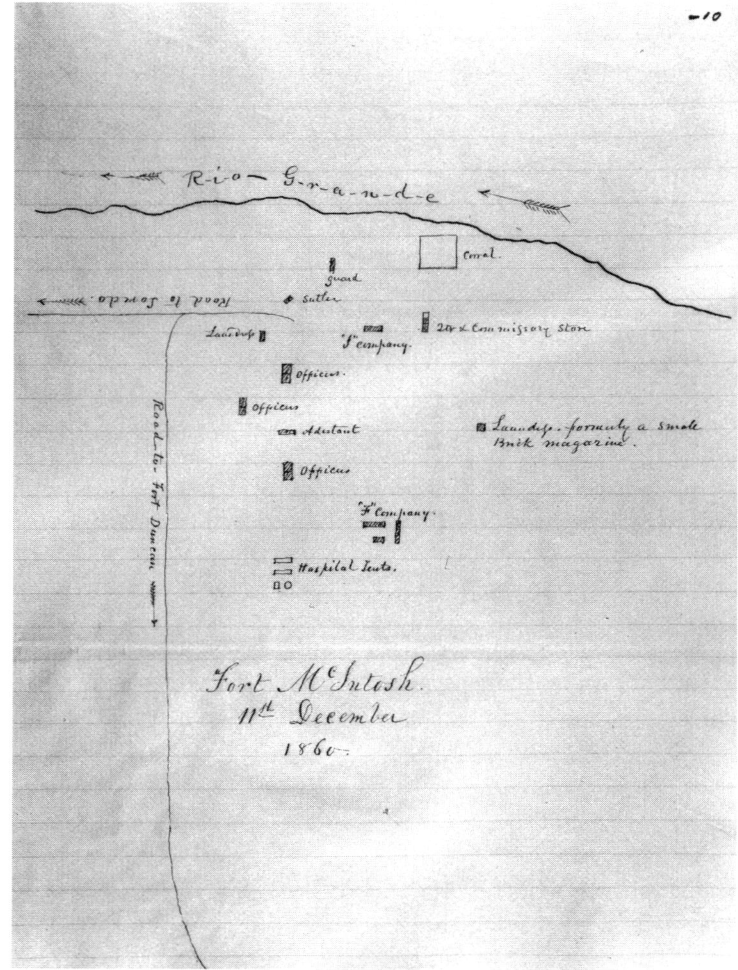

Sketch by Mansfield. (Illustration from LR, AGO, RG 94 courtesy of the National Archives)

a useless expense of labor when our troops were denied in 1856 the means of housing themselves.

It is difficult to say what sustains this town. Some corn, potatoes, onions, & c, are imported [from] across the river, and there is a custom house here & some few goods are retailed in return, and there is some grazing about 6 to 15 miles from the town where cattle & sheep & goats are kept by herders & shepherds for some of the inhabitants of Laredo. There can be but little produce from planting the soil as there is but little land suitable for that purpose. In short the country for miles from the river is a thick chaparral. There is abundant lime & stone but no timber for building purposes. Directly opposite on the Mexican bank of the river is the little town of Nuevo Laredo, grown up since the war with Mexico, & there is a ferry here.[57]

Fort McIntosh was reoccupied between the 27 Dec. & 5th Jan. 1860 by Capt. A. T. Lee of the 8th Inft, and the companies of Capt. C. D. Jorden & R. P. Maclay of the 8th Inft. Capt. J. Trevitt, Co. F of the 3d Inft., relieved Lt. E. D. Blake & company of Capt. Lee of the 8th Inft., 14 Sept 1860.[58] Maj. C. C. Sibley of the 3rd Inft. assumed command on the 27th October 1860, & added to the command. Co. I, Lieut. J. N. G. Whistler, commanding.[59] Accordingly, I found Maj. C. C. Sibley of the 3rd Infantry in command with Cos. F & I of the 3rd Inft, and with a staff of Assistant Surgeon J. J. Gaenslen, and a regular steward, Wm. B. Blair.[60]

These companies with the staff passed in review at quick & double quick time under the command of Maj. Sibley very well and after inspection, Maj. Sibley took them thro' most of the light inft. drill as a battalion, by dividing them into four companies & putting one company under a sergeant's command. This drill was satisfactory as far as it went. The major was ambitious & will in time have these companies well instructed.

Co. "F," Capt. J. Trevitt in command, 1st Lt. M. L. Davis on detached temporary duty at Fort Clark since the 5th Sept. 1860, acting regimental quartermaster and performing the post duty of assistant quartermaster & commissary at that post. 2d Lt. G. W. Holt, acting assistant & commissary of subsistence, 4 sergeants, 3 corporals, 1 musician, 28 privates on inspection parade, 1 quartermaster sergeant, 2 in hospital, 2 cooks for the company, 3 sick in hospital, 5 confined, 4 on guard. Say 2 officers & 53 enlisted men at command. The men on parade were in full uniform, except the pantaloons were of both light & dark blue. The arms & equipments in excellent serviceable order & the knapsacks, canteens, & haversacks good. Four of the muskets of this company had sights different from the standard & were arranged for 100, 300 & 500 yds. only. This is a disadvantageous innovation. The great benefit of the rifle musket is the long & certain range & why cut off its range & efficiency [at] 600 yards. I shall make a special report on the musket at the close of my tour. This company went through about half of the manual (as far as they had been instructed) of the bayonet exercise well. They went thro' the movements of the light infantry drill and at skirmishes pretty well, and at the target 6' x 22," 36 men, one round each, at 100 yards, made 21 hits, say 58⅓ percent; at 200 yards, made 15

Fort McIntosh was named for Colonel James Simmons McIntosh, who died of wounds received at the Battle of Molino del Rey during the Mexican War. Many posts in the Southwest, especially in Texas, were named for officers killed in the conflict. (Photograph courtesy of the Georgia Historical Society)

hits, say 41⅔ percent; at 300 yards, made 6 hits, 16⅔ percent. The tape primer springs did not feed well. Many failed to bring out the primer and many of the caps also failed. This company has only to continue the target practice daily to be proficient. The officers are ambitious & the men enter into the spirit of it. There is a rivalry between the companies.

The books of this company were in good order, and written up. There were 34 discharged in 1860, 2 desertion in 1857, 6 in 1858, 15 in 1859, 3 in 1860. A company fund of 103.85 dolls in the hands of Capt. Trevitt. 4

laundresses accommodated in different places, 80 rifled muskets, 10,000 rifled ball cartridges, 3800 blank cartridges, 5000 caps, 85 knapsacks, 90 canteens, 90 haversacks, 2 wall tents & flys, 5 bell tents, 3 Sibley tents & requisition made for two wall tents & two Sibley tents more.

It is quartered in a frame building clapboarded & shingled, 8 windows, sash & glass taken off & their place supplied with cotton cloth, earthen floor, no chimney nor fireplace, no bunks but clean. Two Sibley tents, 5 men in each, kitchen adobes & thatched, no mess room, a bakery, & orderly sergeant's room, & company store & one laundress in an adobe building thatched. The company bakes its own bread. The baker [is] not one by trade. The oven of adobes & out doors, & most worn out, bread good. This company was last paid to the 31st August by Paymaster F. A. Cunningham.

Co. I, Capt. & Bvt. Lt. Col. D. T. Chandler absent, S.O. 92, Head Quarters Army, since 16th August. 1860. Left the company, 20th August 1858, 1st Lt. J. G. Whistler commanding company, 2d Lt. R. G. Lay acting post adjutant, but attending to company duties, 2 sergeants, 2 corporals, 24 privates on parade inspection, 1 sergt., 1 corporal, 3 privates on guard, 2 sick, 1 cook to company, aggregate at command, 2 officers & 36 privates. No musician to the company. The men on parade were in full uniform, except the pantaloons were both light and dark blue. The arms & accoutrements in excellent serviceable order, but the knapsacks, canteens, & haversacks, much worn, having been in service 3 years.

My attention was called by Lt. Whistler to a defect in the musket of the Harpers Ferry manufacture. The screw that secures the back sight to the barrel penetrates in many instances the bore of the barrel, thereby creating a lump, or impediment to the ball & sometimes to the ramrod. This is a gross oversight of the inspection of the Harpers Ferry armory. My attention was also called to another evil, either the flange of the cap is too large or the nipple sits too close to the Maynard magazine, & the cap cannot be readily put on. These points will be referred to again in my special report on the musket at the close of this tour of inspection. The drill of the company at the light inft. & at skirmishes, & the progress at the manual about equal to that of "F" Co. At the target, 6' x 22," 30 men, one round each, at 100 yards, made 20 hits, say 66⅔ percent; at 200 yards, made 8 hits, say 26⅔ percent; at 300 yards, made 6 hits, say 20 percent. Not so good as Co. "F" but encouraging as the men & officers take a great interest on the rivalry.

The books of the company were in good order. There were 28 discharges in 1860, 1 desertion in 1857, 3 in 1858, 11 in 1859, 7 in 1860. A company fund in the hands of Lt. Whistler, in cash 473. 83 dolls & in the hands of

Bvt. Lt. Col. Chandler 500 dolls, in the aggregate 973.83 dolls. Of course I did not see the 500 dolls in the hands of Lt. Col. Chandler, as he had taken it away to disburse for the company. 80 rifled muskets, 5800 rifle ball cartridges, 1000 caps, 4600 Maynard primers, 4000 blank cartridges, 34 canteens, the knapsacks & haversacks worn out & a requisition made for others, 8 Sibley tents, 6 wall tents, 2 laundresses accommodated indifferently.

The company is quartered in a frame building clapboarded & shingled, & a chimney in the center with two fireplaces, 4 door ways & only one door, wooden floor, glass wanted in the windows. The kitchen tent & no mess room, company property & orderly room in two wall tents. This company does its own baking & uses the same bakery & oven as for "F" Co. The company was paid to the 30th June last in New Mexico.

The guard house is of stone & shingled, a prisoners room, and a guard room. The guard is 1 sergt., 1 corporal, 6 privates strong, 1 sentinel at the guard house & one at commissary & quartermaster's store, 5 prisoners waiting trial (4 for desertion & 1 sleeping on post). One man, Linzenhofer, 5 months confined & waiting trial. He is accused of desertion when bathing in Devil's River. From what I hear of the case & his long confinement, I would recommend to the commanding general to release him. His company officer was disposed to do so but he was ordered to be tried by Col. Bonneville.

The hospital is under the particular direction of Assistant Surgeon J. Y. Gaenslen, who has a regular hospital steward, W. P. Blair. A hospital tent is occupied by the dispensary and store room & steward. The supplies [are] ample of all kinds. Another hospital tent is occupied as a ward & 4 sick in hospital, 10 iron bedsteads, a small tent for a store room, a Sibley tent for a kitchen. Assistant Surgeon Gaenslen relieved Acting Assistant Surgeon Morrow on the 4th May 1860. The books & records were in order but no meteorological records, no thermometer, hygrometer, & c, Post healthy, 1 cook, 1 matron, 1 attendant. The whole condition of this dept. is as well as practicable under tents.

2d Lt. G. W. Holt has been acting assistant quartermaster since 14th Sept., when he relieved Lt. E. D. Blake, and performs the duty well. His supplies are stored in one end of a frame building partly pulled to pieces, and are stored with commissary supplies also and all the care taken of the property practicable under the circumstances. All his papers & returns have been forwarded to date. There was due the U.S., 30th Sept., 8.75 dolls, received in October 2500, expended in Oct. 234.07, received in November 1574.50 dolls, expended in Dec. 1785.09 dolls. Due the U.S., 30th Nov., 2064.09. Expended in Dec., 294.26 dolls, received in Dec. 10.18. Thus showing a balance due the U.S. at date of 1780.01 dolls. This amount is in Maj. D.

H. Vinton's check on Assistant Treasury N. Orleans, 74.50 dolls, in Assistant Treasury N. York 1444.75, in cash in trunk 260.76 dolls. (I will here remark he should be furnished with a small safe). He pays for corn, 2 to 2.25 dolls the bushel, for hay 20 dolls the ton & it is brought from 20 to 30 miles, for mesquite wood 2½ dolls the cord. He keeps an acting quartermaster sergeant, a clerk, 5 teamsters, 1 carpenter as extra duty men, 5 wagons & 34 mules.

Lt. Holt has been acting commissary for the same period & the supplies are stored jointly in the same building with quartermasters supplies. The flour heretofore received from Fort Brown was not good, the hard bread from the same also bad, eaten up by weevils, and none good on hand. He pays for beans from 4 to 4½ dolls the bushel, which is high, for beef 5 cts. in the net. All his papers and accounts have been forwarded to date. On 30th Sept. there was due the U.S., 117.64 dolls, received in Oct., 42.23 dolls, expended in Oct., 106 dolls, received in November, 1497.83 dolls, expended in Nov., 207.39 dolls. Due the U.S., 30th Nov., 1344.81 dolls, expended in Dec., 31.05 dolls. Due the U.S. at date, 1313.26 dolls. This amount is in Paymaster Longstreets check on the Assistant Treasury New York, 300 dolls, cash in hands 1013.26 dolls. The same person as quartermaster sergeant performs the duty of commissary sergt.

The regimental fund on 30th Oct. amounted to 9.50 dolls. Lt. Whistler is the recruiting officer, but has no funds. Hereunto is appended a plan of the post. The buildings occupied by the officers are in a very bad condition. They leak, the plastering is fallen down in part. The doors have been robbed of their locks, they want kitchens & c, & c, and there should be others erected for the subalterns & the surgeon, & the hospital as soon as the soldiers have been made comfortable. There should be about 8000 dolls appropriated for these objects at the present session of Congress.

There is a sutler at the post, B. J. DeWitt, and his supplies are sufficient.[61] He keeps [adequate supplies] in his own store and the soldiers can trade in the town.

As this post, 2d Sgt. James Trumble of "F" Co. applied to me for a situation at a recruiting rendezvous.[62] He is on his 5th enlistment, was at the battles of the 8th & 9th May, was two years in the Florida War, is 46 years old, and an unmarried man.

Also, Pvt. Frederick Reynolds, F Co., on his 5th enlistment, was at the battles of the 8th & 9th May, at Monterey, Vera Cruz, Cerro Gordo, Siege of Mexico, Churubusco, Molino del Rio, an American born.[63] Has a wife & three children. Has acted as drum major & would like a permanent place at a recruiting depot. He is a good fifer.

These men are meritorious & I told them I would recommend them to the General-in-Chief, & I do so cheerfully for positions as drill sergeants & instructor in music at a recruiting depot.

The officers at this post are all highly meritorious & the command in a good state of discipline.

All which is Respectfully Submitted,
Jos. K. F. Mansfield
U.S. Army

RINGGOLD BARRACKS

In Camp 22 miles east
of Ringgold Bks Texas
19th Dec. 1860

Sir:

My last report of inspection was that of Fort McIntosh on the 11th inst. I arrived at Ringgold Barracks & immediately commenced the inspection if that post & have the honor to submit to the General-in-Chief the following result:

Ringgold Barracks was inspected by me in 1856. It was then commanded by Lt. Col. Wait of the 5th Inft.[64] Its position in a military point of view, and as a frontier post, is good & unexceptionable. It is within a half-mile of the little town of Rio Grande City, a place that has improved exceedingly within four years, & is fast being Americanized in manners & customs, and here there is a custom house, and a ferry and a straight road to Camargo. It is about 3 miles below the mouth of the River San Juan, up which the steamers ascend[ed] in the Mexican War with troops & supplies and it is near the head of navigation of steamers on one side of the Rio Grande. It is 121 miles from Fort McIntosh & 115 miles from Fort Brown. There is a post office here kept by the sutler and the mail goes about once a week direct to Corpus Christi, & to Fort Brown, & to Fort McIntosh. Unhappily this post was abandoned about 1857, and in that interval, when the troops were away, depredations were commenced by Cortinez & others, & the buildings, & c., reduced almost to ruins.[65] A new lease has been made out on March, the same terms as before, with Clay Davis the proprietor, only subjected to the approval of the commanding officer of the dept. It provides for 2 years from 7th Dec. 1859, & 10 years more, if desirable, for 600 per annum & the privilege to purchase it for 25,000 dolls. I would certainly recommend its approval.

I look upon this chain of posts along the banks of the Rio Grande in connexion with a foreign nation on the opposite bank, as indispensable to the dignity as well as security of American citizens, so long as the march of progress in settling this unfavored region continues so slow.

The whole country for miles from the river is but continuous cactus, mesquite & chaparral, & all kinds of thorns. Of course there is no grazing here for miles & for want of seasonable rains, no agricultural productions except on spots on the bottom lands of the Rio Grande, & c.

I trust this post will be retained & not abandoned again, even if but a corporals guard be left in it. I propose making a special report to the General-in-Chief on all the military positions of Texas on this frontier, when I shall have completed my tour of inspection.

I found here in command, Lt. Col. E. Backus, with Co. D, 8th Inft, & Co. A, 3d Inft., & 138 recruits, recently received for the 3rd Inft. with a staff of Asst. Surgeon W. A. Carswell, & Lt. A. E. Steen acting adjutant post, & Lt. J. W. Alley acting assistant quartermaster & commissary of subsistence.[66]

This post was reoccupied by Capt. J. B. Ricketts company, 1st Inft., 29th Dec. 1859, Capt. A. T. Lee with his Co. "C," 8th Inft, joined on the 2d April 1860, and Capt. Lee assumed the command. Capt. A. W. Bowman's Co. "A" of the 3rd Inft. arrived on the 2d Nov 1860, from New Mexico. Col. Backus & Capt. Bowman arrived via the Brazos on the 6th November. Col. Backus was sick & did not assume the command till the 12th Nov.

Capt. Lee's company of the 8th Inft. left on the 20th November to relieve Capt. S. D. Carpenter and company at Fort Stockton. Capt. C. D. Jorden's company is under orders to proceed to Fort Hudson to relieve Bvt. Maj. L. Smith's company as soon as Capt. Johns's company of the 3rd Inft. arrives from New Mexico, which will likewise be accompanied by Capt. H. B. Clitz's company.

The post records were in the adjutant's office which is a little square building out of the regimental fund of the 5th Inft. The books were in order & clerk performed the office duties.

On inspection & review, Col. Backus being quite feeble, was not able to command the troops. This duty devolved on Capt. C. D. Jorden of the 8th Inft. The two companies passed in review in common & quick time, ordinarily well. And the recruits were paraded in their knapsacks & in undress.

Co. D, 8th Inft., Capt. C. D. Jorden in command, 1st Lt W. Craig on coast survey duty, S.O. 47, War Dept., 9th March 1860, not joined since promoted, 2d Lt. E. L. Hartz absent since the 9th Nov. 1860 on Genl. Court Martial, Fort Brown, Texas, S.O. 84. Head Quarters, Dept. Texas, 29th Sept. 1860, 3 sergeants, 1 corporal, 1 musician, 29 privates on inspection parade. 1 musician & 1 private detached to San Antonio since 14th

Ringgold Barracks was established at Davis's Ranch or what became Rio Grande City in October 1848. Mansfield criticized the army for abandoning the post in 1859, prior to the Cortina War. In his December 1860 inspection, Mansfield found companies of the Third and Eighth Infantry at the post. (Illustration from William H. Emory, Report on the United States and Mexican Boundary Survey*)*

August 1860, at Head Quarters Regiment with Col Seawell,1 corporal & 5 privates on guard, 3 sick, 1 absent with leave for want of uniform clothes, 3 confined, 1 sergeant as quartermaster sergeant. There were only 2 corporals to the company. In the aggregate one officer & 50 privates at command.

The men on inspection parade were in full uniform, except the pantaloons were both light & dark blue. They, however, appeared on parade without knapsacks, haversacks nor canteens. This was the result of deficiencies. They were neat & in excellent order. Their arms were in good serviceable order, except some few that went off at half cock. This company had made considerable progress in the light inft. drill, and went through the movements well. It, however, could not drill at skirmishes nor at the bayonet exercise (manual). At the target, 6' x 22," at 100 yards, 31 men made 14 hits or 45 percent; at 200 yards, 6 hits or 19⅓ percent; at 300 yards 6 hits or 19⅓ percent. The company books were in order. There were 27 discharges in 1860, 4 desertions in 1857, 5 in 1858, 20 in 1859,14 in 1860. It had a fund of 157 54/100 dolls in the hands of Capt. Jorden, who is also the company recruiting officer, and has 24 dolls due the U.S. at date.

Pertaining to the company were 66 rifled muskets, 10,000 rifled ball cartridges, 2000 caps, 39 tent knapsacks, & 11 knapsacks, 8 haversacks, 48 canteens, 2 wall tents, 5 Sibley tents, 3 laundresses.

It was quartered in a frame building, shingled, rough floor, no chimneys, nor bunks, the same building that was here in 1856, but much dilapidated & dismantled by the abandonment of the post, which gave opportunity to many to carry away what they could. Accordingly there were 12 windows without sash or glass. A little room attached as a shed served for a company store room & orderly, which also contained the ammunition. The kitchen was a miserable small frame building with an earthen floor & the mess room another of the same stamp. The company baked its own bread, which was ordinary. It was last paid to the 31st October 1860 by paymaster Cunningham.

Co. A, 3rd Inft., Capt. A. W. Bowman, 1st Lt. A. E. Steen acting adjutant post, 2d Lt. C. D. Hendren absent without leave since date of his resignation, 30th June 1860, 2 sergeants, 2 corporals, 2 musicians, 29 privates on inspection parade. 1 sergt., 5 privates, on guard, 1 baker, 1 company cook, 1 sergt., 3 sick. In the aggregate, 2 officers & 46 enlisted men at command.

The men on inspection parade were in full uniform, but had no knapsacks, haversacks, or canteens. Their arms were in good order. They went through the movements of the light inft drill and at skirmishes, tolerably well under the command of Lt. Steen, Capt. Bowman being indisposed. They did not know the manual of the bayonet exercise. At the target, 6' x 22," 28 men one round each, at 100 yards, made 14 hits, say 50 percent; at 200 yards, made 3 hits, say 10⅔ percent; at 300 yards, made one hits, say 3½ percent. This is quite poor shooting.

The company books were in order. There were 25 discharges in 1860, 7 desertions in 1857, 2 in 1858, 11 in 1859, 8 in 1860. There was no commissary fund. Capt. Bowman is the company recruiting officer with a fund due the U.S. of about 100 dolls. The account current is away from the post at present.

It had 72 rifled muskets, 5450 rifled ball cartridges, 7876 caps, 550 knapsacks, 50 haversacks, 45 canteens, (I condemned many of these to be dropped as worthless). Two wall tents, 12 bell tents. There were 2 laundresses. This company was similarly quartered to D Co., but not quite as well, in two old frame buildings. The orderly room & company property in one of them, with ammunition. The kitchen, 2 wall tents & fires outside, no bunks. The company bakes its own bread. It was cash paid in New Mexico to the 30th April 1860.

The recruits on parade were formed into two companies temporarily, one 75 strong, of which 68 were present, & 2 sick, 2 cooks, 1 baker, 1 in hospital as attendant, 1 confined. They were neat, but without arms. This company was

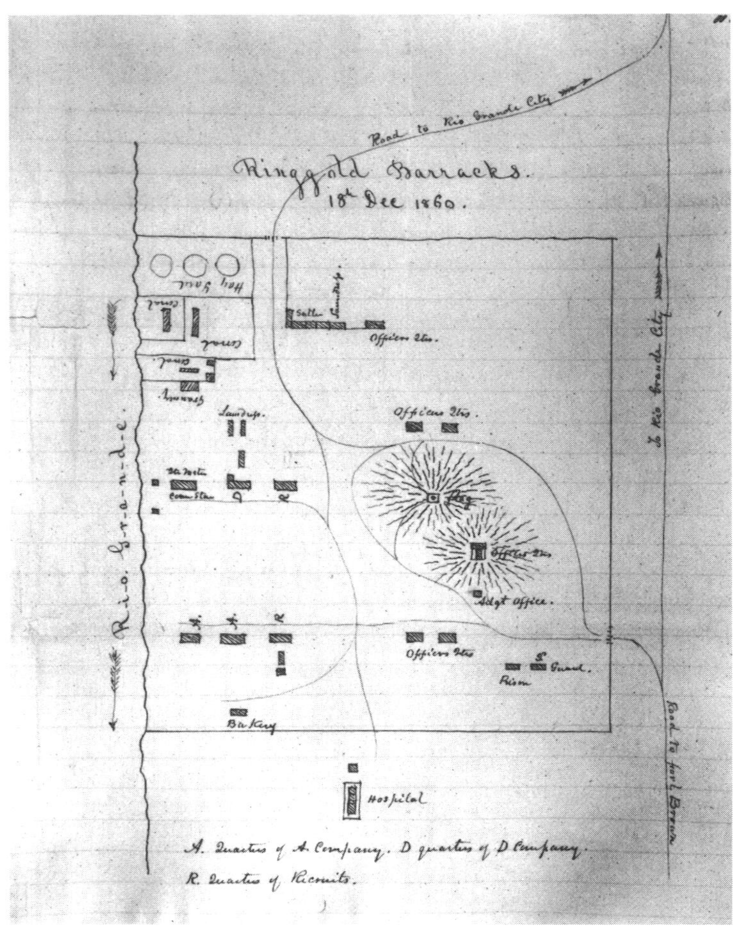

Sketch by Mansfield. (Illustration from LR, AGO, RG 94 courtesy of the National Archives)

under Lt. Alley's immediate charge. The other company was 74 strong, of which 63 were present, 3 sick, 2 confined, 2 cooks, 1 baker, 1 in jail in Rio Grande City for theft, 1 clerk to quartermaster, 1 at commanding officer's quarters. This company was temporarily under Lt. Steen's command.

All these recruits are to be distributed among the companies at this post, & Fort McIntosh. They were a good looking set of men. They were very much crowded in two old frame buildings similar to the quarters of A & D companies. These buildings are marked on the annexed plan R. One of them has 11 windows, but no sash nor glass, wooden shutters, 4 door ways & only two doors, kitchen a similar old building with earthen floor. The other building does not materially differ in character, but the kitchen attached is two bell tents, & a fire outside.

There were no bed sacks on hand, & corn sacks were given the men to make bed sacks of them. These recruits were brought into the department by Lt. Alley (on board of the Star of the South from N.Y., say 582 in all, commanded by Capt. B. H. Hill, 1st Art., left New York, 31st Oct., via Indianola & the Brazos). He represents they were too much crowded on board the ship. They are temporarily crowded here. It is to be regretted that the first impressions a recruit gets in entering the service are to come from such accommodations. I am not surprised at the many desertions in our service.

The guard house is a frame building shingled, rough weather boarded, marked F & a prisoners room within. Also, a prison house of brick and plastered roof adjourning which was formerly the magazine of the post & should be now.

There is a regular by appointed officer of the day & 1 sergeant, 1 corporal, & 9 men is the strength of the guard. One sentinel is placed at the guard-house, one with the prisoners on fatigue, & 1 at quartermaster's corral. There were 8 prisoners, 3 undergoing sentence, 2 for desertion from C Co., 8th Inft., 3 for minor offenses. One of the deserters has irons on & iron shackles to his feet, as he has repeatedly tried to make his escape. He is a German and says he deserted, as the sergeant of his company gave him no peace after he had won from the sergeant, by gambling, about 600 dolls. I think all sergeants that gamble with the privates of their companies should be broke.

Hospital. This building is generally good. It has two chimneys & 4 fire-places, 2 wards, a hall, dispensary, steward's room, a piazza all round it, but in a bad state of repair. It has been pilfered of locks, shelves, & c, & c, and the glass broken during the abandonment of the place. The kitchen a small detached building. There is ample medicines & medical supplies, & 20 iron bedsteads, & c. Assistant Surgeon W. A. Carswell had the charge & control of it since its reoccupation on 29th December 1859, almost a year. He has done his best to put it in proper condition. He has an acting steward, a hospital fund of 3.57 dolls. The books & records are in order, & all his returns but those for November, which are not quite ready in consequence of his having been on leave of absence, have been forwarded. The number of showers of rain from June to November, inclusive, 183 days in 33, two of those in August were heavy. The temperature in June at 2 P.M. ranged from 87° to 103,° in July from 91° to 102,° in August from 71° to 100.° This post in not considered healthy.

In 1856 I gave the opinions of two distinguished surgeons on this point. They were of opinion the garrison should be relieved every two years.

The duty of assistant quartermaster has been performed by Lt. J. W. Alley, who relieved Lt. E. W. H. Reed, 8th Inft., on the 20th November 1860. Lt. Reed left this department with outstanding debts to the amount of 6016.58 dolls, for the paymaster of which no funds have been received by Lt. Alley. His books and papers are in proper condition. He keeps a clerk, quartermaster sergeant, 7 teamsters, 1 smith, 1 herder, 1 carpenter, 1 saddler, as extra duty men. He pays 1.68 dolls the bushel of 56 lbs corn, 20 dolls the ton for hay, brought 10 to 20 miles & has about 135 tons on hand, well stacked, pays for wood, 1.60 dolls the cord delivered of mesquite. He keeps 7 wagons & 42 mules. There are 3 corrals, one for hay, two for mules & horses & wagons with sheds of shelter for the animals & a smith & carpenters shops in them. These are comparatively the best part of the post & are very good. A granary, a large frame building. A store house, a large frame building, 2 stories & braced outside, and the office for quartermaster & commissary on the 2d story, and the building contains stores of both these departments. He is deficient in mule shoes, & lumber costs 80 dolls the [left blank]. His monthly statement for November has been forwarded.

He has receipted for a train of 6 wagons, to transport Capt. Jordan's company to Fort Hudson. He also has a train of 3 wagons that brought Company A from New Mexico, subject to orders from head qts. of the dept. These trains have been on hand sometime. Lt. Alley has also performed the duty of commissary for the same period, having relieved Lt. Reed. Reed who turned over no funds to him, and left no debts to be paid. His monthly statement for November has been forwarded. He has since received 37.08 dolls, which is in a safe & has made no expenditures. He pays for beef 4⅞ cts. the net, delivered, keeps a commissary sergeant, & the office same as for quartermaster, & supplies stored in the same building. There are 51 bbls. flour brought from Brownsville supposed to be worthless, 3963 lbs. hard bread eaten by weevils, 2 bbls. rice worthless, 3 bbls. beans the same. These articles will be sold at auction. The books & records are properly kept. Lt. Alley belongs to "C" Co. 3d Inft. daily expected.

The bakery is a brick building & shingled roof, & brick oven a little too old, but answers well. The bread is only tolerable.

The officers quarters like those of the soldiers have been robbed of the locks & fences, & are in a very bad state of repair.

The sutler, John B. McCluskey, performs that duty well & is also postmaster & occupies his own buildings.[67]

In conclusion, I must recommend that the government make an appropriation of 6000 dollars to erect & repair suitable buildings for a garrison of at least 3 companies for the soldiers, & 2000 dolls for the repair of officers quarters.

At this post, Sgt. Duncan McIntyre of Co. A, 3d Inft., made application to me. He is on his 5th enlistment, was at the battles, 8th & 9th May, at Monterey, Vera Cruz, Cerro Gordo, Contreras, Churobusco, Chapultepec, Garrita & returned with his regiment the 3d Inft.[68] He says he was recommended for a certificate of merit, but did not receive it, & would like to have it. If there be no good reason why he should not receive it, it should be given to him. He is anxious for the appointment to ordnance sergeant [and] has no family. I would recommend that something be done for him. There has never been (he says) but an ordnance sergeant appointed from the 3d Inft. & that Sgt. Bromly of the company.[69] Will the General-in-Chief consider his case?

All of which is Respectfully Submitted,
Jos. K. F. Mansfield
Col. & Inspector Genl.
U.S. Army

FORT BROWN

In Camp en route to San Antonio
120 miles north of Fort Brown[70]
Texas 11th Jan 1861.

Sir:

My last report of inspection in this department was that of Ringgold Barracks. On the 23rd Dec. last, I arrived at Fort Brown. I was detained at that post by Christmas, bad weather, New Years Day, & the necessity of resting my mules till the 4th inst., when I left. My inspection commenced on the 2d & was completed on the 3rd inst., and I have now the honor to report to the General-in-Chief as follows:

Fort Brown, so called, is about 600 yards to the northward of Fort Brown of the Mexican War, and is close adjoining the town of Brownsville. Of course it is a mere locality with quarters, & c, for troops. The old fort is grown over with bushes & trees, & the outline of its grandeur recalls to mind its intrusive value. It is a lovely place where the past can be rehearsed by those living who took part in the exciting scenes of the war, and the patriot can silently mourn for those brave & honored officers, & soldiers, who have done their duty for their country, & are now no more.[71]

This post is 116 miles from Ringgold Barracks, 66 miles below the town of Edinburgh, where there is a custom-house officer.[72] The road all the way to Ringgold Barracks is good for wagons & troops. It is about 30 miles from the Brazos & Point Isabelle & is situated directly opposite to Matamoros.[73] It is about 300 miles from San Antonio by land over a wagon road, which can be travelled in from 10 to 16 days. It has a steamer communication with Ringgold Barracks, & with the Brazos, & thence to New Orleans. Thus it appears its military position is good to control the country in this quarter & where the population is such as the frontier of Texas has, being mostly of Mexican origin & unreliable, as the Cortinez raid has of late proven, it should not again be entirely abandoned.

It has been urged against this post, that it is unhealthy and this is undoubtedly true. It, however, may be greatly alleviated in this particular by proper measures. A great step has already been taken by Bvt. Maj. H. J. Hunt of the 2d Art. by digging a trench, & filling a large lagoon laying between it, & the old fort, during a pocket in the river, & allowing the water to be changed by a corresponding outlet further down the stream. The trenches were then closed, and it is protected, there will be no yellow fever here the coming season. At the time Bvt. Lt. Col. Taylor & 39 men of "L" Co., 1st Art., died. He attempted when this lagoon was very low, to remove the dead fish, & c., then in a state of decomposition, and it is not surprising there should be so much yellow fever. Even now at this post, the sinks are very deep, & offensive, & I doubt not are sufficient in hot weather to produce the yellow fever. Common lime should be used freely, & particular attention paid to trimming trees in the vicinity, to admit a free circulation of air. The buildings too stand about 3 feet above the ground & some of them are not well ventilated underneath, & there are old wooden cisterns in a bad condition, & requiring repairs & cleaning. In short the whole post in order to be healthy & in a suitable condition for this climate, requires a general over hauling & repair. All these matters depend in a great measure on the commanding officer.

While on this subject, I must remark, the buildings all require repair & refitting, as they stand on wooden blocks generally, & are rotting fast, and the corrals for the animals want much due to them. There is no proper nor sufficient stable for the horses of the Light Co. now stationed here & I must remark in relation to this post, for the security of the frontier, there is no necessity for this Light Battery here, and it is wholly unsuitable for its instruction. It is either too dusty, or too muddy, or too hot, and it is not possible for the battery to fire with shot, shell, or canister, without the great probability of either killing persons or animals. In addition, at any such raid in future as that of Cortinez, the battery is worthless & cumbersome in the field along the Rio Grande on account of the chaparral. Further, the frontier is not the proper place for drills of this character that teach a neighboring people like the Mexicans, the full value of such an arm on the field. I reported against this position in 1856 as a suitable place for a field battery & I see no reason to report otherwise now, and trust it will be removed as soon as practicable, & before the sickly season. I have further to remark on this subject that the drills with horses have been suspended for want of full forage.

I found in command at this post Capt. B. H. Hill, 1st Art., with his own company "M," and Light Battery "M," 2d Art., and a staff of Assistant Surgeon L. H. Holden & M. Foster, hospital steward.[74] There was also stationed here Paymaster Cunningham.

Co. "M," 1st Art., Capt. B. H. Hill in command, 1st Lt. L. O. Morris Acting Asst quartermaster & commissary, 1st Lt D. McClure on reextended leave of absence for 12 months from 9th Nov., G.O. 210, Adjt. Genl. Office, 18th Sept. 1861, 2d Lt. W. M. Graham on extended leave of absence until 4th Jan. 1861, S.O. 161, War Department, 7th Aug., 3 sergeants, 1 corporal, 2 musicians, 51 privates on inspection parade, 1 corporal, 8 privates on guard, 4 sick, 3 confined, 1 cook, 1 baker, 1 extra duty, 2 detached service. In the aggregate, 2 officers & 76 enlisted men for duty. There were but 2 corporals & 2 artificers included above. The company passed in review in quick & double quick time. There were many recruits & the movements were imperfect. They could no go thro' the manual of the bayonet exercise, not yet having learned it. They went thro' the manual & movements of the light infantry drill tolerably but could not drill as skirmishers. At the target, 6' x 22," 32 men one round each at 100 yards, made 14 hits or 43¾ percent; at 200 yds., made 10 hits or 31⅓ percent; at 300 yds. made 7 hits or 21° percent. The men on inspection were in full uniform & arms, & c, in good serviceable & good order & the books & records were in good order & the monthly report for Dec. duly to be forwarded. There were 2 discharged & 22 desertions in 1860. There were 81 serviceable rifled muskets, 5 Colts revolvers, 5000 rifled musket ball cartridges, 50 knapsacks, 20 haversacks, 62 canteens, 6 Sibley tents, 2 wall tents. A fund of 1442.41 dolls in the hands of Capt. Hill, as follows, in Lt. Gillem's checks, 1200 & 225 dolls in Assistant Treasury, New Orleans & cash 17.41 dolls. 4 laundresses to the company in temporary buildings.

The company was quartered in a frame building, one story & shingled, one chimney & 2 fire places, neat, bunks made by the men & double tiers, but very inferior & not suitable. Others should be supplied. The mess room was a similar building & one fire place. The kitchen was built

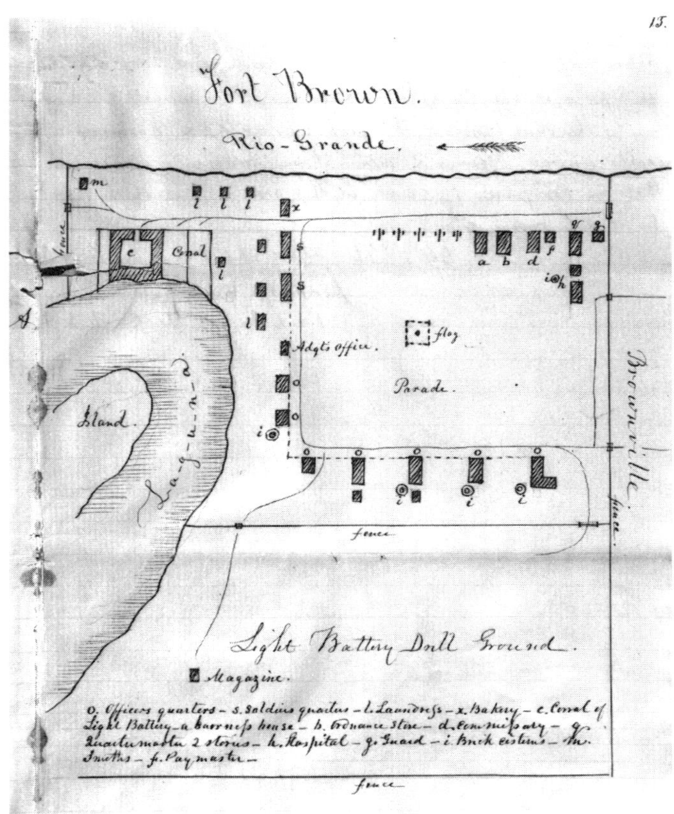

Sketch by Mansfield. (Illustration from LR, AGO, RG 94 courtesy of the National Archives)

by the enlisted men & at their own expense with a good range. The company property & office in the garret even the mess room.

Light Co. "M," 2d Art., Capt. & Bvt. Maj. H. J. Hunt on leave for 60 days, S.O. 98, Head Quarters, Dept. Texas, 26 Nov., and left 13th Dec 1860, 1st Lt. E. R. Platt in command, 1st Lt. T. R. Thompson sick, 2d Lt. G. D. Bailey sick, 4 sergeants, 1 bugler, 1 guidon, 24 drivers, 31 cannoneers inclusive of 4 corporals & 54 horses on parade inspection, 1 on guard, 1 cook, 1 extra duty for hay, 2 in hospital, 2 sick. In the aggregate, 3 officers & 69 enlisted men at command. Included in this number are attached from the Ordnance Department, 1 smith & 2 carriage makers. One musician only to the company.

This company was armed with four light 12-pounders, with a battery wagon & travelling forge, and passed in review on the walk & trot well. The guns, harness, implements, horses & men, were neat & in excellent order, and were well drilled by Lt. Platt, and gave satisfaction. His two subalterns at terms were sick. There could be no target firing in this locality. There was a great want of convenience for [a] harness house & corral and sheds for the horses, & the place as I before stated, is not suited to the battery. The horses being on half forage were now unable to drill in future & the hay they received was of a worthless character hardly fit for litter. The weather had been for several days stormy, and the corral was ankle deep in mud. There were no feed troughs & no lumber allowed to make them of & of course the half allowance of forage was in part wasted on the ground. The harness was placed in a building adjoining the commissary store, say 600 yards from the corral, & inconveniently, & the battery wagon & forge in the same & in good state of preservation.

This company was quartered like the other in a separate building, with bunks made by the men & with a separate messroom & kitchen constructed at the expense of the enlisted men & by them. 4 laundresses quartered in temporary huts.

The company property was in a good state of preservation, 84 sabres, 15 Colts pistols, 2 Adams pistols, 128 fixed round 12-pr. shots, 98 shells for 12-pr., 92 spherical case for same, 540 blank 12-pr. cartridges, 1200 Colts pistol ball cartridges, 1504 friction primers, 5 wall tents, 2 bell tents, 5 Sibley tents. The books were in order & kept in part of the building of the adjutant's office, 2 discharges in 1860, 14 desertions in 1859, & 9 in 1860. There was a fund of 89.35 dolls in the hands of Lt Platt. The stable guard consisted of two non-commissioned officers & 6 men, which also herded the horses & policed the corral.

The post guard was under the direction of an officer of the day, 1 corporal, 1 lance corporal, 6 privates, 1 orderly. A sentinel is kept at the gate where the guard house stands & one at the magazine. There were 10 prisoners, one for desertions & 9 for drunkenness. Some of those for drunkenness had only the day before been released under the orders of Gen. Twiggs, releasing the prisoners generally of the department from the sentences imposed by courts. And here I must remark, that when a soldier has been condemned to be indelibly marked, & shaved, & drummed out of camp or dishonorably discharged, he should never be permitted to enter the ranks again & stand by the side of a soldier, and I have to call the attention of the General-in-Chief particularly to this point. In such cases of the man be released he should be discharged. There is no use in retaining such a fellow in the service to lower the standard of the private soldier. There were several such cases here & I think three of them belonged to Capt. Stoneman's Co., 2d Cavalry. The guard house was a frame building with a guard room & a prisoners room & no cells.

The hospital has been under the direction of Assistant Surgeon L. H. Holden since the 20th November 1859 when reoccupied, with a steward Max Foster as his aid. It is a large frame building near the quartermasters store & guard house. Is ample as to size & supplies & accommodations, a dispensary & stewards room, store room, and a large ward, a kitchen, & c, & 20 iron bedsteads, all in good order. There were 5 sick in hospital & it is healthy here in winter & sickly in summer, one attendant, one cook, one matron. The books & records in order & a fund of 31.15 dolls. From May to December 1860, 245 days, there were 32 showers, 3 of them in August last heavy. In June the temperature ranged from 86° to 95° at 2 P.M., in July from 77° to 102° & in August from 80° to 100°. All the returns have been duly forwarded.

The post bakery is a frame building with oven of brick & good, a regular baker & good flour & bread.

The duty of assistant quartermaster has been performed by Lt. L. O. Morris, 1st Art. since 1st Dec 1860, when he relieved Lt. A. C. Gillem of the 1st Art. who turned over no funds but a certificate of indebtedness of 1879.07 dolls. As yet no returns have been required of him. His papers will be in readiness to forward according to the regulations. He has received for sales 162.20 dolls & from Maj. D. H. Vinton, 4800 dolls. Expended to Dec. 31st 4708.61 dolls. Due U.S. at date 254.20 dolls in cash on hand in safe.

His office & store house is a large frame two story building. It also comprises his saddler's shop. His operations extend to the employment of a citizen clerk at the Brazos for whom he pays 85 dolls per month, & of two laborers there for which he pays 30 & 20 dolls respectively per month, & the three each receive a ration per day. He keeps generally a quartermaster's sergeant, a smith, a carpenter, 5 teamsters, & a clerk in common with the commissary department as extra duty men, 33 mules, 5 wagons, pays for corn, 1.24 dolls the bushel for oats, .94 dolls the bushel of 32 lbs for hay, 13. 95 dolls the ton, which would be reasonable if it were good, for wood 2.50 dolls the cord for mesquite. Lieut. Morris is attentive & competent & performs this duty well.

Lt. Morris has also been acting commissary of subsistence since 1st Dec. 1860, and relieved Lt. Gillem from this duty, who turned over to him 764.26 dolls. He received in New York for recruits 300 dolls, received for sales 34.89 dolls. Expended transferred & disbursed since, 869.06 dolls, due the U.S. at date 230.09 dolls. This amount is in the Assistant Treasury, N. Orleans. His office is the same as that of the quartermaster's and his clerk the same. His supplies are kept in a one-story frame building adjourning the quartermasters. He has no sugar on hand but purchases daily at the prices of the department. He keeps a commissary sergeant, pays for beef 4½ cts net, sugar 10 cts.

His accounts & papers are all properly kept & will be forwarded according to the regulations. There are a number of bbls. of hard bread unfit for use & some flour, & c, which I recommended to be condemned & sold at once.

Lt. Morris also performs this duty well. Lt. Morris is also post treasurer, but has had no funds since 31st Dec. He has been without a fire in his office in consequence of their being no chimney & denied a stove. I regard this as unjust & injurious.

This post has been under the command of Capt. B. H. Hill, 1st Art., since 19th Nov 1860. He joined with recruits from New York. Of course he has had but little time to advance the drills of the two companies here. On the 5th Nov., Assistant Surgeon Holden requests that drills be discontinued during the epidemic & that morning drills of the Light Battery from May to November be abolished. Thus, 6 months of the year the rank & file are not to be instructed. Hence, this is not a post to instruct soldiers & an additional argument against the Light Battery here, with horses not to be used for 6 months at a time in the battery. However, Capt. Hill has had regular drills since the 9th Nov., two per day for the foot company & one for the Light Battery. But the last drill has taken place for the Light Battery in consequence of the half forage to the horses.

There is no post fund, no sutler at the post, & none needed as the enlisted men can trade in the town.

The books are all in order, kept in the adjutant's office which is a small frame building. Here I saw the late order of Gen. Twiggs of the 20th Dec 1860, No. 21, releasing prisoners of the department, and returning to the ranks some who were condemned to be shaved & marked, & drummed out of service, & whose punishment had been commuted to dishonorable discharge. There were 3 men of Co. "L," 1st Art., stationed at Fort Duncan here from such a sentence & sent to the ranks.

Capt. Hill is accountable for the post ordnance, as the ordnance sergeant has been temporarily detached to the Brazos by the chief of the ordnance corps. There are on parade mounted 2 howitzers 24-prs., 4 guns 12-prs., 2 guns 6-prs., 1 battery wagon, 1 travelling forge with limbers & caissons complete in good order. I recommended a piece of board be put under each wheel, to move it from the ground, which was done immediately. There was a quarterly of ordnance property, harness, & c, in a building adjoining the harness house of the Light Battery, a part of which the soldiers had converted into a theater, a very healthy recreation for the men.

A magazine of brick & slated roof was about 400 yds. from the buildings, in the Light Battery drill ground. This was full of ammunition, & c, and contained the following: 96 shells for 24-pr. howitzers, 64 spherical case for 24-pr. guns, 176 spherical case for 12 pr. guns, 88 spherical case for 6-pr., 8 spherical case for 12-pr. howitzer, 20 grape for 24-pr. guns, 28 grape for 12-pr. guns, 33 canister for 24-pr. howitzer, 160 canister for 12-pr. guns, 70 canister for 6-pr. guns, 560 shot for 12-pr. guns, 269 shot for 6-pr. guns, 315 blank cartridges for 24-pr. guns, 100 blank cartridges for 6-pr. guns, 10,000 Sharps carbine ball cartridges, 4000 colts ball cartridges, 1000 muskets ball cartridges, 4000 musketoon lock and ball cartridges, 115,000 rifled musket ball cartridges of caliber .58, 10,000 Harpers Ferry rifle ball cartridges, 300 cartridge bags, 600 friction primers, 100 percussion primers, 50,000 musket caps, 7 bbls. damaged & condemned powder used for blank cartridges.

These articles were in good state of preservation and the magazine dry. It was provided with double doors, but should be surrounded on this locality by a wall fence.

I refer to the plan, herewith, for the distribution of the quarters which are ample if in a good state of repair for two companies. The water used is principally from cisterns & there are 5 brick cisterns all of which leak, since the blowing up of a store in Brownsville and there are a number of wooden cisterns out of repair. The water of the Rio Grande is reported as offensive when at its lowest stage in hot weather. But at present that water is used & a wagon employed to haul it, & supply the quarters.

I would recommend an appropriation of 3000 dolls for repairs of soldiers quarters & bunks & corral, and 2000 dolls for repairs of offices quarters & cisterns & store houses.

The discipline of the post was good & harmony exists among officers & men. I am, however, of opinion that one company is ample at this post & that it should be relieved every year.

All which is Respectfully Submitted
Jos. K. F. Mansfield
Col. & Inspt. Genl.
U.S.A.

PAYMASTER F. A. CUNNINGHAM, FORT BROWN

In camp "en route" for San Antonio
Texas 14th Jan 1861.

Sir:

The last inspection report I closed was that of Fort Brown. Maj. F. A. Cunningham of the pay department was stationed at this post & I now have to report to the General-in-Chief my inspection of that officer as follows:

Paymaster Cunningham was stationed at this post from 1st Feb. 1857, to 15th Sept 1858, and after that time, San Antonio till the 15th Sept 1860.[75] He pays all posts below Fort Duncan on the Rio Grande & is able to do so every two months. He generally leaves Fort Brown on a steamer for Ringgold Barracks, then he takes government transportation of 4 mules to his own spring wagon, & with an escort of 10 men, & two wagons, & a wagon for his specie, & c.

His bond for 4 years from 5th December 1860 has been renewed & approved. On the 30th November 1860, there was due the U.S., 23,156.96 dollars. Expended since 11,542.27, due U.S. at date, 11,614.69 dolls. Of this there is in the Asst. Treasury at New Orleans, 1,104.75 dolls, & in Asst. Treasury at New York 258.36 dolls, and in coin on hand 10,251.58 dolls.

There is nothing but a travelling safe to keep his money in at the post. The check books on Assistant Treasury at New York & New Orleans appear well kept, and properly balanced. The large safe formerly used at this post by Paymaster Wagner was removed to San Antonio & never returned.

His office is a frame building near the guard house, but [it] has no chimney, nor a stove & in cold weather, in winter, it is impracticable to sit & write there. A stove should be furnished here, but as yet it has been denied by the quartermaster's department.

The unexpected balance of 11,614.69 dolls should be paid out, & his accounts closed before any further funds be sent to him. This is due to his present bondsmen as a business transaction, and I would call the attention of the paymaster general to it.

Maj. Cunningham keeps a clerk who seems to be competent in every respect, and the duty is well performed by the major.

All which is Respectfully Submitted
Jos. K. F. Mansfield
U.S. Army

CAPTAIN GEORGE STONEMAN'S COMPANIES E & G, 2d CAVALRY

In camp "en route"
to San Antonio, Texas
17 Jan. 1861
Lt. Col. Lorenzo Thomas
Asst. Adjt. Gen.
Head Quarters Army.

Sir:

My last inspection report was that of Paymaster Cunningham, stationed at Fort Brown. I left that post on the 4th inst. and arrived at the camp of Capt. Geo. Stoneman the same day & now have the honor to report to the General-in-Chief the result of my inspection of that command, as follows:

It appears that Capt. Stoneman was put in command of Company "G," 2d Cavalry, in addition to his own Co. "E" and required to occupy positions from time to time between Ringgold Barracks & Fort Brown & he has accordingly shifted his camp. These orders were probably issued in consequence of the Cortinez raid. One great difficulty exists in these movements & that is the want of sufficient grass along the river which is not owned & required, by the rancheros. In his present camp on the open prairie some 5 miles from the Rio Grande, he has been applied to for pay for occupying the ground & using the grass. He is now pleasantly encamped on a prairie & resaca with wood, water & grass ample. He will not probably have to change his camp for a month. This is certainly the best mode of feeding his horses (as the grass costs nothing & corn is had cheapest at Brownsville), and keeping them in order. But it is questionable if these two companies should now be thus employed. It is my opinion they should be stationed at two of the posts on the Rio Grande & relieve two companies of the artillery for sea coast service.

Co. E, 2d Cavalry, Capt. Geo. Stoneman, 1st Lt. J. B. Witherell recently promoted to the company, 2d Lt. J. F. Minter on duty as regimental quartermaster at regt. head quarters, since 14th Sept. 1856, 4 sergeants, 2 corporals, 2 buglers, no farrier, 33 privates, on inspection parade, 1 confined at Fort Brown, 1 cook, 1 sick, 1 orderly, 3 on police (being the men released from sentences by order of Gen. Twiggs), aggregate 2 officers present, 47 enlisted men & 57 serviceable horses & 3 unserviceable. This company passed in review at a walk & a trot, tolerably, & the horses looked well. It was neat & arrived with Sharps carbines, Colts pistols, & the sabre, & the arms were in good serviceable order. The carbines were new, but the hind sights to some were broken off. This sight is too delicate for mounted men. The leaf sight is much more durable. The ball cartridges of the carbines were entirely too small by some mistake of the ordnance department, & therefore the target trial was not practicable. The pistol practice was dispensed with on account of the same. This company was taken thro' the drill of the platoon & the sabre exercise, which were indifferent. There were no valises, no haversacks, no sword knots, no saddle blankets, & the men used their own blankets for saddles, and the headstalls were deficient. The new steel bridle bit was too narrow for the horses' jaw, and the attention of the ordnance department should be called to this fact. There were several kinds of saddles, but the Hope Tree is preferred here. There is yet nothing fixed or settled as to the saddle & bridle belts, & it is well to try all kinds for the experiment. The books & records were in order, 20 desertions in 1858, 3 in 1859, 13 in 1860. There were 3 discharges in 1858, 1 in 1859, 28 in 1860. It was supplied with 49 Sharps carbines, 40 Colts navy size pistols, 74 sabres, 59 serviceable saddles & 25 unserviceable bridles, 6500 Sharps ball cartridges, 6500 pistol ball cartridges, 1 travelling forge with tools, 32 canteens, 4 Sibley tents, 2 wall tents. There was no company fund & the company property was in tents. There were three laundresses to this company.

The discipline of the company is good, but Capt. Stoneman was unwell & Lieut. Witherell but recently promoted to this company. It was not sufficiently instructed in the drills. Capt. Stoneman was the recruiting officer & had on hand at date, 276 dolls in the Assist. Treasury in New Orleans.

Co. G, 2nd Cavalry, Capt. W. R. Bradfute absent in arrest at Fort Belknap, Texas, since 25 Nov 1858, by order of the Secretary of War, and turned over to the civil authority for trail, 1st Lt. K. Garrard on duty with detachment of recruits from Carlisle Barracks for Texas, S.O. 119, Head Quarters Army, 2d Lt. J. M. Kemmel in command of company, 3 sergeants, 3 corporals, 2 buglers, 1 farrier, 40 privates, 50 horses on inspection parade, 11 privates without horses, 1 on detached service at Fort Mason, 1 at Carlisle Barracks with recruits, 1 sick at Fort Inge.[76] In the aggregate, one officer and 69 men at command. These men were clean, but no uniformity as to drills & armament, many hats without trimmings, only 5 valises, no saddles blankets, the men used their own blankets for the saddles, saddles & bridles of all patterns, armed with Harpers Ferry rifles, old, & inferior, same old carbines with the swivel-ram-rod, some holster pistols & some Navy size. There were many recruits in the ranks & they passed in review at the walk & trot in a very indifferent manner. Some of the gun slings had no ties &

their arms accordingly carried on the shoulder & many of the recruits had not yet learned to ride properly. The drills were very imperfect & incomplete. In short the company required drilling & sitting up. I could not with such arms attempt target trial even if it had the practice. I condemned all the rifles & carbines as unsuitable & to be turned in and Sharps carbines supplied in stead, but it will depend on the commanding officer of the department to say if it should be done. It is folly to put the Harpers Ferry rifle, and that worthless carbine into the hands of cavalry as an arm suitable.

Lt. Hemmel is a highly meritorious young officer, but it will take him sometime to instruct this company as it should be. It requires another officer to it & Lt. Garrard should soon arrive.

I must remark Capt. Bradfute is under arrest for shooting a soldier. Is not that a military offence & should he not be tried by a military court? Will the General-in-Chief investigate this point?

The books & records of this company were in order. There were 79 sabres, 18 swivel-rod-carbines, 56 Harpers Ferry rifles, 46 Colts Navy & 19 Colts holster pistols, 4000 rifle ball cartridges, 4,000 Colts navy & 4500 Colts holster size ball cartridges, 19 saddles of the Campbell pattern, 10 Grimsely pattern, 50 Hope's pattern, 82 bridles, 6 Sibley tents, 2 wall tents, 33 knapsacks, 60 canteens, 73 haversacks.[77] There were 12 desertions in 1858, 10 in 1859, 16 in 1860, 1 discharged in 1858, 0 in 1859, 28 in 1861. A company fund of 64.79 dolls in the hands of Lt. Kemmel.

Lt. Kemmel is the recruiting officer & has on hand at date, 130 dolls in the Assistant Treasury at New Orleans.

These companies were each provided with 6 wagons, & 6 mules to each wagon, & 6 mules to the travelling forge & can move at will. The corn for horses & mules & other supplies are received via Brownsville.

Lt. Kemmel has been acting commissary of subsistence since 1st Dec. 1860. His returns & accounts all forwarded to date and there was due the U.S. at date, 229.35 dolls, which is in the Asst. Treasury at New Orleans. The supplies of flour & bacon were wormy & hard bread weevilly & all unfit for use, but they could readily be returned to the commissary at Fort Brown for others.

All which is Respectfully Submitted
Jos. K. F. Mansfield
Col. & Inspector Genl.
U.S. Army

DEPARTMENT OF TEXAS

Middletown, Connecticut
22d February 1861.

Sir:

Agreeably to my plan adopted for the inspection of the Department of Texas, to defer the inspection of the Head Quarters and its branches at San Antonio till I had completed the inspection of the line of posts from San Antonio to El Paso and thence down the frontier of the Rio Grande, I now know the honor to report that I arrived at San Antonio conformably thereto from Fort Brown on the 19th January last, and on Monday the 21st, commended the inspection of Head Quarters of the Department of Texas, & have to submit the General-in-Chief the following:

Bvt. Maj. Gen. D. E. Twiggs assumed the command of this department on 27th Nov. 1860, and thereby relieved Bvt. Col. R. E. Lee, 2d Cavalry, who was temporarily in command. Lt. T. A. Washington, 1st Inft, and Lt. J. M. Jones of the 8th Inft, were aids to Genl. Twiggs since 13th December. Capt. & Bvt. Major W. A. Nichols, the assistant adjutant general, jointed this department on 1st Dec. 1860. These officers all perform their inspection duties, and Lt. Jones is also the adjutant of the 8th Inft.

The Adjutant General's Department occupy three rooms in a large brick block, with other buildings of a square, rented by the government for the various heads of departments, & store-houses, and one company of infantry which guards the whole. It is on the east side of the river and within the city limits.[78] There are 3 clerks inclusive of the orderly in the office, 2 from the 2d Cav., and one from the 1st Inf., on extra duty. The records were properly kept and the duty properly performed. There were 21 officers absent from this department on leave, and the whole strength of the command was 206 officers & 2659 men (see the plan of the Brick Block, & c, rented by the government herewith). This block contains the paymaster's offices, the chief quartermaster's office, the chief commissary's office, the commissary of the post office; the topographical office, the office of the head quarters of the 8th Inft., the office of the medical director, & a hospice apartment of the clerks of the adjutant genl's office, and one vacant room on the 2d-story. On the 1st-story are under the east end a clothing room, & the residue the commissary store room. Within the enclosure are commissary & quartermasters & medical directors, stores, & the quarters of one infantry company inclusive of a kitchen & a guard house.

The Commissary Department

Capt. W. B. Blair is the chief of this department. He was the chief when I inspected it in 1856. All funds to the various posts in Texas on this account pass thro' his hands and his books & records are properly kept, & his accounts to the 31st December forwarded. There was then due the United States, 18,651.47 dolls. Expended since, 4304 dolls. Due the U.S. at date, 14,347.47 dolls. Of this amount there is in Assist. Treasury, New Orleans, 9471 dolls & in specie, 4,876.47 dolls in a safe. He keeps one clerk at 75 dolls & one laborer at 20 dolls & a ration. The supplies of flour & beans are preserved in Texas except at Fort Brown & Ringgold Barracks, where they come from New Orleans. The northwestern posts are supplied with flour from wheat raised on the Trinity. The past year, however, that wheat was injured by smut and New Orleans flour substituted accordingly.

There is a subordinate branch of this department here to supply the forces of the city. Lt. Thos. G. Williams, 1st Inft., has performed the duty of post commissary, and relieved Capt. T. G. Pitcher, 8th Inft., on the 1st April 1859. Has change of all the supplies in store, & they are all in a good state of preservation & well stored. He keeps a clerk at 90 dolls, a receiving and forwarding clerk at 50 dolls and a ration, a commissary sergeant at 60 dolls, a cooper at 40 dolls, 3 laborers at handling, & c, at 18 and a ration.

Most of the supplies come from New Orleans. Fresh beef costs 5 cts the pound net. The posts in the interior have been supplied for 5 months by transportation thro' the quartermaster's department.

All his books, records and accounts are properly kept. His accounts to the 31st Dec. have been forwarded, and there was then due the U.S., 257.55 dolls. Received since of Capt. Blair, 250, and for sales, 28.50. Expended in January, 209.29 dolls. Due U.S. at date, 326.76 dolls. Of this amount, 219.25 is in cash & 107.50 in the Assistant Treasury in Baltimore.

The duties of this department are well performed.

Medical Department

Surgeon E. H. Abadie has been on duty as chief of this department as medical director & purveyor and attending surgeon at head quarters since 5th May 1860. He has 19 medical officers under him in this department, and one citizen, employed at Camp Verde. All the posts get their supplies from him. He keeps one clerk at 50 dolls per month & one laborer at 20 dolls in the purveying branch. He has a large supply of medical stores & supplies, well stored in a one story building and in good order. His accounts are in order & all his papers have been forwarded to the 31st Dec. 1860, at which date there was due the U.S., 325.04 dolls in cash on hand.

The hospital is pleasantly located on the river, and hired for that purpose at the rate of 40 dolls per month, or 480 dolls per annum, a high price. It is a two story building well managed and ample for all the purposes required, a dispensary, stewards' room with a fireplace in each, a small ward, a store room. [There are] 4 small rooms on the first floor, the second floor, two ward-rooms, a fire place in each, & two small reserve rooms. There was also a kitchen and mess room in a shanty detached, with ample yard enclosed.

He had a steward, cook, attendant, & matron, with ample supplies. The books & records were well kept. The place healthy, only 4 sick in hospital.

The temperature in June 1860 at 2 P.M. ranged from 87° to 108°, in July from 91° to 103°, in August from 75° to 101°. In 8 months from May to December, 245 days there were 38 showers of rain. One very heavy rain in August. The others light. From 1st May to the middle August there were but 4 slight showers & the grass all dried up.

Pay Department

Major S. Maclin is the chief of three paymasters in this department, and is stationed here. He pays all the northwestern posts, to wit, Camps Verde & Colorado & Cooper, and Fort Mason and Chadbourne in addition to head quarters, as often as once in two months. To effect these payments the U.S. furnished him four mules to his private ambulance, and an escort of ten men and four 6 mule wagons & teams. His accounts were forwarded to the close of November according to the regulations. At that date there was due the U.S., 2967.42 dolls. He has disbursed since 1124.80 dolls to the 31st Dec, and in January, 243.99, leaving a balance due the U.S., at date, of 1593.63 dolls. Of this amount, 1203 is in the Assistant Treasury of New York & 278.19 dolls in the Assist. Treasury, New Orleans, & 117.44 dolls cash on hand. He keeps one clerk & occupies one room of the Brick Block on the 2d-story.

Paymaster D. McClure is also stationed at head quarters & pays the posts from San Antonio on the route to El Paso as far as Fort Davis & also Fort Duncan and Camp Wood. He also keeps a clerk and occupies a room on the 2d-floor of the Brick Block, and is provided the same means of transportation to make his payments & pays the posts as often as once in two months generally. At present he is absent in New Orleans for funds.

Topographical Department

Maj. C. Graham has been on this station but has been absent since 27th Oct. His assistant, Lt. W. H. Echols, is now in command & has recently

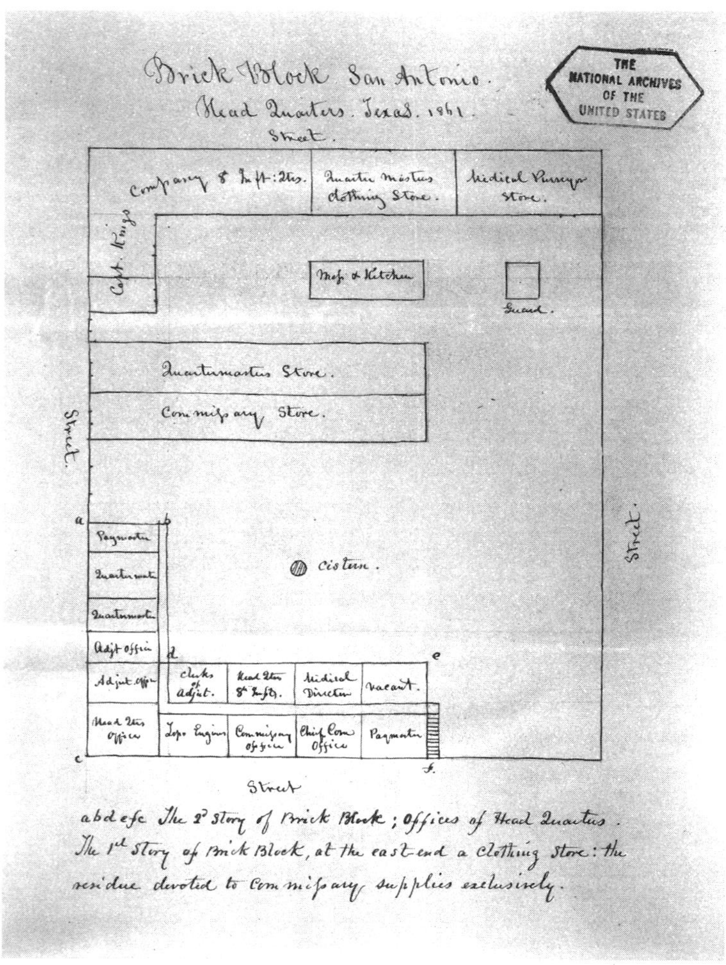

Sketch by Mansfield. (Illustration from LR, AGO, RG 94 courtesy of the National Archives)

been joined by Lieut. N. Bowen. It seems this department has been exploring in the Big-Bend of the Rio Grande the past annum & have completed their mapping and are now doing nothing. A room has been assigned to them on the 2d-floor of the Brick Block, but is not used enough to air it. I would recommend these young officers be ordered to some place where they can be of service to the country.

Quartermaster Department

Maj. David H. Vinton assumed command as chief of this department, 5th Jan. 1857, when he relieved Bvt. Lt. Col A. C. Myers.[79] He supplies all the posts of this department with funds & quartermaster stores either directly or indirectly thro' the various subordinates. There is an officer at each military post in Texas acting as assistant quartermaster. All contracts are approved or made by him. He occupies 1½ rooms in the Brick Block for offices and keeps two clerks at 100 & 75 dolls per month respectively, and one messenger at 25 dolls, and the three receive in addition a ration each. His books, papers, & accounts are all properly kept, and duly forwarded. There was due the U.S. on the 31st last, 30,615.29 dolls, and due at date, 29,609.29 dolls. Of this sum 14,634.50 dolls is in Assistant Treasury at N. Orleans & 13,691.64 dolls in the Assist. Treasury at New York & 2303.13 dolls in cash.

His expenditures for the year 1860 amounted to 531,673.32 dolls. This amount includes the transfers of funds to subordinates of the department, as the amount actually disbursed by him was 4787.38 dolls in that period.

In this office is kept the books of the estimates for clothing, requisitions, inspections, & boards of surveys, abstracts, accounts & summary statements of subordinate posts, and the contracts for transportation & for rents, & c, & c, throughout the Department of Texas.

It appears that a new system for transporting supplies has been adopted, and a new contract entered into accordingly. The depot at Indianola has been broken up and the property ordered to be sold and the government supplies are all received under the new contract (with James Duff) at New Orleans for the year 1861 and shipped to Indianola & transported by him to all the posts at the following rates, to wit. From N. Orleans to Indianola, 87 cents the barrel of 5 cubic feet and 75 cts. for 100 lbs. for 100 miles to San Antonio. Thence to Forts Inge, Clark, Wood, Hudson, Duncan, Lancaster, Stockton, Verde, Mason, Chadbourne, Colorado, Cooper, 92 cts. for 100 lbs. for 100 miles. Thence to Forts Davis, & c, 100 cts. for 100 lbs. for 100 miles. Thence Forts Quitman, Bliss, Fillmore, 122 cts. for 100 lbs. for 100 miles. The contractor to receive on one days notice to San Antonio not exceeding 20,000 lbs & an 10 days notice not exceeding 200,000 lbs., & 20 days notice not exceeding 500,000 lbs. He to receive and store at Indianola all articles for which he is to be paid 17 cts. the barrel of 5 cubic feet, and to keep at Indianola all supplies of feed & forage sufficient to meet the wants of the quartermaster's department and to be paid the market price for them. In the transportation ox teams are to make 12 miles per day & mule teams 18 miles.

The amount paid to 13 individuals in San Antonio for rent for building

Brigadier General David E. Twiggs commanded the Department of Texas from San Antonio during Mansfield's inspection and Texas secession. A native of Georgia, Twiggs was dismissed from the army after he surrendered his department to the state of Texas without firing a shot. (Photograph courtesy of the Library of Congress)

accounts to 1038 dolls per month, or to 12436 dolls per annum. Of this 7500 is paid to Vance & Brother for the use of the Brick Block, & c, of a square. I think about 1500 dolls too much is paid to this concern. Six thousand per annum would pay them well in my opinion. There is also 9060 dolls per annum paid for the hire of sites for military posts to 13 individuals for land in this state, that otherwise would not yield anything at all. Of this amount, a new lease was made, 30th April 1860, with Geo. T. Howard for land at the rate of 600 dolls per annum for a new post near Fort Inge which should never be built for a school of artillery practice.[80] This I consider a superfluity & should be cut off.

A subordinate branch of this department is here under the command of Capt. A. W. Reynolds, assistant quartermaster. This is indispensable for the current service. Capt. Reynolds relieved Capt. E. E. McLean on 1st April 1860 in this duty. The means of transportation, and the change of the quartermaster's workshops, & c, are under his immediate orders. He occupies the building & locality called the Alamo. The first floor of the Alamo is used as a granary and the second floor by the military store keeper (see plan herewith). The building fronting the common is two stories and used for offices, storerooms, packing rooms, saddler's shop, harness room, & wagon shed, and in the corral are mule sheds. On the east side of the street is the corral for wagons & the carpenter's shop and smith's shop & hay yard. About 4 miles out of the city on the river is another corral where all the supernumerary trains, & c, not in use are kept & the mules grazed. These arrangements seem to be all proper & correct.

There are the following person employed, one clerk at 91.66 dolls, 1 at 83.33 dolls per month, 1 store-keeper at 75 dolls per month, 1 assistant military store-keeper at 66.66 dolls, 1 messenger at 25 dolls per month, 4 store-house laborers at 25 dolls, 5 wheelrights one at 50 dolls & 4 at 40 dolls per month, 3 smiths at 50, 40, & 35 dolls per month, 3 saddlers at 50, 45 & 40 dolls per month, 1 yard master at 40 dolls per month, 3 watchmen at 18 dolls per month, 1 cook for mechanics & teamsters at 18 dolls per month, 1 overseer in charge of all the mules at the corral at 40 dolls per month, 3 wagon masters at 58.60 dolls per month, 72 teamsters at 20 dolls per month, 1 cart driver & 9 laborers & ostlers at 18 dolls per month, 1 chief herder at 35 dolls per month, 12 herders at 18 dolls per month, 1 forage master at 58.60 dolls per month. The above named employees, with the exception of the assistant military store-keeper & the wagon masters, all receive a ration each.

One wagon & forage master appointed by the quartermaster genl. under the law of Congress at 89.54 dolls per month. One express man to Camp Colorado with the mail & one wagon & two mules per contract 248.95 dolls per month. This contract is not to be renewed unless ordered.

He keeps 1 horse, 820 mules, 192 wagons, 1 hospital ambulance, 3 carts, 2 spring wagons.

Under the present contract for forwarding supplies to the posts, the number of employees here seem to me unnecessarily large. It appears to me the assistant mail store keeper might be dispensed with, also 2 wheelwrights,

1 smith, 1 sadder, 5 laborers & ostlers & 6 herders, as the teamsters should herd the animals & the duty of forage & yard master might I think be done by one person. The number of mules & teamsters appear to me very large, as the posts have their regular teams, & there is no great change of troops contemplated.

Capt. Reynold's books & records are all in order and his quarterly returns of property to the 30th Sept. have been forwarded & the like returns of the 31st Dec. will be forwarded within a month. The summary statement & all monthly papers to the 31st Dec. have been forwarded, showed a balance due the U.S. of 4585.72 dolls at that date. And his quarterly accounts to the 31st Dec. will be forwarded to the 25th instant. He received from Major Vinton in January, 9539.35 dolls & expended in January, 8743.05 dolls, leaving a balance due the U.S. at date, 5382.02 dolls. Of this amount there is in the Assistant Treasury, New York, 139.85 dolls and in the Assist. Quartermaster Lieut. M. L. Davis on the Assist Treasury of New Orleans, 904.97 dolls, and in a check of Paymaster Van Ness, 5.32 dolls. The residue, 4317.38 dolls, was in cash, which was counted out of several little bags in his safe in small amounts. He pays for hay 12.47 dolls the ton and has about 60 tons on hand, 2 dolls the bushel for corn of which he has about 2090 bushels on hand.

Connected with this department is the military store keeper R. M. Potter. He has charge of the camp & garrison & clothing stores & occupies the 2d-story of the Alamo and two store rooms on the square of the Brick Block. These store rooms are generally full and contain at least one year's supply for five regiments. His books are properly kept & his property returns to the 31st Dec. made out complete for forwarding except the fair copy.

A large amount of property having been destroyed by fire not long since. The department is now provided with a fire engine.

Company I, 1st Inft.

There is quartered on the square of the Brick Block of head quarters, Co. I, 1st Inft., Capt. John H. King, 1st Lt. J. A. Washington detached as aid to Gen. Twiggs since 16 Dec. 1857, 2d Lt. J. H. Holman absent since 28th Dec. 1860, S.O. 106, Head Quarters Dept. Texas, 16th Dec. 1860, for 60 days with permission to apply for an extension, 3 sergeants, 1 corporal, 1 musician, 53 privates for duty, 2 in hospital as attendants, 3 learning music, 1 post baker, 1 sergeant & 2 privates sick, 3 privates in jail in San Antonio for violation of the city ordnance, 1 musician & 1 private at Fort Chadbourne since 20th Oct. 1860, on duty 1 corporal & 8 privates at Columbus, Texas, since 7th Jan. 1861, as an escort to Paymaster McClure, absent in New

Orleans for funds, 1 corporal & 5 privates at Fort McIntosh since 7th Jan. 1861, as escort for Assist. Surgeon Byrne. In the aggregate, 37 enlisted men.

This company is particularly engaged as escorts to paymasters, & c, to the various posts, in addition to the guard of the public stores, & c, 11 of them were with me for 3½ months, constantly on the road. The weather was very unpleasant, wet, & muddy, when I was in San Antonio & this company was not turned out for inspection, I, however, examined the books of the company and found them all as they should be & Capt. King is a very competent officer. There were four desertions in 1860 & 9 discharges. There was a company fund of 306.93 dolls in the hands of Capt. King & he also had a recruiting fund of 185.35 dolls. It was supplied with 87 knapsack, 88 haversacks, 84 canteens, 6 Sibley tents, and was armed with 82 rifled muskets, 11 Colts navy size pistols, 10 Sharps carbines, 5000 rifled muskets ball cartridges, 4000 blank cartridges, 2000 Sharps carbine cartridges, 1500 Colts pistol cartridges.

Head Quarters, 8th Inft.

The Head Quarters of the 8th Inft. is in San Antonio & the office in the Brick Block. The field officers of the regiment are all absent. Lt. T. M. Jones, the adjutant, was present but acting as aid to Gen. Twiggs also. Bvt. Maj. Larkin Smith arrived with his company from Fort Hudson on the 19th Jan. 1861, and assumed command of head quarters & the post, inclusive of Co. "I," 1st Inft., Capt King. This company was inspected by me at Fort Hudson and it is now quartered in one of the buildings of the ordnance department to protect it. The guard posted in the city is one non-commissioned officer & six privates strong for the day guard and an additional guard of 1 non-commissioned officer & 12 men for the night guard. One sentinel is at the guard-house, one at the quartermaster's depot, & two at ordnance depot & yard.

Lt. W. McE. Dye is the regimental quartermaster & absent on leave for 6 months from 5 Dec. 1860. The sergeant major, regimental quartermaster sergeant & 13 of the band were present. All the regimental books & records were in order & the companies were distributed as follows: "A" at San Antonio, "B" at El Paso, "C" at Fort Stockton, "D" at Fort Hudson, "I" & "E" at Fort Bliss, "F" at Fort Quitman," G" (broken up), "H" at Fort Davis, "K" under orders.

Lt. T. M. Jones is the recruiting officer here & has 522.25 dolls on hand in cash at date. There is one clerk here on duty, corporal of A Co., 8th Inft.

Arsenal of San Antonio

The ordnance department here has been under the direction of Capt. R. H. K. Whiteley of the ordnance corps since 1st July 1858. At present the ordnance stores, supplies, ammunition, & c, & c, are distributed as follows: There is a magazine, an old stone building and adobe cover & shingled roof, with 5 doors in it, in front of the quartermaster depot, (see plan herewith), and the Alamo. For this he pays 18 dolls per month or 216 dolls per annum & it is good for nothing else. It is full of the fixed ammunition, & c. A lower magazine, 1½ miles out of the city, is three stories high with powder, & cartridges. On the west side of the river, just over the bridge from the Brick Block, there is a lot, on which stands a store house, & office, & armory, & gun shed, with mounted guns, & c, for which he pays 200 dolls per month or 2400 per annum, a very high price (see plan herewith).

To do away [with] these rents, & concentrate his supplies, & c, the U.S. have purchased a 16 acre tract of land with a good house on it, suitable for quarters of the officer in charge, in an eligible position, at a cost inclusive of 585.25 for council fees, 18,028.98 dolls and an office has been built & a magazine, mostly completed on the premises, up to the 31st Dec. when the works were suspended for want of funds. There was, however, out of appropriations this object, amounted to 96,500 dolls, an unexpended balance of 45,010.93 dolls still in treasury.

The store house at the depot is 3 stories high & a basement. The 2d-story is the office. The 1st-story is filled with small arms in chests & horse equipments. The basement is a general store room. The store room above the office is filled with new parts. Above one of the gun sheds is a store room for old arms, & unserviceable articles.

He now has in his employ two clerks at 2 dolls each per day. One store keeper at 2.25 dolls per day, two laborers & one ostler at 1.25 dolls per day, in all, 11 employees. He keeps two mules for lobbing.

His accounts are all in excellent order & his property returns nearly all ready to be forwarded to the 31st Dec. There was then due the U.S., 2533.44 dolls. Expended in January, 524.88 dolls. Due at date, 2008.46 dolls. Of this amount there was in the Assistant Treasury, New Orleans, 107.07 dolls and in Asst. Treasury, New York, 776.16 dolls and in cash 1125.23 dolls.

He has the following named serviceable ordnance & stores on hand, in good order:

Field Guns Mounted Complete

10, 6-pr. brass guns; 4, 12-pr. brass howitzers, 3 of these mounted complete; 8, 12-pr. brass howitzers not mounted; 2, 6-pr. iron guns in Gribeauval carriages; 4, 12-pr. mountain howitzers carriages; 7, 12-pr. mountain howitzers carriages (prairie); 4, 12- pr. howitzer caissons; 7, 6-pr. caissons; 2 traveling forges, complete; 3 portable forges, complete; 4 battery wagons, complete.[81]

Cannon Balls

179, 24-pr. cannon balls; 119, 18-pr. cannon balls; 12, 12-pr. cannon balls; 48, 6-pr. cannon balls.

Fixed Ammunition

400, 12-pr. shots; 2110, 6-pr. shots; 160, 12-pr. spherical case shots; 81, 12-pr. canister; 620, 6-pr. canister; 16, 32-pr. howitzer canister; 42, 24-pr. howitzer canister; 467, 12-pr. howitzer canister; 424, 12-pr. howitzer canister; 128, 32-pr. howitzer shells; 138, 24-pr. howitzer shells; 959, 12-pr. howitzer shells; 407, 12-pr. mountain howitzer shells; 96, 32-pr. howitzer spherical case shots; 78, 24-pr. howitzer spherical case shots; 1118, 12-pr. howitzer spherical case shots; 756, 12-pr. mountain howitzer spherical case shots; 691, 6-pr. spherical case shots.

Small Arms

862 rifle musket caliber 58; 732 Harpers Ferry rifles; 18 Colts Navy size pistols; 385 Colts Navy size pistols; 213 Sharps carbines; 78 rifle carbines; 171 horse artillery sabers; 412 cavalry sabres.

Powder

Cannon, musket & rifle powder, 5761 pounds.

Cartridges for small arms.

467,000 rifle musket cartridges, caliber 58; 372,760 musket buck & ball cartridges; 126,000 rifle cartridges; 113,000 rifle carbine cartridges; 110,000 Colts pistol army size cartridges; 230,000 Colts, Navy size.

Capt. Whiteley is a highly meritorious & distinguished officer of the ordnance department & performs his duty well.

I have now closed my final report of my inspections of the Department of Texas.

All which is respectfully submitted
Jos. K. F. Mansfield
Col. & Inspt. Genl.
U.S. Army

This daguerreotype shows Joseph K. F. Mansfield at the time of the Mexican War. As a captain in the Corps of Engineers, Mansfield supervised the construction of Fort Brown during the conflict. (Photograph courtesy of the Middlesex County Historical Society, Connecticut)

CONCLUSION

Of those officers mentioned by either Johnston or Mansfield in their inspection reports, eighty-five (60 percent) went on to serve in the Union Army while forty-four (31 percent) cast their future with the defiant Confederacy. Most of those who served in the Southern Army resigned late in 1860 or early 1861, not long after Mansfield completed his inspection of the Department of Texas. A few of the officers who joined the Confederacy never bothered to resign and were dismissed. At least eight officers who either retired or resigned prior to the Civil War did not serve in the war. The fates of those who did serve are as various as the war itself. A surgeon, Irish-born Bernard John Dowling Irwin, earned the Medal of Honor as a result of the Bascom Affair in February 1861 at Apache Pass, Arizona. In fact, Irwin is credited with earning the very first Medal of Honor and the only one earned for the antebellum Indian Wars, although he did not receive the medal until January 24, 1894. Others were not so fortunate: nine of the officers mentioned by either Johnston or Mansfield died in the war. One officer, Pennsylvania-born Edward H. Fitzgerald, a captain in the First Dragoons, died on January 9, 1860, only four months after Lieutenant Colonel Johnston saw him at Fort Fillmore.

The story of Texas's participation in the Civil War shows how history sometimes unfolds slowly, then all at once. Only days after Mansfield completed his inspection of Department Headquarters in San Antonio, a Secession Convention assembled in Austin on February 1, 1861. As Mansfield departed Texas for his home in Connecticut, the convention voted 166 to 8 to present a secession ordinance to the people of Texas, a decision that made the Lone Star state one of only two states in the South to submit the crucial question directly to the people. On February 23, Texans voted 46,129 to 14,697 for disunion. Events were moving fast. On March 5, without hesitation, the convention declared Texas independent and voted to join the Confederate States of America.

At Department Headquarters in San Antonio, Gen. David Emanuel Twiggs, seventy-one and in ill health, was known to be sympathetic to the South but proud and protective of his command. On February 16, 1861, Col. Benjamin McCulloch, a veteran of the Texas Revolution and the Mexican War who had been appointed a colonel of cavalry by a committee of the Secession Convention, swarmed into San Antonio's Main Plaza with 250 men and quickly occupied the rooftops of buildings housing Federal supplies and men. Carrying the Lone Star flag, McCulloch vowed that he would force General Twiggs to surrender. After ten days of tense negotiations, state commissioners persuaded Twiggs, who was said to have wept like a child, to turn over all Federal property in Texas. "If an old woman with a broomstick should come with full authority from the state of Texas to demand the public property," Twiggs was heard to say, "I would give it to her."[1] Twiggs's disgraceful surrender resulted in his dishonorable dismissal from the army. Mercilessly vilified, he was replaced by a loyal New York Unionist with a long record of distinguished service in the army, Col. Carlos Adolphus Waite. Colonel Waite rode into San Antonio from Camp Verde to find that chaos had engulfed the army command in San Antonio. Maj. Sacfield Maclin, who had gone over to the Texan Rebels, forced Colonel Waite to surrender after a heated and lengthy confrontation and debate.[2] In the confusion, Corp. John C. Hesse was able to conceal and carry off the flag of the Eighth Infantry, which had been carried through the Mexican War. The flag, which Hesse had concealed around his body, was placed in Lt. Edward A. Hartz's trunk and taken to Washington. Hesse, who went on to become a colonel, later received the Medal of Honor for his patriotic deed.[3]

Col. Robert E. Lee, who had commanded the Department of Texas for eight months in 1860, arrived in San Antonio only hours after the Twiggs surrender under orders to report to Washington. When Lee drew his ambulance in front of the Read House, he was surrounded by a crowd of curious men on whose coats Lee observed a crude red insignia. Told they were state troops and that Twiggs had surrendered, Lee's eyes clouded with tears.[4] "Has it come to this," he was heard to whisper.[5] The Virginian later told a friend that, if he had been in command of the Department of Texas at the time of the Twiggs surrender, he would have resisted.[6] If Lee had indeed been in command, the Civil War might well have begun in San Antonio instead of Fort Sumter eight weeks later.

In the meantime, confusion and uncertainty gripped the frontier posts in Texas. On March 3, 1861, in distant Fort Quitman, First Lt. Zenas R. Bliss was joined by Lt. Royal T. Frank and Company E of the Eighth Infantry, who were on their way to Fort Davis. After evacuating the post and receiving conflicting orders, Bliss returned to Fort Quitman to await the arrival of Lt. Col. Isaac Van Duzer Reeve and the troops from Fort Bliss. At El Paso, the bespectacled Lieutenant Colonel Reeve turned the post and public property over to Samuel Magoffin, a local secessionist.[7] After Magoffin had also received the public property at Fort Quitman, Reeve headed for San Antonio on April 4, 1861.

On the long trek east, Reeve's force was reduced by desertion, sickness, and drunkenness, its number shrinking from 347 to 270.[8] When the column finally went into camp at San Lucas Spring at the base of Adams's Hill, fifteen miles west of San Antonio, Reeve was confronted by Col. Earl Van Dorn and 1,370 Texans, most of them mounted and anxious for a fight. Fatigued, outnumbered, and intimidated, Reeve surrendered his small force.[9] "I have taken all the U.S. Troops in Texas prisoners of war, and now lean back in my chair and smoke my pipe in peace," boasted Van Dorn, a hard-living Mississippian.[10] Although the officers were paroled within days, many of the enlisted men spent the next twenty-two months in Texas, some at Camp Verde in the heart of the hill country, waiting to be exchanged. "Separated from their officers, divided into squads, and removed to different posts on the frontiers of Texas . . . they were subjected to degrading labors, supplied with scanty food and clothing, and sometimes chained to the ground or made to suffer other severe military punishments," a Union officer claimed.[11]

At Fort McIntosh, Massachusetts-born Maj. Caleb Chase Sibley, a loyal Unionist, received orders from Department Headquarters to turn the post over to authorities of the state. He evacuated the fort on March 12 with rations for twenty-five days, taking up the 230-mile march for Fort Brown.[12] Sibley was hoping to find transportation to the North and, if necessary, even move down the coast to Tampico to catch a ship from a Mexican port. Changing directions to Indianola, Sibley was joined by troops from other posts in Texas. However, when Major Van Dorn arrived from Galveston with more than a thousand zealous Texans, the group was forced to surrender at Saluria on April 25, 1861.[13]

At noon on March 20, Capt. O. L. Shepherd gave up the post at Fort Duncan and marched for Fort Brown.[14] At Fort Brown in the meantime, Capt. R. H. Hill, in consultation with Capt. George Stoneman, who had arrived with his two companies of the Second Cavalry, refused to surrender the post to commissioners for the state of Texas. Moreover, Captain Hill ordered forty of Stoneman's cavalry to Brazos Santiago to spike the guns and destroy the large quantity of ordnance at the depot. First Lt. James

Thompson of the Second Artillery, however, had already surrendered the depot.[15] At Fort Brown, Hill remained defiant. Col. John S. "Rip" Ford, newly appointed commander of the Confederate Department of the Rio Grande, arrived at Brazos Santiago on February 23, 1861, and, with a force that would eventually number some fifteen hundred Texans, reported that Hill was "determined at first to fight and not to yield."[16] Stoneman had gone as far as to say that "with his two companies of cavalry he would march all over Texas."[17] Many feared the Federals would attack the Texans and inaugurate a horrible civil war, which, Ford said, "we may not see the end of."[18] When Lt. Col. Electus Backus arrived from leave and assumed command, arrangements were made for the state troops to assume control. On March 20, 1861, the Stars and Stripes were saluted and lowered; as six companies of Texans marched into the fort, the Federals left by boat for Brazos Santiago, there to find transportation to the North.[19] Tragically, on the way down the river, First Lt. James Bonaparte Witherell of the Second Cavalry stepped overboard and drowned.[20] Colonel Ford perhaps put it best when he recalled, "the future was full of uncertainty, dark, and lowering."[21]

At Camp Colorado, eighty miles south of Fort Belknap, Capt. Edmund Kirby Smith refused to surrender to Col. Henry E. McCulloch and several companies of state troops. Smith went as far as to tell Colonel McCulloch that he would "never, under any circumstances, give up my arms and horses, or negotiate upon terms that would dishonor the troops under my command."[22] If McCulloch persisted, Smith threatened to "endeavor to cut my way through any force opposed to me."[23] In time, Smith managed to negotiate with McCulloch, and leave Camp Colorado with his troops. Later, he would become a lieutenant general in the Confederate Army and, between 1863 and 1865, command the Trans-Mississippi Department.

Throughout the Southwest, a number of other officers resigned to cast their fortunes with the infant Confederacy. Realizing the seriousness of the secession crisis, many took leave to await the troubling national events elsewhere. In New Mexico at Fort Union, Major Henry H. Sibley and Col. William Wing Loring, two southerners, plotted to take their commands into Texas. The specific details of the Sibley-Loring conspiracy are unclear, but the two veterans appear to have also considered seizing the forts and supplies in the southern part of the territory. The egotistical Loring, who had lost his left arm at Belén Gate on the outskirts of Mexico City, had assumed command of the department in March 1861, and appears to have deliberately held on to his position as long as possible.[24]

In New Mexico, secession fever engulfed Tucson and the Mesilla Valley where southern sympathizers created considerable excitement. By the summer of 1861, Lt. Col. John Robert Baylor, an aggressive and egotistical Texan, not only had occupied Fort Bliss with less than four hundred ragged and ill-equipped troops but thrust north into the Mesilla Valley. After occupying Mesilla, Baylor fought off a meager Federal attempt to drive him out and forced the evacuation of Fort Fillmore. Learning that Baylor was bringing forward artillery and believing the post indefensible, an aging Maj. Issac Lynde decided to flee eastward through the Organ Mountains to the safety of Fort Stanton. Under a hot New Mexico sun, Baylor caught up with the fleeing Federals, who had filled their canteens with whiskey, as they faltered near the steep summit of St. Augustine Pass. With fewer than two hundred men, Baylor captured most of the Seventh Infantry and the regimental band.[25]

Many officers who commanded the various posts in Texas and New Mexico were promoted within weeks after the commencement of hostilities, and a few went on to command great armies. Those who remained loyal included Arthur T. Lee, who was breveted a lieutenant colonel for gallantry at Gettysburg.[26] New York-born Isaac Van Duzen Reeve, whom Johnston had found sick at Fort Buchanan and who surrendered to Federal forces outside San Antonio, became a colonel in the Thirteenth United States Infantry. He was breveted a brigadier general for faithful and meritorious service during the war and died on December 31, 1890.[27]

Predictably, many died in the arising conflict. One of the first to die was the young artillery officer Douglas Ramsay, whom Colonel Mansfield had seen at Fort Duncan. Ramsay was killed on July 21, 1861, while gallantly defending the Federal guns at First Bull Run.[28] New York-born Guilford Dudley Bailey, a young second lieutenant in the Second Artillery whom Mansfield found sick at Fort Brown in January 1860, was killed at the Battle of Fair Oaks outside Richmond, Virginia, on May 31, 1862, in the same battle where Gen. Joseph E. Johnston was wounded.[29]

Of those who remained loyal and served in the Union Army, none were more distinguished than William "Wild Bill" Hazen. The Vermont-born Hazen, who lay severely wounded when Johnston visited Fort Inge in November 1859, recovered and was assistant instructor of infantry tactics at West Point when the war started. Through the assistance of a boyhood friend, Lt. Col. James A. Garfield, Hazen secured the colonelcy of an Ohio infantry regiment and commanded a brigade at Shiloh, there leading a gallant charge against Confederate lines. It was at Stones River, Tennessee, however, that he won national attention. The next year, Hazen erected the first Civil War battlefield monument on the spot where his brigade had suffered heavy casualties. Hazen was at Chickamauga, helped to raise the siege of Chattanooga, and was among the first to reach the summit of Missionary Ridge. After the fall of Atlanta, he led a division in Sherman's "March to the Sea," ending the war as a major general of volunteers. In addition, Hazen fought in the Indian Wars, observed the Franco-Prussian War, and became a brigadier general in the regular army and chief signal officer. He died in Washington, D.C., in 1887.[30]

George Stoneman, whom Mansfield found in camp on the Rio Grande with two companies of cavalry in the wake of the Cortina War, was made a major general of volunteers and chief of cavalry in the Army of the Potomac. Stoneman was in the Union debacle at Fredericksburg and in the Chancellorsville campaign five months later. In the latter, he created great consternation in Richmond by operating in the Confederate rear with ten thousand cavalry. During the Atlanta campaign, he directed the Cavalry Corps of the Army of the Ohio and was captured on July 31, 1864, while trying to free the prisoners from the notorious Andersonville. Exchanged, he ended the war in North Carolina with Sherman. Stoneman returned to the Southwest to command the Department of Arizona and, in 1882, was elected governor of California. He died at Buffalo, New York, on September 5, 1894.

A gallery of other Union soldiers reflects the diversity of the Union Army. Tennessee-born Alvan Cullom Gillem, who was at Fort Clark commanding a company of the First Artillery in 1860, also remained loyal to the Union. He fought at Shiloh and rose from captain to brigadier general. Gillem returned to Texas during Reconstruction and was later in the Modoc Indian War in the lava beds of Northern California. He died in Tennessee on December 2, 1875.[31]

Henry Jackson Hunt, whom Mansfield saw at Fort Brown during Christmas 1860, fought bravely at First Bull Run. He later became an artillery colonel in the Army of the Potomac and commanded several batteries of Union guns that repulsed Lee's Army of Northern Virginia at Malvern Hill. Promoted to brigadier general and chief of artillery, Hunt was at Antietam and Fredericksburg. At Gettysburg, he commanded seventy guns on Cemetery Hill that hurled back Gen. George Pickett's fateful charge. He died in Washington, D.C., on February 11, 1889.

James Brewerton Ricketts, who with his artillery company had reoccupied Ringgold Barracks during the Cortina War, commanded an artillery battery at First Bull Run. Wounded four times and captured, he was exchanged in January 1862 and received a commission as brigadier general. Ricketts was at Cedar Mountain and Second Bull Run. At Antietam, he had a horse killed under him and was seriously injured when a second horse that was killed fell on him. As a major general, he was shot in the chest at Cedar Creek in the Shenandoah Valley campaign of 1864. After he recovered, he fought at the Battles of the Wilderness, Spotsylvania, Cold Harbor, and Petersburg. Ricketts died at Washington, D.C., on September 22, 1887.[32]

Thomas Gamble Pitcher, a Hoosier who was depot commissary at Fort Bliss when the war began, rode east to fight at Cedar Mountain, where he was severely wounded in the knee. He ended the war as provost general for the state of Indiana. Pitcher died of tuberculosis at Fort Bayard, New Mexico, on October 21, 1895.[33]

Andrew Porter, grandson of a revolutionary general and first cousin of the mother of Mary Todd Lincoln, fought at First Bull Run and was provost marshal of the Army of the Potomac during the Peninsular Campaign. In bad health, he resigned in 1864, moved to France, and died at Rue de Coliseé, outside Paris, on January 3, 1872.[34]

Daniel Henry Rucker, who was quartermaster at the Albuquerque depot in August 1859, was promoted to major at the beginning of the war and served in the Quartermaster Department. Rucker died at Washington, D.C., on January 6, 1910, less than four months short of his ninety-eighth birthday. He was buried at Arlington National Cemetery.[35]

Zenas R. Bliss, who had spent much time in the Trans-Pecos, was promoted to colonel in command of the Tenth and later the Seventh Rhode Island Infantry. In 1898, he was awarded the Medal of Honor for heroism at the Battle of Fredericksburg, where he rose to his feet in the midst of a withering enemy fire to encourage the neophyte men of the Seventh Rhode Island to attack. After the war, Bliss was promoted to major general and died on January 2, 1900.[36]

Many of the officers in the Department of New Mexico who stayed on in the territory played crucial roles in 1862 in turning back the Texan invasion. James Lowry Donaldson, chief quartermaster at Fort Marcy at the time of Johnston's inspection, helped to destroy or remove much of the public property in the Rio Grande Valley following the Texan victory at Valverde, including the destruction of the Albuquerque depot, one of the largest in the territory. In command of the Military District of Santa Fe, Donaldson was also instrumental in removing most of the Federal supplies from Santa Fe only days prior to the Texan occupation of the capital. Donaldson was later breveted a major general of volunteers for faithful and meritorious services during the Atlanta campaign. He died on November 4, 1885.[37]

Gabriel René Paul, the grandson of an officer of Napoleon and assistant adjutant in New Mexico in 1860, became acting inspector general of the Department of New Mexico in April 1861 and colonel of the Fourth New Mexico Infantry. He held Fort Union at the time of the Rebel invasion and was later in charge of the District of Southern New Mexico. In the east, he commanded a brigade at Fredericksburg, Chancellorsville, and Gettysburg. In the last, he was severely wounded by a rifle ball that entered his right temple and passed through his left eye, rendering him totally blind. Paul lived twenty more years, dying in Washington, D.C., on May 5, 1886.[38]

Stone-faced Benjamin S. Roberts, age fifty when Johnston saw him in command of a company of the First Dragoons at Fort Fillmore in September 1859, commanded the Fifth New Mexico Volunteers at the Battle of Valverde and was promoted to colonel. Summoned east, he was made inspector general and then chief of cavalry in Gen. John Pope's Army of Virginia. In a sensational investigation following Second Bull Run, Roberts pressed charges against Gen. Fitz John Porter that led to Porter's ruin. After Porter's trial, Roberts and Pope were sent to Minnesota to fight Indians. After the war, he became professor of military science at Yale and died in Washington, D.C., on January 29, 1875.[39]

Of all the heroes in the small Union Army in the territory, the most notable was Alexander MacRae, a North Carolina loyalist in the Mounted Rifles who died while bravely defending an artillery battery at Valverde. Prior to the war, MacRae had served at Forts Merrill, Ewell, and Inge in Texas and at Fort Union, Cantonment Burgwin, and Fort Craig in New Mexico.[40] "Pure in character, upright in conduct, devoted to his profession, and of a loyalty that was deaf to the seductions of family and friends, Captain MacRae died, as he had lived, an example of the best and highest qualities that man can possess," Gen. Edward R. S. Canby wrote.[41] Five years after MacRae's death, his body was disinterred, placed in a casket, and given a hero's escort across New Mexico and the Great Plains on the way to burial at West Point. As his remains passed through Albuquerque on April 20, 1867, the procession was led by a cavalry horse draped in mourning "with boot in stirrup," followed by a detachment of United States Infantry and three hundred citizens.[42] Fort MacRae, downriver from Valverde, was named in his honor in 1863.[43]

First Lt. Kenner Garrard, a Kentuckian who was escorting troops to Texas during the secession crisis, remained loyal and fought at Gettysburg, after which he was made a brigadier general of volunteers. After commanding a cavalry division in Sherman's Georgia campaign, Garrard fought at both Nashville and Franklin. After resigning from the army in November 1866, he dabbled in real estate and died at Cincinnati, Ohio, on May 15, 1879.[44]

Lt. William Henry French, whom Mansfield found in command of Co. K of the First Artillery at Fort Clark, was a brigadier general of volunteers in the Peninsula Campaign and the Seven Days before Richmond. Commanding a division at Antietam, he was promoted to major general and saw action at Fredericksburg and Chancellorsville. Criticized for his lackluster leadership at Gettysburg, he never saw field service again and died at Washington, D.C., on May 20, 1881.[45]

William James Hamilton White, whom Mansfield saw at Fort Clark in late November 1860, became medical director of the Sixth Corps of the Army of the Potomac and was killed while leading a reconnaissance in the East Woods at Antietam, only a stone's throw from where Mansfield was mortally wounded.[46]

Stephen Decatur Carpenter, who had been reluctant to give up Camp Cooper when Texas seceded, was killed instantly when he received six mortal wounds in the Union ranks at Stones River, Tennessee, on December 31, 1862.[47] George L. Willard, who was commanding a company in the Eighth Infantry at Fort Stanton in September 1860, rose to the rank of colonel in the Union Army and was killed on July 2, 1863, while leading the 125th New York Infantry at the Battle of Gettysburg.[48] Assistant Quartermaster Lewis Owen Morris, who was at Fort Union in 1859, was killed in the bloodbath at Cold Harbor, Virginia, on June 3, 1864.[49] Vermont-born Henry Raymond Selden, who was at Fort Davis in October 1859, died on February 2, 1865, while in command of the First New Mexico Volunteers, only months before the end of the war. Three months later, Fort Selden was established at the southern end of the *Jornada del Muerto*, twelve miles above the village of Doña Ana.[50]

From the elite Second Cavalry, most of whom were in North Texas and not mentioned in either Mansfield's or Johnston's reports, came one-half of the Confederacy's full generals. They included Albert Sidney Johnston, Robert E. Lee, E. Kirby Smith, and John Bell Hood. William J. Hardee, as well, became a lieutenant general in the Confederate Army. Other Rebel generals who came out of the Second Cavalry included Nathan G. Evans, Charles W. Field, Earl Van Dorn, George B. Cosby, James P. Major, Fitzhugh Lee, and George Burgwin Anderson, who died of wounds received at Antietam.

With the exception of Robert E. Lee and Albert Sidney Johnston, the most respected Rebel general who served on the Texas frontier was John Bell Hood. Hood, who had been on leave when Mansfield visited Camp Wood in September 1860, resigned his commission on April 16, 1861, three days after the surrender of Fort Sumter. Dissatisfied with the neutrality of his native Kentucky, he declared himself a Texan and was commissioned a captain in the Confederate cavalry. Appointed a colonel six months later, he was placed in charge of the Fourth Texas Infantry, Hood's Texas Brigade, that fought at Second Bull Run, Antietam, Fredericksburg, and Gettysburg, where he received a severe wound in the left arm. Hood's division played a crucial role in the Battle of Chickamauga, where Hood lost his left leg. Hood, who replaced Joseph E. Johnston, led the Army of Tennessee in the final weeks of the Atlanta campaign. Following his disastrous defeat at Franklin and Nashville, Hood retreated into Georgia, along the way having to be strapped to his saddle because of his two wounds. After the war, he moved to New Orleans where he, his wife, and his eldest daughter died of yellow fever in August 1879.[51]

Another prominent officer who resigned to join the Confederacy was Richard Stoddert Ewell, a serious, bold, and imaginative fighter who was one of the most deeply admired and respected officers in the antebellum army.[52] With a physical appearance bordering on the grotesque, "Old Bald Head" Ewell became one of only seventeen men to attain the rank of lieutenant general in the Confederate Army. He fought in many major battles in the east and was wounded in the leg at Groverton at the beginning of the Second Bull Run campaign on August 28, 1862. Following the death of Stonewall Jackson, Ewell, fitted with a wooden leg, took command of the Second Corps of the Army of Northern Virginia and fought at Gettysburg, the Wilderness, and Spotsylvania, where he lost almost half his corps. He died of pneumonia on January 22, 1872.[53]

Other Confederate soldiers are as interesting as their counterparts on the Union side. First Lt. James Edwin Slaughter, great-nephew of President James Madison, who was sick at Fort Duncan when Mansfield saw him in late 1860, did not bother to resign and was dismissed on May 14, 1861. As a Confederate captain of artillery, Slaughter survived the Federal bombardment of Pensacola early in the war and was commissioned a brigadier general, briefly serving under Gen. Joseph E. Johnston. In April 1863, Slaughter transferred to Galveston as chief of artillery and spent the latter part of the war in command on the Rio Grande. He died while visiting Mexico City on January 1, 1901.[54]

Assistant quartermaster of the depot at Indianola in September 1860, Virginia-born Alexander Welch Reynolds, also left the army without resigning. Reynolds went on to command a brigade at Vicksburg. Exchanged, he won a brigadier general's commission and was at Chattanooga and in the

Atlanta campaign, where at New Hope Church in May 1864 he was severely wounded. In 1869, Reynolds accepted a commission as a colonel in the army of the khedive of Egypt. Continually feuding with former Union officers who were also in the service of the khedive, Reynolds died in Alexandria, Egypt, on May 26, 1876.[55]

Certainly the most notorious former officer to join the Confederacy was Gen. David Emanuel Twiggs. "Old Davey," as he was known in the frontier army, was seventy-two and in ill health when Mansfield last saw him.[56] After surrendering the Department of Texas, Twiggs was known in the North as "Traitor Twiggs." Despised and dismissed from the army, he became the oldest officer of the antebellum army to declare for the Confederacy. Appointed a major general and placed in command of the District of Louisiana, which included the defenses of New Orleans, he was never active in the Confederate cause and died in July 1862.[57]

Fifty-three-year-old Lt. Col. John Breckinridge Grayson, who was chief commissary officer for the Department of New Mexico when Johnston inspected Fort Marcy, resigned from the army on July 1, 1861, to cast his lot with the Confederacy. As a brigadier general in command of the Confederate Department of Middle and Eastern Florida, Grayson was consistently in bad health. Relieved of command, he died in Tallahassee of tuberculosis on October 21, 1861.[58] Alexander Early Steen, who became a brigadier general in the Missouri State Guard and a colonel in the Rebel Army, was killed in a desperate fight at Cane Hill near Prairie Grove, Arkansas, on December 7, 1862.[59]

JOHNSTON, MANSFIELD & THE CIVIL WAR

After his New Mexico and Texas inspections, Johnston left for Washington, D.C. Along with his wife Lydia, the couple traveled on to New York to attend the wedding of Capt. George B. McClellan, a longtime friend. Back in Washington in June 1860, Johnston learned that Gen. Thomas Sidney Jesup, quartermaster general of the army for forty-two years, was dead. Within three weeks, Johnston had been chosen over Robert E. Lee, Albert Sidney Johnston, and Charles F. Smith for the coveted position with the rank of brigadier general.

Life in Washington was pleasant and everyone agreed that General Johnston brought a renewed energy to the Quartermaster Department. The national crisis triggered by the election of Abraham Lincoln and the secession of South Carolina dictated, however, that the Johnstons' tenure in Washington would be short.[60] Yet Johnston, who commanded the nation's storehouse of war materials, continued his daily walks to the War Department and tried to remain above the increasingly intensive debate that was sweeping the nation. Anguished over the succession crisis, he thought the defenders of slavery and the advocates of secession foolish. Visitors to his office found him distracted. One person recalled having to speak to Johnston "several times before he could be jolted from his private thoughts to acknowledge the visitor's presence."[61] One thing was clear to Johnston: his loyalty was to Virginia, and, if the state left the Union, he would have to resign. Realizing this, Gen. Winfield Scott tried to convince him to remain loyal.

In the first week of February 1861, Johnston watched anxiously as the citizens of Virginia went to the polls to select delegates to a state convention. Among those selected was his oldest living brother, Peter, who wrote that most of the delegates were willing to give the Lincoln administration a chance.[62] Fort Sumter and Lincoln's call for seventy-five thousand volunteers, however, dealt a death knell to hopes of keeping Virginia in the Union, and, on April 17, Peter and a majority of the Virginia delegates voted to take the commonwealth out of the Union. The news reached Washington two days later, and, on Monday morning, April 22, Johnston walked to the War Department and, with his head bowed and tears in his eyes, submitted his letter of resignation to Secretary of War Simon Cameron. Although the United States had "educated me and clothed me with honor," he said, "I must go with the South."[63] Leaving behind all their personal belongings, including his professional books and the mementos of three decades in the army, Johnston left Washington with his wife for Richmond by train the next day.

In the newly established Confederate capital, Johnston was named a major general in command of the state army and, although later reduced in rank to brigadier general, was sent to command the Southern forces gathering at Harpers Ferry. Within days he concluded that Harpers Ferry could not be defended and evacuated the town. In July 1861, he brought his army by rail through the Blue Ridge Mountains, and, as ranking officer of the Confederate Army, took command of the Southern army at Manassas, where he skillfully commanded the Rebels in the first great battle of the war.

Back in Richmond, Johnston continued to quarrel with President Jefferson Davis and the Confederate government about his rank. Historians have speculated that Davis and Johnston had long been personal rivals and that the quarrel may have had something to do with their wives.[64] Other historians have argued that Davis supported another officer for quartermaster general when Jesup died in 1860. On the other hand, Davis may have simply distrusted Johnston's abilities and wanted to make sure that he would never exercise command over Albert Sidney Johnston or Robert E. Lee.[65] Regardless, an increasingly bitter and heated correspondence characterized their relationship for the remainder of the war. By the summer of 1862, Johnston was clearly identified with the opponents of President Davis.

In command of the Confederate Army, Johnston was seriously wounded during the Peninsular Campaign at Seven Pines on May 31, 1862. Late in the afternoon, Johnston was setting astride his horse on a small rise when he was struck in the shoulder by a musket ball. While he was still mounted, Johnston was struck in the chest and thigh from an artillery shell that burst nearby. Johnston fell hard from his horse, and several of his staff, who at first thought he was dead, carried him from the field.[66] Conscious and in great pain, Johnston was placed in an ambulance and hurried to Richmond. Although his wounds were not fatal, Johnston remained inactive for six months and was replaced by Gen. Robert E. Lee.

Returning to duty in November 1862, Davis sent Johnston to command Confederate forces in Tennessee and Mississippi. By the early summer of 1863, Johnston was given command of the forces aimed to raise the siege of Vicksburg. Johnston's inability to relieve the besieged city resulted in Vicksburg's surrender on July 4, 1863. Consequently, Johnston fell into an unseemly quarrel over who was responsible for the defeat, and he went several months without a command. However, when President Davis had to find a new commander for the Army of the Tennessee, Johnston's career was resurrected. Johnston found the dispirited and hungry Army of Tennessee in late 1863 camped around Dalton, Georgia. Although Davis urged Johnston to advance and reestablish Confederate control over Tennessee, Johnston, outmanned and outgunned two to one by Gen. William T. Sherman, remained on the defensive, skillfully falling back into the heart of Georgia. Despite Davis's displeasure, a leading Civil War scholar has characterized Johnston's retreat from Dalton to Atlanta as "a model of operational strategy."[67] By July 1864, Johnston had retreated to the defenses of Atlanta, and Davis removed him from command, replacing him with Gen. John Bell Hood. Johnston's removal has been characterized as "Davis's greatest single blunder of the war."[68] At any rate, Davis once again recalled Johnston in February 1865 to active service to command Confederate troops in the Carolinas in a futile effort to halt Sherman's march north toward Virginia. Three weeks after Appomattox, Johnston surrendered his army to Sherman at a farmhouse in North Carolina.

During Reconstruction, Johnston lived in Virginia, Alabama, and Washington, D.C. From 1879 to 1881, he served as a representative for Virginia in the United States House and dabbled in national politics. Much of his time and energy went into writing a *Narrative of Military Operations Directed During the Late War Between the States*, which was published in 1874. As was the case with almost all Civil War memoirs, the study was self-serving, presenting a one-sided view of events such as the Vicksburg campaign.[69] Johnston, who continued his vendetta against Jefferson Davis through the years, spent more and more of his time unveiling Confederate statues and attending funerals. When Davis died in 1889, though, Johnston did not mourn.

In the winter of 1891, Johnston went north to New York as an honorary pallbearer at the funeral of his old adversary, Gen. William T. Sherman. On a cold and raw February afternoon, as Johnston stood silent, a mourner leaned forward to urge the old general to put on his hat lest he get sick. "If I were in his place and he were standing here in mine," Johnston remarked, "he would not put on his hat."[70] Johnston caught a cold, continued to weaken, and died in Washington, D.C., on March 21, 1891. Of all the epitaphs and newspapers accounts of Johnston's life, it was that by Sam Watkins, a Rebel infantryman from Tennessee, that was most appropriate. He wrote in his classic *"Co. Aytch,"* "Farewell, old fellow! We privates loved you because you made us love ourselves."[71]

Before departing Texas in 1861, Col. Joseph King Fenno Mansfield had originally intended to inspect the entire Department of Texas.[72] Undeniably, the secession crisis hastened his departure. Although there is no mention or even hint of the secession crisis in his reports, he is certain to have been privy to the growing and heated debate that characterized the increasingly angry discourse among the military in the Southwest.[73] There is also no doubt that he realized the severity of the crisis. In a letter to a Connecticut friend, he warned that the whole South was likely to go out of the Union and that war was inevitable.[74] By the time Mansfield left Texas, six southern states had left the Union. In fact, Mansfield departed San Antonio within days of the vote of the Texas Secession Convention. As the secession crisis continued to rage, he returned to Middletown, Connecticut, to his red brick, two-story, Federal-style home on Main Street. Either he or Louisa clipped an article from the *New York Times* on General Twiggs's surrender.

Just as Johnston was committed to Virginia, Mansfield remained intensely loyal to the Union and was horrified at how the country seemed to be approaching the brink of destruction. Writing in February 1861 to John H. B. Latrobe, a West Point classmate, Mansfield offered hope that the situation was not entirely lost. "We have," he wrote, "not yet gone so far that our steps can not be retraced."[75] As Mansfield waited in Middletown, the future continued to grow increasingly dark. He feared that the old Union he loved so dearly might be gone forever and the Union and Confederacy would be forced to exist side by side as two separate nations.[76] Too many people were "at work destroying the best government in the world."[77] To Mansfield, disunion was like a bad dream. "I awake," he wrote, "and rub my eyes, and yet it is there. Oh that it were a dream! And I could exclaim, Thank God it is nothing but a phantom! Alas it is too true!"[78] He encouraged his friend Latrobe to "come forward and hang out your colors for the Great North American Republic."[79]

Only days after Fort Sumter, Mansfield hurried west to Columbus, Ohio, to oversee the enlistment and mustering of volunteers who were rallying to the Stars and Stripes by the thousands.[80] Not long after arriving in Columbus, he was quickly ordered to Washington, D.C.[81] In Washington on May

14, 1861, Mansfield was promoted to brigadier general by President Lincoln, who placed him in charge of the capital's defenses. In that capacity, Mansfield urged Gen. Winfield Scott to occupy the Virginia bank of the Potomac River. On May 24, 1861, the day after Virginia left the Union, he sent Federal troops to occupy Alexandria and Arlington Heights, only two miles from the government buildings in the city.[82] Eight weeks later, Mansfield watched as Gen. Irvin McDowell marched out to humiliating defeat at First Bull Run. Then, in the wake of the Union disaster, Mansfield helped to reorganize the disorganized and demoralized Federals.[83]

After again returning for a brief visit to Middletown, Mansfield returned to Washington to dine with Gen. Winfield Scott on the anniversary of the fall of Mexico City.[84] There were rumors he would be sent to California or Missouri, but instead he remained in Washington as president of a retiring board. Finally in October 1861, orders came that transferred him to Fortress Monroe, Virginia, where he was placed under another aging general, Gen. John Wool. Mansfield would remain in Virginia, mostly at Suffolk, for almost a year. Much of his time would be occupied in arresting citizens he judged seditious and dangerous and in defending and protecting free blacks and runaway slaves.[85]

In Virginia, Mansfield became exceedingly restless as he watched officers many years his junior assume command of great armies. He particularly resented Gen. George B. McClellan's promotion to command the Army of the Potomac and was not surprised when, in the summer of 1862, McClellan ran "aground" outside of Richmond. For months, Mansfield, who had served in the army twenty-four years longer than McClellan, consistently complained that "Little Mac" had not "exhibited one sign [of] a generous feeling towards me."[86] Then, when Gen. John Pope was given command of the Union Army of Virginia, Mansfield complained to his wife that Pope was "a man of no sound moral principles."[87] He was also miffed at the appointments of Henry W. Halleck and John C. Fremont, for both had served as second lieutenants under his command in the Mexican War. In addition, General Scott was "too old to effect anything."[88] He pleaded with influential friends in Washington, including Secretary of the Treasury Salmon P. Chase, that he had been wronged.[89]

In the cold and rainy Virginia winter, Mansfield confessed he was "disgusted with the management of the military affairs of the country."[90] In a letter to Louisa during a "terrible stormy day" in January 1862, he despondently asserted that both Scott and McClellan were "little in every sense of the word" and that McClellan was so "conceited" he would "probably burst up out of sheer self-esteem."[91] Though he remained desperate for a command, Mansfield found the war, as he wrote in July 1862, "extremely irksome."[92] Indeed, he wrote General Wool, "I am ready to march with any force from a company to ten thousand men."[93] There were some happy moments in Virginia, however, especially when his son, Samuel Mather, graduated toward the top of his class at West Point and was assigned to the Corps of Engineers. Moreover, Lieutenant Mansfield joined his father as aide and chief engineer.[94]

With General Lee's Rebel army across the Potomac River into Maryland, Mansfield's break came on September 10, 1862, when he was ordered to join General McClellan's army. From Willard's Hotel only hours before leaving Washington for McClellan's headquarters near Frederick, Maryland, Mansfield wrote an ominous and nostalgic letter "in great haste" to his old West Point professor Sylvanus Thayer. "This is only to say if I never see you again, that I have not forgotten your inestimable favors to me. May God bless you in your old age & finally receive you into his glorious Kingdom of Heavenly Peace."[95] Mansfield also took time to scribble a note to son Samuel: "Fill your pockets with sandwiches and follow me."[96]

On Saturday, September 13, at four o'clock in the afternoon, with his Connecticut-born aid, Capt. Clarence Hopkins Dyer, and a black body servant, Mansfield departed Washington by horseback. He reached McClellan's headquarters at Middletown, Maryland, two days later and was immediately assigned to the command of the 10,000-man Twelfth Corps. The next day, as McClellan's army moved west to confront Lee's Rebel army, Mansfield received an urgent order: "The Major General commanding desires that you hold your command in readiness to move at a moment's warning."[97] Early on the morning of Wednesday, September 17, 1862, near Sharpsburg, Maryland, after crossing Antietam Creek before midnight and after only a few hours of sleep on the bare ground, Mansfield rose before daylight in the foggy and misty half-light of early dawn and led his corps into battle. In support of Gen. Joseph Hooker's First Corps, Mansfield, following his training at West Point decades earlier, ordered his small army to move forward in columns so the officers could maintain control.

In the battle that followed, the tall white-bearded and white-haired general seemed to be everywhere, dashing about with vigor and enthusiasm, bringing up regiment after regiment, all the time "displaying enthusiasm and fatherly assurance."[98] A Maine soldier remembered Mansfield riding forward, tall and erect in the saddle: "Bullets from the enemy began to whiz over and around us . . . 50 to 100 Confederates were strung along the fence firing at us . . . it was an awful morning, our comrades went down one after another pierced with bullets."[99] Advancing at the head of Brig. Gen. Samuel Crawford's brigade, mostly Pennsylvania and Maine boys, Mansfield was fired on from less than fifty yards by what turned out to be men of the Fourth Alabama. Just as he turned and attempted to go through a fence, his horse hesitated and was struck several times. Mansfield attempted to dismount and lead the wounded horse through a small gate, but he was struck in the chest with a minie ball, the bullet ripping open his coat and passing through his right lung.[100]

As he fell, Mansfield was caught by several men of the Tenth Maine. Bleeding profusely, he was attended by a surgeon from a Pennsylvania regiment and carried back a quarter mile to the rear, where he was placed in an ambulance that took him another mile to a makeshift Union hospital in an old farmhouse.[101] For the next twenty-four hours, he emerged in and out of consciousness. When told that his wound was certain to be mortal, he calmly remarked, "It is God's will, it is all right."[102] Attended by three surgeons, Mansfield conversed freely for hours. Told that both Gen. Ambrose E. Burnside and Gen. Joseph Hooker were dead, he lifted his hands in the air and exclaimed, "Too bad. Too Bad. Poor Fellows. Poor Fellows."[103] Later informed that both had actually survived, Mansfield appeared "much gratified and relieved."[104] Although opiates eased his pain, he grew weaker and weaker. Although his speech became slurred, it was evident he was in prayer as occasionally such phrases as "My Lord," "Father in Heaven," and "into thy hands," were discernible. At ten minutes after eight on the morning of Thursday, September 18, 1862, Mansfield died. The old general was fifty-eight.

Mansfield's body was carried in an ambulance to Monocacy Station on the Baltimore and Ohio Railroad and placed in a railroad car for Baltimore, where a casket was obtained. There, Capt. Samuel Mansfield joined Captain Dyer for the journey to Middletown. An escort of cavalry escorted the general's remains through Baltimore. In New York City, a request by city fathers that his remains lie in state in the city hall, at least for a day, was denied. The body continued by the midnight train to Meriden, Connecticut, and then by carriage to Middletown. In Middletown, Mansfield's body first lay in state at the town hall. Guarded by a regiment of Connecticut soldiers, the coffin was covered in an American flag, on top of which was placed bouquets of white flowers alongside the general's sword, sash, and chapeau. For two days, hundreds of Middletown's finest citizens filed past to view the remains. Public buildings, as well as businesses and private homes, were all decorated with black mourning and flags flew at half mast.[105]

On the day of Mansfield's funeral, after a brief ceremony at the family home on Main Street, the remains were carried to North Church. There, a photograph and a steel engraving were placed at the entrance. Eulogies were delivered by Rev. Ebenezer Jackson, Sen. James Dixon, and Gov. William A. Buckingham, after which a long procession wound its way to Mortimer Cemetery. Several hundred soldiers from Connecticut's twin capitals of New Haven and Hartford were followed by Captain Dyer, Mansfield's body servant leading a horse, and the Mansfield family in carriages. Next came politicians, aldermen, members of the local bar, and faculty and staff from Wesleyan University and Berkeley Divinity School. In addition, there were hundreds of schoolchildren and citizens, young and old.[106] Bells tolled and a volley was fired at the grave site by a local militia unit, the Mansfield Guards. Mansfield's remains were later transferred to Indian Hills Cemetery, which overlooked the town. Later, a sober brownstone monument was erected, its crest carved to represent an officer's sword, hat, and the American flag. In May 1900, the state of Connecticut erected an impressive granite monument near the East Woods on the Antietam battlefield where Gen. Mansfield fell on that fateful and bloody day in September 1862.[107] Today, far from the lush green Connecticut countryside, Mansfield is best remembered for his meticulous and numerous inspections of military posts and depots in the American West.

ABBREVIATIONS

AAG	Assistant Adjutant General
AAAG	Acting Assistant Adjutant General
AGO	Adjutant General's Office
Asst. Sur.	Assistant Surgeon
Batt.	Battalion
Brig.	Gen. Brigadier General
CAH	Center for the Study of American History, University of Texas at Austin
Capt.	Captain
Co.	Company
Col.	Colonel
Corp.	Corporal
CQM	Chief Quartermaster
DNM	Department of New Mexico
DT	Department of Texas
DRT	Library of the Daughters of the Republic of Texas at the Alamo, San Antonio, Texas
First Lt.	First Lieutenant
LC	Manuscript Division, Library of Congress, Washington, D.C.
Lt.	Lieutenant
Lt. Col.	Lieutenant Colonel
LS	Letters Sent
LR	Letters Received
Maj.	Major
Maj. Gen.	Major General
MCHS	Middlesex County Historical Society, Middletown, Connecticut
NYHS	New York Historical Society, New York, New York
NA	National Archives, Washington, D.C.
PR	Post Returns
Pvt.	Private
QM	Quartermaster
Reg.	Regiment
Second Lt.	Second Lieutenant
Sgt.	Sergeant
USMA	United States Military Academy Archives, West Point, New York

APPENDIX

Department Commanders

Texas

Eighth Military Department

Brigadier and Brevet Major General David Emanuel Twiggs, Nov. 1, 1848, Headquarters at Galveston
Colonel and Brevet Major General William Jenkins Worth, Dec. 26, 1848, Headquarters at San Antonio[1]
Colonel and Brevet Brigadier General William Selby Harney, May 14, 1849
Colonel and Brevet Major General George Mercer Brooke, July 7, 1849
Colonel and Brevet Brigadier General William Selby Harney, Mar. 9, 1851
Colonel and Brevet Major General Persifor Frazer Smith, Sept. 16, 1851, Headquarters at Corpus Christi as of Dec. 1, 1852
Colonel and Brevet Brigadier General William Selby Harney, Dec. 3, 1852
Colonel and Brevet Major General Persifor Frazer Smith, May 11, 1853

Department of Texas

Colonel and Brevet Major General Persifor Frazer Smith, Nov. 23, 1853; Headquarters at San Antonio as of Oct. 1, 1855
Colonel Albert Sidney Johnston, Apr. 1, 1856
Brigadier and Brevet Major General David Emanuel Twiggs, May 18, 1857
Colonel Henry Wilson, Mar. 24, 1858
Colonel and Brevet Major General David Emanuel Twiggs, June 1, 1858
Lieutenant Colonel Washington Seawell, Dec. 7, 1859
Lieutenant Colonel and Brevet Colonel Robert Edward Lee, Feb. 20, 1860
Brigadier and Brevet Major General David Emanuel Twiggs, Nov. 27, 1860
Colonel Carlos Adolphus Waite, Feb. 19, 1861[2]

New Mexico

Ninth Military Department

Brigadier General Stephen Watts Kearny, Aug. 13, 1846; Headquarters at Santa Fe[3]
Brigadier General of Volunteers Sterling Price, June 11, 1847
Lieutenant Colonel of Volunteers A. R. Easton, Aug. 29, 1847
Brigadier General of Volunteers Sterling Price, Dec. 11, 1847
Major and Brevet Lieutenant Colonel Benjamin Lloyd Beall, Aug. 27, 1848
Major and Brevet Lieutenant Colonel John Macrae Washington, Oct. 11, 1848
Colonel and Brevet Major General William Jenkins Worth, Dec. 26, 1848[4]
Major and Brevet Lieutenant Colonel John Macrae Washington, May 1849
Major and Brevet Colonel John Munroe, Oct. 23, 1849
Lieutenant Colonel and Brevet Colonel Edwin Vose Sumner, July 19, 1851; Headquarters at Fort Union; Santa Fe as of May 3, 1852; Albuquerque as of Aug. 31, 1852
Lieutenant Colonel Dixon Stansbury Miles, June 1, 1853
Lieutenant Colonel and Brevet Colonel Edwin Vose Sumner, June 3, 1853
Lieutenant Colonel Dixon Stansbury Miles, July 1, 1853
Colonel and Brevet Brigadier General John Garland, July 20, 1853

Department of New Mexico

Colonel and Brevet Brigadier General John Garland, Jan. 1, 1854; Headquarters at Santa Fe as of Sept. 6, 1854
Colonel Benjamin L. E. Bonneville, Oct. 11, 1856
Colonel and Brevet Brigadier General John Garland, May 12, 1857
Colonel Benjamin L. E. Bonneville, Sept. 16, 1858
Colonel Thomas Turner Fauntleroy, Oct. 25, 1859
Colonel William Wing Loring, Mar. 22, 1861
Colonel Edward Richard Sprigg Canby, June 23, 1861

Military Personnel Named in the Reports

Officers

In the inspection reports by Lt. Col. Joseph E. Johnston and Col. Joseph K. F. Mansfield, the names of 144 officers appear. Of those listed, four died before the Civil War, one officer drowned (James B. Witherell) and another was killed (George McLane) during the 1859–1860 Navajo Expedition. Fifteen of the men listed were surgeons. A few were on leave at the time or had already left the army. Excluding surgeons, the vast majority of the officers, ninety-three (72 percent) were graduates of the United States Military Academy.

The following list includes all the officers named by Johnston or Mansfield. Following the officer's name is the state of that individual's birth. USMA indicates that the officer graduated from West Point and the number in parentheses is his class rank. The date given is the year the cadet entered the Academy and not the year of graduation, which in most instances was four years later, although a few cadets took five years to complete their course of study. USA indicates that the officer remained loyal to the Union; CSA, that he served with the Confederacy. The next rank given is the highest attained regular rank at the time of the inspection, whereas Johnston and Mansfield, as was the custom, often refer to the brevet rank of the officer. k. refers to those who were killed during the Civil War; d. refers to the date of death, if known. Most of the information is taken from Francis B. Heitman, *Historical Register and Dictionary of the United States Army*; Robert M. Danford, ed., *Register of Graduates and Former Cadets, United States Military Academy*; and *Army Register*, 33d Cong., 2d sess., *House Executive Document* 58. Also used was Ezra J. Warner's *Generals in Blue: Lives of the Union Commanders* and his *Generals in Gray: Lives of the Confederate Commanders*, as well as various Civil War encyclopedias and biographies.

Abadie, Eugene Hilarian: France. Major Surgeon (July 24, 1853). USA: Major Surgeon. d. Dec. 22, 1874.

Abbott, Robert Osborne: Pennsylvania. Asst. Sur. (Nov. 23, 1849). USA: Major Surgeon. d. June 16, 1867.

Alley, John W.: Maine. USMA (32) 1846. First Lt. (Dec. 31, 1856) Third Infantry. USA: Capt. Dismissed (Oct. 20, 1863). d. Feb. 5, 1890.

Anderson, William Wallace: South Carolina. Asst. Sur. (June 29, 1849). Resigned (Apr. 20, 1861). CSA: Surgeon.

Backus, Electus: New York. USMA (28) 1820. Lt. Col. (Jan. 19, 1859) Third Infantry. USA: Col. d. June 7, 1862.

Bailey, Guilford Dudley: New York. USMA (17) 1852. Second Lt. (July 1, 1856). USA: Col. k. Fair Oaks, Va. (May 31, 1862).

Beauregard, Pierre Gustavus Toutant: Louisiana. USMA (2) 1834. Capt. (Mar. 3, 1853) Topographical Engineers. Resigned (Feb. 20, 1861). CSA: General. d. Feb. 20, 1893.

Blair, William B.: Virginia. USMA (11) 1834. Capt. (Sept. 27, 1850) Second Artillery. Resigned (May 14, 1861). CSA: Maj. d. Mar. 23, 1883.

Blake, Edward D.: South Carolina. USMA (37) 1843. Capt. (Oct. 17, 1860) Resigned (June 11, 1861). CSA: Lt. Col. d. Nov. 29, 1882.

Bliss, Zenas Randall: Rhode Island. USMA (41) 1850. First Lt. (Oct. 17, 1860). USA: Col. Retired as Maj. Gen. (May 22, 1897). Awarded Medal of Honor (Dec. 3, 1898) for service at Battle of Fredericksburg (Dec. 13, 1862). d. Jan. 2, 1900.

Bomford, James Voty: New York. USMA (34) 1828. Maj. (Oct. 17, 1860) Sixth Infantry. USA: Col. d. Jan. 6, 1862.

Bonneau, Richard Vanderhorst: South Carolina. USMA (42) 1847. Second Lt. (Mar. 3, 1855) Third Infantry. Resigned (Mar. 2, 1861). CSA: Maj. d. Jan. 28, 1899.

Bonneville, Benjamin L. E.: France. USMA (35) 1813. Col. (Feb. 3, 1855) Third Infantry. Retired (Sept. 9, 1861). d. June 12, 1878.

Bowen, Nicolas: New York. USMA (4) 1855. Brevet Second Lt. (July 1, 1860) Topographical Engineers. USA. Capt. d. July 11, 1871.

Bowman, Andrew W.: Pennsylvania. USMA (40) 1837. Capt. (June 6, 1852) Third Infantry. USA: Lt. Col. d. July 17, 1869.

Brackett, Albert Gallatin: New York. Capt. (Mar. 3, 1855) Second Cavalry. USA: Maj. d. June 25, 1896.

Bradfute, William R.: Tennessee. Capt. (Mar. 3, 1855) Second Cavalry. CSA: Col.

Brodie, Robert Little: South Carolina. Asst. Sur. (May 15, 1854). Resigned (May 7, 1861). CSA: Surgeon.

Brooks, William Thomas Harbaugh: Ohio. USMA (46) 1837. Capt. (Nov. 10, 1851) Third Infantry. USA: Brig. Gen. d. July 19, 1870.

Caldwell, James Nelson: Ohio. USMA (25) 1836. Capt. (Oct. 26, 1850) First Infantry. USA: Maj. d. Mar. 12, 1866.

Carpenter, Stephen Decatur: Maine. USMA (35) 1836. Capt. (Oct. 17, 1851) First Infantry. USA: Maj. k. (Stone's River, Tenn. (Dec. 31, 1862).

Carswell, William A.: South Carolina. Asst. Sur. (Nov. 29, 1859). Resigned (Mar. 25, 1861). CSA: Surgeon. d. Sept. 8, 1886.

Chandler, Daniel T.: District of Columbia. Capt. (Sept. 21, 1846) Third Infantry. Retired (Feb. 27, 1862). CSA: Lt. Col. d. Oct. 14, 1877.

Childs, Frederick Lynn: Maine. USMA (9) 1851. Second Lt. (June 14, 1855) First Artillery. Resigned (Mar. 4, 1861). CSA: Lt. Col. d. June 10, 1894.

Clary, Robert Emmet: Massachusetts. USMA (13) 1823. Capt. (July 7, 1838) Fifth Infantry. USA: Col. d. Jan. 19, 1890.

Clitz, Henry Boynton: New York. USMA 936) 1841. Capt. (Dec. 6, 1858) Third Infantry. USA: Col. d. Oct. 30, 1888.

Closson, Henry Whitney: Vermont. USMA (8) 1850. First Lt. (Oct. 31, 1856) First Artillery. USA: Capt. Retired (June 6, 1896). d. July 15, 1917.

Cogswell, Milton: Indiana. USMA (11) 1845. First Lt. (Aug. 15, 1855) Eighth Infantry. USA: Col. d. Nov. 20, 1882.

Craig, William: Indiana. USMA (52) 1849. First Lt. (Oct. 19, 1859) Eighth Infantry. USA: Capt. d. May 27, 1886.

Cunningham, Francis A.: South Carolina. Major Paymaster (Mar. 2, 1849). USA: Maj. d. Aug. 14, 1864.

Davis, Matthew L.: North Carolina. USMA (21) 1848. First Lt. (Jan. 14, 1858) Third Infantry. Resigned (May 13, 1862). CSA: Col. d. Apr. 23, 1862.

Dawson, Samuel Kennedy: Pennsylvania. USMA (22) 1835. Capt. (Mar. 31, 1853) First Artillery. USA: Lt. Col. d. Apr. 17, 1889.

De Leon, David Camden: South Carolina. (August 21, 1838). Major Surgeon (Aug. 29, 1846). Resigned (Feb. 19, 1861). CSA: Surgeon. d. Sept. 3, 1872.

Donaldson, James Lowry: Maryland. USMA (15) 1832. Capt. (Aug. 20, 1847) First Artillery. USA: Col. d. Nov. 4, 1885.

Dye, William McEntire: Pennsylvania. USMA (32) 1849. First Lt. (Feb. 1, 1856) Eighth Infantry. USA: Col. d. Nov. 13, 1899.

Echols, William Holding: Alabama. USMA (4) 1854. Brevet Second Lt. (July 1, 1858) Topographical Engineers. Resigned (Mar. 21, 1861). CSA: Col. d. Nov. 13, 1909.

Elliott, Washington Lafayette: Pennsylvania. Capt. (July 20, 1854) Mounted Rifles. USA: Brig. Gen. d. June 29, 1888.

Ewell, Richard Stoddert: Virginia. USMA (13) 1836. Capt. (Aug. 4, 1849) First Dragoons. Resigned (May 7, 1861). CSA: Lieutenant General. d. Jan. 25, 1872.

Fitzgerald, Edward H.: Pennsylvania. October 26, 1839. Capt. (Sept. 8, 1847) First Dragoons. d. Jan. 9, 1860.

Freedley, Henry William: Pennsylvania. USMA (24) 1851. Second Lt. (Sept. 30, 1853) Third Infantry. USA: Capt. d. Nov. 3, 1889.

Freeman, William Grigsby: Virginia. USMA (15) 1830. Capt. (Sept. 13, 1847) Fourth Artillery. Resigned (Mar. 31, 1856). d. Nov. 12, 1866.

French, William Henry: Maryland. USMA (22) 1833. Capt. (Sept. 22, 1848) First Artillery. USA: Maj. Gen. d. May 20, 1881.

Garrard, Kenner: Kentucky. USMA (8) 1847. First Lt. (Mar. 3, 1855) Second Cavalry. USA: Brig. Gen. d. May 15, 1879.

Ghiselin, James Thomas: Maryland. Asst. Sur. (June 1, 1855). USA: Major Surgeon. d. Mar. 2, 1896.

Gillem, Alvan Cullom: Tennessee. USMA (11) 1847. First Lt. (Mar. 3, 1855) First Artillery. USA: Brig. Gen. d. Dec. 2, 1875.

Gordon, William Hamilton: Virginia. Capt. (Sept. 21, 1846) Third Infantry. Retired (Mar. 15, 1862). d. Dec. 7, 1865.

Graham, Campbell: Virginia. USMA (9) 1817. Maj. (Dec. 9, 1857) Topographical Engineers. Retired (Sept. 9, 1861). d. Nov. 8, 1866.

Graham, William Montrose: District of Columbia. (June 7, 1855). Second Lt. (June 7, 1855) First Artillery. USA: Col. Retired (Sept. 28, 1898).

Granger, Robert Seaman: Ohio. USMA (28) 1833. Capt. (Sept. 8, 1847) First Infantry. USA: Brig. Gen. d. Apr. 25, 1894.

Grayson, John Breckinridge: Kentucky. USMA (22) 1821. Maj. (Oct. 21, 1852) Second Artillery. Resigned (July 1, 1861). CSA: Brig. Gen. d. Oct. 21, 1861.

Greene, James B.: New York. USMA (41) 1847. First Lt. (Feb. 11, 1856) First Infantry. d. June 24, 1861.

Hartz, Edward L.: Pennsylvania. USMA (24) 1851. Second Lt. (Aug. 15, 1855) Eighth Infantry. USA: Capt. d. Nov. 11, 1868.

Haskell, Alexander McDonald: District of Columbia. Second Lt. (June 27, 1856) First Infantry. Resigned (May 1, 1861). CSA: Maj.

Hazen, William Babcock: Vermont. USMA (28) 1851. Second Lt. (Sept. 4, 1855) Eighth Infantry. USA: Maj. Gen. d. Jan. 16, 1887.

Hendren, Cornelius D.: Virginia. Second Lt. (Feb. 21, 1857) Third Infantry. Resigned (June 30, 1860). d. Nov. 17, 1894.

Hill, Bennett Hoskin: District of Columbia. USMA (21) 1833. Capt. (Jan. 12, 1848) First Artillery. USA: Lt. Col. d. Mar. 24, 1886.

Holden, Levi H.: Rhode Island. Major Surgeon (Apr. 23, 1860). USA: Major Surgeon. d. May 12, 1874.

Holman, J. H.: Tennessee. Second Lt. (Feb. 21, 1857) First Infantry. Resigned (Apr. 17, 1861). CSA: Lt. Col.

Holt, George Waller: Alabama. USMA (31) 1853. Second Lt. (Sept. 28, 1857). CSA: Lt. Col. d. Jan. 23, 1876.

Hood, John Bell: Kentucky. USMA (44) 1849. First Lt. (Aug. 18, 1858) Second Cavalry. Resigned (Apr. 16, 1861). CSA: General. d. Aug. 30, 1879.

Howland, George Washington: Rhode Island. USMA (38) 1844. First Lt. (Mar. 3, 1855) Mounted Rifles. USA: Capt. d. Dec. 21, 1886.

Hunt, Henry Jackson: Michigan. USMA (19) 1835. Capt. (Sept. 28, 1852) Second Artillery. USA: Brig. Gen. d. Feb. 11, 1889.

Irwin, Bernard John Dowling: Ireland. Asst. Sur. (Aug. 28, 1856. USA: Major Surgeon. Awarded Medal of Honor for action against Chiricahua Apaches at Apache Pass, Ariz. (Bascom Affair) on Feb. 13 and 14, 1861. Retired (June 28, 1894).

Jackson, William Hicks: Tennessee. USMA (38) 1852. Second Lt. (Dec. 30, 1856) Mounted Rifles. Resigned (May 16, 1861). CSA: Brig. Gen. d. Mar. 30, 1903.

Jenkins, Walworth: New York. USMA (23) 1849. First Lt. (Feb. 16, 1856) First Artillery. USA: Capt. d. May 17. 1874.

Johns, William Brooke: District of Columbia. USMA (39) 1836. First Lt. (Nov. 26, 1845) Third Infantry. Dropped (Apr. 11, 1861). d. Oct. 18, 1894.

Jones, John Marshall: Virginia. USMA (39) 1837. Capt. (Mar. 3, 1855) Seventh Infantry. Resigned (May 27, 1861). CSA: Brig. Gen. k. Spotsylvania Courthouse, Va. (May 10, 1864).

Jones, Samuel: Virginia. USMA (19) 1837. Capt. (Dec. 24, 1853) First Artillery. Resigned (Apr. 27, 1861). CSA: Maj. Gen. d. July 31, 1887.

Jones, Thomas Marshall: Virginia. USMA (47) 1849. First Lt. (July 19, 1858) Eighth Infantry. Resigned (Feb. 28, 1861). CSA: Brig. Gen. d. Mar. 7, 1913.

Jones, Walter: District of Columbia. First Lt. (Oct. 31, 1857) First Infantry. Resigned (May 10, 1861). CSA: Capt.

Jordan, Charles Downes: Massachusetts. USMA (44) 1838. Capt. (May 15, 1851) Eighth Infantry. USA: Maj. d. Jan. 5, 1876.

Kimmel, Manning Marius: Missouri. USMA (22) 1853. Second Lt. (Aug. 18, 1858) Second Cavalry. Resigned (Aug. 14, 1861). CSA: Maj. d. Feb. 27, 1916.

King, John Haskell: Michigan. Capt. (Oct. 31, 1846) First Infantry. USA: Col. d. Apr. 7, 1888.

Langdon, Loomas Lyman: New York. First Lt. (July 30, 1860) First Artillery. USA: Capt. Retired (Oct. 25, 1894).

Langworthy, Elisha Perkins: New York. Asst. Sur. (May 16, 1850). Resigned (Apr. 30, 1861). CSA: Surgeon. d. Mar. 8, 1862.

Lay, Richard Gregory: District of Columbia. Second Lt. (June 30, 1859) Third Infantry. USA: Capt.

Lee, Arthur Tracy: Pennsylvania. Capt. (Jan. 27, 1848) Eighth Infantry. USA: Maj. d. Dec. 29, 1879.

Lee, Robert Edward: Virginia. USMA (2) 1825. Lt. Col. (Mar. 3, 1855) Second Cavalry. Resigned (Apr. 25, 1861). CSA: General-in-Chief. d. Oct. 12, 1870.

Lynde, Richard Douglass: Michigan. Asst. Sur. (Aug. 29, 1856). Resigned (Aug. 31, 1862). USA: Surgeon. d. Feb. 12, 1876.

Maclay, Robert Plunket: Pennsylvania. USMA (32) 1836. Capt. (Jan. 22, 1849) Eighth Infantry. Resigned (Dec. 31, 1860). CSA: Brig. Gen. d. May 20, 1903.

Maclin, Sacfield: Tennessee. Major Paymaster (Mar. 2, 1849). Resigned (March 1, 1861). CSA: Maj.

Major, James Patrick: Missouri. USMA 923) 1852. Second Lt. (Dec. 1, 1856) Second Cavalry. Resigned (Mar. 21, 1861. CSA: Brig. Gen. d. May 8, 1877.

McClure, Daniel: Indiana. USMA (21) 1845. Major Paymaster (Oct. 23, 1858). USA: Major Paymaster. d. Oct. 31, 1900.

McLane, George: Delaware. Capt. (Dec. 30, 1856) Mounted Rifles. k. Black Rock, New Mexico Territory, in action against Navajo Indians (Oct. 13, 1860).

McLean, Eugene Eckel: District of Columbia. USMA (47) 1838. Capt. (Aug. 29, 1855) First Infantry. Resigned (Apr. 25, 1861). CSA: Maj. d. Jan. 4, 1906.

Minter, Joseph F.: Virginia. Second Lt. (Mar. 3, 1855) Second Cavalry. Resigned (Mar. 31, 1861). CSA: Maj. d. Aug. 15, 1885.

Morris, Lewis Owen: New York. First Lt. (Dec. 23, 1847). USA: Col. k. Cold Harbor, Va. (June 4, 1864).

Myers, Abraham C.: South Carolina. USMA (32) 1828. Capt. (Feb. 16, 1847). Resigned (Jan. 28, 1861). CSA: Col. d. June 20, 1889.

Nichols, William Augustus: Pennsylvania. USMA (19) 1838. First Lt. (June 1, 1844) Second Artillery. USA: Col. d. Apr. 8, 1869.

O'Bannon, Laurence W.: South Carolina. First Lt. (Sept. 30, 1856). Resigned (Mar. 31, 1861). CSA: Lt. Col. d. June 2, 1882.

Oakes, James: Pennsylvania. USMA (34) 1842. Capt. (Mar. 3, 1855) Second Cavalry. USA: Lt. Col. d. Nov. 27, 1910.

Perin, Glover: Ohio. Asst. Sur. (Dec. 4, 1847). USA: Major Surgeon. d. Dec. 15, 1890.

Peters, DeWitt Clinton: New York. Asst. Sur. (June 23, 1860). USA: Asst. Sur. d. Apr. 22, 1876.

Pitcher, Thomas Gamble: Indiana. USMA (40) 1841. Capt. (Oct. 19, 1858). USA: Brig. Gen. d. Oct. 19, 1895.

Platt, Edward Russell: Vermont. USMA (13) 1845. First Lt. (Oct. 8, 1853) Second Artillery. USA: Lt. Col. d. June 17, 1884. The 1860 Cameron County census lists Platt's birthplace as "unknown."

Pope, John: Kentucky. USMA (17) 1838. Capt. (July 1, 1856) Topographical Engineers. USA: Maj. Gen. d. Sept. 23, 1892.

Porter, Andrew: Pennsylvania. Capt. (May 15, 1847) Mounted Rifles. USA: Brig. Gen. d. Jan. 4, 1872.

Ramsay, Douglas: District of Columbia. Second Lt. (June 7, 1855) First Artillery. USA: First Lt. k. Bull Run, Va. (July 21, 1861).

Read, Edwin W. H.: Ohio. Second Lt. (June 27, 1856). USA: Capt. d. Nov. 11, 1875.

Reeve, Isaac Van Duzer: New York: USMA (45) 1831. Capt. (June 18, 1846) Eighth Infantry. USA: Col. d. Dec. 31, 1890.

Reynolds, Alexander Welch: Virginia. USMA (35) 1833. Capt. (Aug. 5, 1847) First Infantry. Dismissed (Oct. 8, 1855). Reinstated (Mar. 29, 1858). Dropped (Oct. 4, 1861). CSA: Brig. Gen. d. May 26, 1876.

Ricketts, James Brewerton: New York. USMA (16) 1835. Capt. (Aug. 3, 1852) First Artillery. USA: Brig. Gen. d. Sept. 22, 1887.

Roberts, Benjamin Stone: Vermont. USMA (53) 1830. Capt. (Feb. 17, 1847) Mounted Rifles. USA: Brig. Gen. Breveted colonel for gallantry and meritorious service at Valverde, New Mexico Territory (Feb. 21, 1862). d. Jan. 29, 1875.

Robinson, James Watts: Virginia. USMA (13) 1848. First Lt. (Mar. 3, 1855). Resigned (May 15, 1861). d. Sept. 9, 1918.

Royall, William Bedford: Virginia. First Lt. (Mar. 3, 1855) Second Cavalry. USA: Maj. d. Dec. 13, 1895.

Rucker, Daniel Henry: New Jersey. Capt. (Aug. 23, 1849) First Dragoons. USA: Brig. Gen.

Ruff, Charles Frederick: Pennsylvania. USMA 944) 1834. Maj. (Dec. 30, 1856) Mounted Rifles. USA: Lt. Col. d. Oct. 1, 1885.

Schroeder, Henry Belt: Maryland. USMA (22) 1839. Capt. (May 31, 1857) Third Infantry. Resigned (May 30, 1861). d. Dec. 21, 1904.

Seawell, Washington: Virginia. USMA (20) 1821. Col. (Oct. 17, 1860) Sixth Infantry. Retired (Feb. 20, 1862). d. Jan. 8, 1888.

Selden, Henry Raymond: Vermont. USMA (31) 1839. Capt. (Oct. 18, 1855) Fifth Infantry. USA: Col. d. Feb. 2, 1865.

Shaaff, John Thomas: District of Columbia. USMA (38) 1847. First Lt. (May 1, 1856) Second Cavalry. Resigned (Feb. 22, 1861). CSA: Capt. d. July 2, 1877.

Shepherd, Oliver Lathrop: New York. USMA (33) 1836. Capt. (Dec. 1, 1847) Third Infantry. USA: Col. d. Apr. 15, 1894.

Sherburne, John P.: New Hampshire. Second Lt. (June 27, 1856). USA: Col. d. Jan. 9, 1880.

Sibley, Caleb Chase: Massachusetts. USMA (29) 1825. Maj. (Jan. 19, 1859) Third Infantry. USA: Col. d. Feb. 19, 1875.

Silvey, William: Ohio. USMA (6) 1845. First Lt. (Oct. 31, 1853) First Artillery. USA: Capt. d. Oct. 23, 1875.

Slaughter, James E.: Virginia. First Lt. (Aug. 3, 1852) First Artillery. Dismissed (May 14, 1861). CSA: Brig. Gen. d. Jan. 1, 1901.

Smith, Joseph Rowe: New York. USMA (22) 1819. Maj. (June 11, 1851) Seventh Infantry. Retired (Sept. 25, 1861). d. Sept. 3, 1868.

Smith, Leslie: Ireland. Sgt. (July 27, 1849). USA: Capt.

Sprague, John Titcomb: Massachusetts. Capt. (Sept. 21, 1846) Eighth Infantry. USA: Lt. Col. d. Sept. 16, 1878.

Steen, Alexander Early: Missouri. First Lt. (Sept. 28, 1857) Third Infantry. Resigned (May 10, 1861). CSA: Brig. Gen. k. Cane Hill, Ark. (Dec. 7, 1862).

Stevens, Walter Husted: New York. USMA (4) 1844. Capt. (Mar. 3, 1855) Topographical Engineers. Dismissed: (May 2, 1861). CSA: Brig. Gen. d. Nov. 12, 1867.

Stoneman, George: New York. USMA (33) 1842. Capt. (Mar. 3, 1855) Second Cavalry. USA: Maj. Gen. Governor of California, 1883–1887. d. Sept. 5, 1894.

Sutherland, Charles: Pennsylvania. Asst. Sur. (Aug. 5, 1852). USA: Major Surgeon. d. May 10, 1895.

Sykes, George: Maryland. USMA (39) 1838. Capt. (Sept. 30, 1855) Third Infantry. USA: Maj. Gen. d. Feb. 8, 1880.

Taylor, John Gibson: Kentucky. Second Lt. (June 7, 1855). Resigned (June 7, 1861). CSA: Lt. Col. k. White Oak Swamp, Va. (June 30, 1862).

Thompson, James: New York. USMA (6) 1847. First Lt. (Aug. 16, 1854) Second Artillery. USA: Capt. d. Feb. 14, 1880.

Tilford, Joseph Green: Kentucky. USMA (40) 1847. First Lt. (June 14, 1858) Mounted Rifles. USA: Capt. d. Feb. 24, 1911.

Trevitt, John: New Hampshire. USMA (12) 1840. Capt. (Dec. 31, 1846). Resigned (Apr. 17, 1861). d. Mar. 24, 1893.

Twiggs, David Emanuel: Georgia. Brig. Gen. (June 30, 1846) Second Dragoons. Dismissed (Mar. 1, 1861). CSA: Maj. Gen. d. July 15, 1862.

Van Bokkelen, William Kimble: New York. USMA (27) 1818. Maj. (Mar. 3, 1847). USA: Col. d. Feb. 21, 1877.

Van Horn, James Judson: Ohio. USMA (14) 1854. Second Lt. (July 19, 1858) Eighth Infantry. USA: Capt. d. Aug. 30, 1898.

Vinton, David Hammond: Rhode Island. USMA (14) 1818. Maj. (Mar. 3, 1847). USA: Col. d. Feb. 21, 1877.

Waite, Carlos Adolphus: New York. Lt. Col. (Nov. 10, 1851) Fifth Infantry. USA: Col. d. May 7, 1866.

Walker, John George: Missouri. Capt. (June 30, 1851) Mounted Rifles. Resigned (July 31, 1861). CSA: Maj. Gen. d. July 20, 1893.

Washington, Thornton Augustus: Virginia. USMA (33) 1845. First Lt. (Dec. 8, 1855). Resigned (Apr. 8, 1861). CSA: Maj. d. July 10, 1894.

Whistler, Joseph Nelson Garland: Wisconsin. USMA (47) 1842. First Lt. (June 6, 1852) Third Infantry. USA: Col. d. Apr. 20, 1899.

White, William James Hamilton: District of Columbia. Asst. Sur. (Mar. 12, 1850). USA: Major Surgeon. k. Antietam, Md. (Sept. 17, 1862).

Whiteley, Robert Henry Kirkwood: Maryland. USMA (13) 1826. Capt. (Mar. 27, 1842) Second Artillery. USA: Lt. Col. d. June 9, 1896.

Whiting, Charles Jarvis: Massachusetts. USMA (4) 1831. Capt. (Mar. 3, 1855) Second Cavalry. USA: Maj. d. Jan. 8, 1890.

Wilkins, John Darragh: New York. USMA (46) 1842. First Lt. (Nov. 10, 1851) Third Infantry. USA: Maj. d. Feb. 20, 1900.

Willard, George L.: New York. First Lt. (Dec. 31, 1853) Eighth Infantry. USA: Col. k. Gettysburg, Pa. (July 2, 1863).

Williams, George Augustus: New York. USMA (34) 1848. First Lt. (Feb. 11, 1856) First Infantry. USA: Capt. d. Apr. 2, 1889.

Williams, Thomas Greenhow: Vermont. USMA (32) 1845. First Lt. (Aug. 7, 1855) First Infantry. Resigned (Mar. 15, 1861). CSA: Col. d. Jan. 22, 1885.

Witherell, James Bonaparte: Michigan. Second Lt. (Mar. 3, 1855) Second Cavalry. Drowned (Mar. 20, 1861).

Wood, William Henry: Massachusetts: USMA (37) 1841. First Lt. (Sept. 9, 1851) Third Infantry. USA: Lt. Col. d. Jan. 1, 1887.

NOTES

Introduction

1. William B. Skelton, *An American Profession of Arms: The Officer Corps, 1784–1861* (Lawrence: University of Kansas Press, 1992), 198; Francis B. Heitman, *Historical Register and Dictionary of the United States Army, From its Organization, September 29, 1789, to March 2, 1903*, 2 vols. (Washington D.C.: Government Printing Office, 1903), 1:578, 688. (Unless otherwise noted, all references to Heitman will be to vol. 1.)

2. Craig L. Symonds, *Joseph E. Johnston: A Civil War Biography* (New York: W. W. Norton and Company, 1992), 3.

3. Letter of Jared Mansfield, Aug. 25, 1817; Jared Mansfield to [James Monroe], June 15, 1817; and Jared Mansfield to [James Monroe], June 15, 1817; all in West Point Application Files, Adjutant General's Office, Record Group 92, National Archives, Washington, D.C.

4. Heitman, *Historical Register*, 688.

5. *Memorial of Gen. J. K. F. Mansfield, United States Army, Who Fell in Battle at Sharpsburg, Md., Sept. 17, 1862* (Boston: T. R. Marvin and Son, 1862), 65.

6. Tombstone data, Indian Hills Cemetery, Middletown, Connecticut.

7. Heitman, *Historical Register*, 688.

8. Mansfield to Louisa Mansfield, Aug. 15, 1846, Mansfield Papers, USMA.

9. Mansfield to Louisa Mansfield, Sept. 25 and Oct. 4, 1846, USMA.

10. Heitman, *Historical Register*, 688.

11. Henry Washington Benham, *Recollections of Mexico and the Battle of Buena Vista, Feb. 22 and 23, 1847, by an Engineer Officer, on its Twenty-Fourth Anniversary* (Boston: n.p., 1871), 11.

12. Mansfield to Louisa Mansfield, Feb. 24, 1847, USMA.

13. Heitman, *Historical Register*, 688.

14. David A. Clary and Joseph W. A. Whitehorne, *The Inspectors General of the United States Army, 1777–1903* (Washington, D.C.: Office of the Inspector General and Center for Military History, United States Army, 1987), 191.

15. Ibid.

16. Symonds, *Joseph E. Johnston*, 10.

17. Ibid., 11–13.

18. Ibid., 34.

19. Ibid., 42.

20. Ibid., 40.

21. Ibid., 59–61.

22. Heitman, *Historical Register*, 578.

23. Ibid.

24. Symonds, *Joseph E. Johnston*, 65–66.

25. Quoted in Ibid., 74.

26. Nyle H. Miller, ed., "Surveying the Southern Boundary of Kansas: From the Private Journal of Col. Joseph E. Johnston," *Kansas Historical Quarterly* 18 (February 1932): 104–39.

27. Symonds, *Joseph E. Johnston*, 85.

28. J. K. F. Mansfield to Mary Mansfield, Oct. 8, 1860, Mansfield Papers, Archives, USMA.

29. Ibid.

30. In 1853, for example, it took Mansfield twenty-four days to make the trip from El Paso to San Antonio. Although a number of Mansfield's letters to his family survive from his previous inspections, only a single personal letter was located from the 1860–1861 inspection of the Department of Texas.

31. Floyd left office on Dec. 19, 1860. President James Buchanan replaced him with Joseph Holt who served from Jan. 18, 1861, to Mar. 5, 1861, at which time President Abraham Lincoln appointed Simon Cameron.

32. Darlis A. Miller, *Soldiers and Settlers: Military Supply in the Southwest, 1861–1885* (Albuquerque: University of New Mexico Press, 1989), 3.

33. Larry Durwood Ball, "The United States Army on the Interwar Frontier, 1846–1861" (Ph.D. diss., University of New Mexico, 1994), 139.

34. Robert W. Frazer, ed., *Mansfield on the Condition of the Western Forts, 1853–54* (Norman: University of Oklahoma Press, 1963), 20.

35. Military Department No. 9 was often referred to, however, as the Department of New Mexico in official documents.

36. Charles Conrad to Edwin Sumner, Apr. 1, 1851, in Annie Heloise Abel, ed., *The Official Correspondence of James S. Calhoun While Indian Agent at Santa Fe and Superintendent of Indian Affairs in New Mexico* (Washington: Government Printing Office, 1915), 383–84. See also Ball, "United States Army on the Interwar Frontier," 217–18. Sumner was the cousin of Charles Sumner, the outspoken abolitionist senator from Massachusetts and the victim of Preston Brooks's vicious 1856 caning that drew national attention.

37. Frazer, *Mansfield*, xvi; Robert W. Frazer, *Forts and Supplies: The Role of the Army in the Economy of the Southwest, 1846–1861* (Albuquerque: University of New Mexico Press, 1983), 62.

38. Ibid., 22.

39. Frazer, *Mansfield*, 30.

40. George P. Hammond, ed., *Campaigns in the West, 1856–1861: The Journal and Letters of Colonel John Van Deusen Du Bois with Pencil Sketches by Joseph Heger* (Tucson: Arizona Pioneers Historical Society, 1949), 47.

41. Edwin Sumner to Roger Jones, Oct. 24, 1851, Calhoun Correspondence, 417. See also Robert M. Utley, *Frontiersmen in Blue: The United States Army and the Indian, 1848–1865* (New York: Macmillan Publishing Co., 1967), 67; and Chris Emmett, *Fort Union and the Winning of the Southwest* (Norman: University of Oklahoma Press, 1965), 15–19.

42. Frazer, *Mansfield*, 15.

43. Lawrence R. Murphy, "Cantonment Burgwin, New Mexico, 1852–1860," *Arizona and the West* 15 (spring 1973), 22–46.

44. Post Returns, Cantonment Burgwin, 1852, AGO, RG 393, NA.

45. Ibid., 7–8; Frazer, *Mansfield*, 16.

46. Frazer, *Mansfield*, 50.

47. Robert W. Frazer, *Forts of the West: Military Forts and Presidios and Posts Commonly Called Forts West of the Mississippi up to 1898* (Norman: University of Oklahoma Press, 1965), 40.

48. Frazer, *Forts and Supplies*, 67.

49. Frazer, *Mansfield*, 18.

50. James A. Bennett, *Forts and Forays: A Dragoon in New Mexico, 1850–1856*, ed. Clinton E. Brooks and Frank D. Reeves (Albuquerque: University of New Mexico Press, 1996), 23.

51. Frazer, *Mansfield*, 40.

52. Frazer, *Forts of the West*, 36–37.

53. PR, Fort Defiance, 1851, AGO, RG 393, NA.

54. William Woods Averell, *Ten Years in the Saddle: The Memoir of William Woods Averell, 1851–1862*, ed. Edward K. Eckert and Nicholas J. Amato (San Rafael: Presidio Press, 1978), 155–56.

55. Frazer, *Mansfield*, 22; Frazer, *Forts and Supplies*, 93.

56. Frazer, *Mansfield*, 23–34.

57. Ibid., 22.

58. Ibid., 24.

59. Ibid.

60. PR, Fort Craig, 1851, AGO, RG 393, NA.

61. Averell, *Ten Years in the Saddle*, 123.

62. Bennett, *Forts and Forays*, 64.

63. Frazer, *Forts of the West*, 99; PR, Fort Fillmore, 1851, AGO, RG, 393, NA.

64. Lydia Spencer Lane, *I Married a Soldier or Old Days in the Old Army* (Albuquerque: Horn and Wallace, 1964), 65.

65. Rick Hendricks and W. H. Timmons, *San Elizario: Spanish Presidio to Texas County Seat* (El Paso: Texas Western Press, 1998), 70–71.

66. Frazer, *Mansfield*, 28.

67. Lane, *I Married a Soldier*, 68.

68. PR, Fort Stanton, 1854, AGO, RG 393, NA.

69. Lane, *I Married a Soldier*, 65.

70. PR, Fort Webster, 1852, AGO, NA; Frazer, *Forts and Supplies*, 65.

71. Bennett, *Forts and Forays*, 35–36.

72. Ibid.

73. Frazer misplaced the new fort some fifteen miles to the northwest. Frazer, *Mansfield*, xvii.

74. Frazer, *Mansfield*, 25; E. Backus to Mansfield, Dec. 20, 1853, Mansfield Papers, MCHS.

75. Frazer, *Forts of the West*, 104–5.

76. Quoted in Frazer, *Forts and Supplies*, 89.

77. B. Sacks, "The Origins of Fort Buchanan, Myth and Fact," *Arizona and the West* 7 (autumn 1960), 207–20.

78. Report of N. H. Davis, Apr. 26, 1864, Letters Received, Department of New Mexico, RG 393, NA.

79. Frazer, *Forts of the West*, 6–7.

80. Frazer, *Mansfield*, xx–xvi.

81. Thomas T. Smith, *The Old Army in Texas: A Research Guide to the U.S. Army in Nineteenth-Century Texas* (Austin: Texas State Historical Association, 2000), 102.

82. Edward M. Coffman, *The Old Army: A Portrait of the American Army in Peacetime, 1784–1898* (New York: Oxford University Press, 1986), 141.

83. Janet Schmelzer, "Fort Worth," in Ron Tyler, et al., eds., *New Handbook of Texas*, 6 vols. (Austin: Texas State Historical Association, 1996), 2:1, 124–25 (hereafter cited as *NHT*).

84. Sandra L. Myer, "Fort Graham," *NHT*, 2:1, 102–3.

85. Art Leatherwood, "Fort Ewell," *NHT*, 2:1, 100.

86. Martin L. Crimmins, ed., "W. G. Freeman's Report on the Eighth Military Department," *Southwestern Historical Quarterly* 51 (January 1948), 252.

87. Ibid., 256.

88. Ibid., 258.

89. Ibid., 252.

90. Ibid. (July 1949), 71–72.

91. Frederick Law Olmsted, *A Journey Through Texas; or, A Saddle-Trip on the Southwestern Frontier* (New York: Dix, Edwards & Co., 1857), 285–86.

92. Ibid.

93. Lane, *I Married a Soldier*, 30–31.

94. Vivian Elizabeth Smyrl, "Fort McKavett," *NHT*, 2:1, 111.

95. Jim W. Corder, *Hunting Lieutenant Chadbourne* (Athens: University of Georgia Press, 1993), 4.

96. Beatrice Grady Gay, "Camp Colorado," *NHT*, 1:932.

97. Ibid.

98. Charles G. Davis, "Camp Cooper," *NHT*, 1:932–33.

99. PR, Camp Verde, 1856, AGO, RG 393, NA.

100. J. Marvin Hunter, *Old Camp Verde, the Home of the Camels: A Romantic Story of Jefferson Davis' Plan to Use Camels on the Texas Frontier* (Bandera: Frontier Times, 1936).

101. Martin L. Crimmins, ed., "W. G. Freeman's Report on the Eighth Military Department," *Southwestern Historical Quarterly* 52 (July 1948), 101–4.

102. Caleb Coker, ed., *The News from Brownsville: Helen Chapman's Letters from the Texas Military Frontier, 1848–1852* (Austin: Texas State Historical Association), 130.

103. R. B. Marcy to Nellie Marcy, Nov. 15, 1856, McClellan Papers, Library of Congress, Washington, D.C.

104. Ibid.

105. Marcy to My Precious Child, Dec. 14, 1856, McClellan Papers, LC.

106. Crimmins, "W. G. Freeman's Report," 52:105; Coker, *News from Brownsville*, 67, 73, 100, 108, 113, 187, 193. Also, PR, Fort Brown, 1848–1853, RG 393.

107. PR, Ringgold Barracks, 1848, AGO, RG 393, NA.

108. Teresa Griffin Viele, *Following the Drum: A Glimpse of Frontier Life* (Lincoln: University of Nebraska Press, 1984), 129.

109. Crimmins, "W. G. Freeman's Report," 52:231, 233.

110. Ibid., 231.

111. Crimmins, ed., "Colonel J. K. F. Mansfield's Report of the Inspection of the Department of Texas in 1856," *Southwestern Historical Quarterly* 42 (October 1938), 130.

112. Ibid., 228.

113. Ibid., 130.

114. Voucher, "Defensive Works Rio Grande," March 3, 1854; "Report of Persons Employed," November 1854; "Report of persons Employed," November 1854; all in Richard Delafield Papers. Manuscript Collections, NYHS.

115. Lane, *I Married a Soldier*, 25.
116. Ibid., 42.
117. Ibid., 42.
118. Olmsted, *Journey Through Texas*, 452.
119. Crimmins, "Colonel J. K. F. Mansfield's Report," 131.
120. Ibid. 234–44.
121. Marcy to Nellie Marcy, July 14, 1856, George B. McClellan Papers, LC.
122. Ibid.
123. James E. Slaughter to Robert Jones, Aug. 8, 1855, Brackett Papers, Library of the Daughters of the Republic of Texas, San Antonio, Texas.
124. Albert G. Brackett to Charles Brackett, June 8, 1857, Brackett Papers, DRT.
125. Ibid.
126. Ibid., 445.
127. Crimmins, "Colonel J. K. F. Mansfield's Report," 131.
128. R. W. Johnson, *A Soldier's Reminiscences in Peace and War* (Philadelphia: J. B. Lippincott, 1886), 64.
129. Lane, *I Married a Soldier*, 28.
130. David A. Clary, ed., "'I Am Already Quite a Texan': Albert J. Myer's Letters from Texas, 1854–1856," *Southwestern Historical Quarterly* 82 (July 1978), 31.
131. Ibid., 31.
132. Ibid., 35.
133. Olmsted, *Journey Through Texas*, 314.
134. Ibid., 286.
135. Jerry Thompson, ed., *Fifty Miles and a Fight: Major Samuel Peter Heintzelman's Journal of Texas and the Cortina War* (Austin: Texas State Historical Association, 1998), 81.
136. Ibid., 80.
137. Joseph E. Chance, ed., *My Life in the Old Army: Reminiscences of Abner Doubleday* (Fort Worth: Texas Christian University Press, 1998), 179.
138. PR, Fort Clark, 1852, AGO, RG 393, NA.
139. Crimmins, "W. G. Freeman's Report," 51:71.
140. Crimmins, "Colonel J. K. F. Mansfield's Report," 131.
141. PR, Fort Davis, 1854, AGO, RG 393, NA; Robert Wooster, *Fort Davis: Outpost on the Texas Frontier* (Austin: Texas State Historical Association, 1996).
142. Ibid., 44.
143. Clary, "'I Am Already Quite a Texan,'" 48.
144. Ibid.
145. Ibid., 356.
146. PR, Fort Lancaster, 1855, AGO, RG 393, NA; Lawrence John Francell, *Fort Lancaster: Texas Frontier Sentinel* (Austin: Texas State Historical Association, 1999), 1.
147. Ibid., 76.
148. Crimmins, "Colonel J. K. F. Mansfield's Report," 131.
149. Ibid.
150. Thomas T. Smith, *The U.S. Army and the Texas Frontier Economy, 1845–1900* (College Station: Texas A&M University Press, 1999), dedication page.
151. Ibid., 132.
152. PR, Fort Quitman, 1858, AGO, RG 393, NA.

153. Lane, *I Married a Soldier*, 169.

154. George Ruhlen, "Fort Quitman: 'The Worst Post at Which I Ever Served,'" *Password* 11 (fall 1966), 107; Zenas R. Bliss, "Memoirs, 1854–1894" unpublished manuscript, typescript, Center for the Study of American History, University of Texas at Austin, 220.

155. Bliss, "Memoirs," 241.

156. Edward L. Hartz to Dear Father, Jan. 4, 1856, Hartz Papers, LC.

157. Ibid.

158. Marcy to Nellie Marcy, Aug. 2, 1855, McClellan Papers, LC.

159. Chance, *My Life in the Old Army*, 175.

160. Clary, "'I Am Already Quite a Texan,'" 33.

161. Olmsted, *Journey Through Texas*, 318–19; Ben E. Pingenot, "Jack Woodland: Forgotten Frontiersman," *The Journal of Big Bend Studies* 8 (1996), 51–60.

162. Johnson, *Soldier's Reminiscences*, 63.

163. Ibid.

164. Lane, *I Married a Soldier*, 27.

165. Galveston *Tri-Weekly News*, Nov. 1, 1859. For the impact of the army on the Texas economy, see Smith, *U.S. Army and the Texas Frontier Economy*.

166. Galveston *Tri-Weekly News*, Nov. 1, 1859.

Johnston and Mansfield Inspections

1. Colonel Bonneville commanded the Department of New Mexico from Oct. 11, 1856, to May 11, 1857, and again from Sept. 16, 1858, to Oct. 24, 1859. Raphael P. Thian, comp., *Notes Illustrating the Military Geography of the United States, 1813–1880*, ed. John M. Carroll (Austin: University of Texas Press, 1979), 79.

2. William Rawle Shoemaker was military storekeeper at the Fort Union arsenal, before, during, and after the Civil War. He retired in June 1882, and, for his long dedication to the army, Shoemaker and his wife were given permission to retain their quarters. Emmett, *Fort Union*, 101, 227, 395.

3. On March 31, 1854, a serious defeat was inflicted on two companies of the First Dragoons in the Battle of Cieneguilla in the Picauris Mountains, some fifteen miles southwest of Taos and nine miles west-southwest of Cantonment Burgwin. The rout, in which twenty Dragoons perished, was the most serious defeat suffered by the army at the hands of Native Americans in the history of New Mexico Territory. For the remainder of the year, the army relentlessly pursued the Jicarillas in a series of battles and skirmishes. In August 1855, after Chief Chacon had come into Santa Fe to sue for peace, Gov. David Meriwether concluded a treaty with the Jicarillas in which they were given a tract of land west of the Chama River. Morris F. Taylor, "Campaign Against the Jicarilla Apache, 1854," *New Mexico Historical Quarterly* 44 (1969), 269–91; Morris F. Taylor, "Campaign Against the Jicarilla Apache, 1855," *New Mexico Historical Quarterly* 45 (1970), 119–36; Veronica E. Velarde Tiller, *The Jicarilla Apache Tribe: A History, 1846–1970* (Lincoln: University of Nebraska Press, 1983), 35.

4. Kentucky-born Col. John B. Grayson, fifty-three, is listed on the 1860 census with real estate of fifty-six thousand dollars and personal property of thirty-five hundred dollars. In Grayson's personal hire were two Hispanic servants. Eighth Census (1860), Santa Fe County, New Mexico Territory, NA.

5. Maj. James Lowry Donaldson, assistant quartermaster and forty-six, was born in Maryland. He brought his Maine-born wife, Harriet, thirty-nine, to New Mexico. Donaldson listed his real estate at fifteen hundred dollars and his personal property at thirty-five hundred dollars. Eighth Census (1860), Santa Fe County, New Mexico Territory, NA.

6. The Maynard tape primer, an invention of Edward Maynard, a dental surgeon from Washington, D.C., consisted of a narrow strip of varnished paper of double thickness having deposits of fulminating compound between the two strips. The strip was coiled in a recessed magazine in the lock plate of the arm of the weapon and was pushed up by a toothed wheel when the hammer was cocked. The Maynard primer system had been applied not only to the manufacture of new arms, but to the modification of older weapons. Dr. Maynard sold his patent rights to the government in 1854 for fifty thousand dollars, and some twenty thousand flintlock muskets were altered to the system. Arcadi Gluckman, *United States Muskets, Rifles and Carbines* (Buffalo: Otto Ulbrich, 1948), 224–25.

7. The Rio Puerco drains the northern and eastern slopes of the San Mateo Mountains and 11,301-foot Mt. Taylor. The stream, which is dry most of the year except for the monsoon season in late summer and during the spring snow melt when it is intermittent, converges with the Rio Grande at Bernardo.

8. Delaware-born Capt. George M. McLane, thirty-four, with personal property valued at twenty-five hundred dollars, is listed on the 1860 census at Albuquerque. McLane's wife, Maryland-born Serena, thirty, and their three children, George Jr., Louis, and Henry B., were all living in Albuquerque at the time. McLane, who had been breveted for bravery at Contreras and Churubusco during the Mexican War, was killed five months later at Black Rock north of Wheatfield Creek during the 1860 Navajo campaign. Eighth Census (1860), Bernalillo County, New Mexico Territory, NA; Frank McNitt, *Navajo Wars: Military Campaigns, Slave Raids, and Reprisals* (Albuquerque: University of New Mexico Press, 1972), 400, 403.

9. Prior to his arrival at Fort Fillmore, Assistant Surgeon James Cooper McKee was assigned to Fort Defiance. A Pennsylvanian by birth, Cooper is best remembered today for his account of Maj. Issac Lynde's surrender of Federal forces at St. Augustine Pass in the Organ Mountains in July 1861. Cooper rose to become a major surgeon during the Civil War and a lieutenant colonel of surgery in 1887. He retired in June 1891 and died on Dec. 11, 1897. Post Returns, Fort Defiance and Fort Fillmore, 1858–1859, AGO, RG 393, NA; James Cooper McKee, *Narrative of the Surrender of a Command of U.S. Forces at Fort Fillmore, New Mexico in July, a.d., 1861* (Houston: Stagecoach Press, 1960); Heitman, *Historical Register*, 671.

10. When the Mexican War created a demand for revolvers, Samuel Colt was approached by the government to resume the manufacture of Colt arms. Colt proceeded to contract with Eli Whitney for the manufacture of pistols at the latter's armory at Whitneyville, Connecticut. After the first order for one thousand revolvers was received in January 1847, Colt equipped a factory at Hartford, Connecticut, and completed another thousand revolvers known as the Model 1848. Although the Model 1848 revolver continued to be manufactured with some minor variations, a new .36-caliber navy model was brought out in 1851. During the Civil War, the Colt Armory furnished the United States government with 386,417 revolvers, about

7,000 revolving rifles and carbines, and 113,980 muzzle-loading rifle muskets. Arcadi Gluckman, *United States Martial Pistols and Revolvers* (Harrisburg: Stackpole Company, 1960), 157–59; William Hosley, *Colt: The Making of an American Legend* (Amherst: University of Massachusetts Press, 1996), 50–68, 82–89.

11. Dragoon Springs was located just east of the San Pedro River, some 220 miles west of Mesilla, 85 miles east of Tucson, and 34 miles west of Apache Pass. The spring was located in a deep ravine with a rock-walled stage station nearby. Donald Howard Couchman, *Cooke's Peak—Pasaron Por Aqui: A Focus on United States History in Southwestern New Mexico* (Las Cruces: Bureau of Land Management, 1988), 263.

12. Major Reeve arrived to take command on March 28, 1859, and left the post on May 17, 1859. Ewell, forty-three, with real estate of six thousand dollars and a personal estate of ten thousand dollars, is listed on the Aug. 23, 1860 census. Ewell, one of the most popular officers in the frontier army, was frequently on scout against Apaches and left on detached service to Fort Bliss on Sept. 20, 1860. PR, Fort Buchanan, 1859, AGO, NA; Eighth Census (1860), Arizona County, New Mexico Territory, NA; and James S. Hutchins, "Bald Head Ewell: Frontier Dragoon," *Arizoniana: The Journal of Arizona History* 3 (spring 1962), 20–21.

13. A musketoon was a short musket used by cavalry, artillery, or special troops. Lieutenant Colonel Freeman reported in 1853 that the musketoon was "worthless." Samuel Colt was largely responsible for developing the first practicable and working firearm equipped with a mechanically operated cylinder. Colt manufactured a number of models of various barrel lengths and calibers ranging from .22 to .50, many of which won instant popularity in Texas prior to the Mexican War. In 1839, Colt, at the request of the Texas government, produced at his Paterson, New Jersey, foundry a martial .44 caliber revolver, the famous Walker pistol, named for Capt. Samuel H. Walker of the Texas Rangers, who was to die in the Mexican War at the Battle of Humantla. Colt brought out a .44 caliber, six shot, single action model in 1847 and a similar model in 1848. In 1851, he issued his .36 caliber navy model that was six shot, single action. A .44 caliber, six shot, side hammer model was issued in 1855 along with a .36 caliber, six shot, side hammer. Gluckman, *United States Martial Pistols and Revolvers*, 154–81; Crimmins, "W. G. Freeman's Report," 51:208.

14. The June 12, 1860, census lists Pitcher, thirty, with personal property of two thousand dollars along with his wife, Alabama-born Mary, twenty-eight, and two children, Louis, age seven, and John, five, both born in Texas. Eighth Census (1860), El Paso County, Texas, NA.

15. Simeon Hart, a New York-born civil engineer, came to the Southwest as an adjutant in the Missouri Cavalry during the Mexican War. In 1849, along with his bride, Jesusita Siqueiros, daughter of a wealthy Chihuahua flour miller, Hart settled at the Pass of the North. There, he established a flour mill, El Molino, and signed his first contract with the army in March 1850, for which he agreed to furnish flour at eleven cents a pound to the army at Doña Ana, the post opposite El Paso del Norte and San Elizario. In 1851, he provided the United States Boundary Commission with flour for a year at 12½ cents a pound. In 1860, with real and personal property valued at 350,000 dollars, he was the wealthiest man in the area. Much of his wealth was lost during the Civil War when Hart cast his fortune with the Confederacy. W. H. Timmons, "Simeon Hart," *NHT*, 3: 492; Smith, *U. S. Army and the Texas Frontier Economy*, 83, 107, 260.

16. Rhett, thirty-six and with personal property of two thousand dollars, was still at Fort Bliss on June 12, 1860. He is enumerated on the census along with his Virginia-born wife, Frances, thirty-one, and their two children, James, ten, and Frances, five. Eighth Census (1860), El Paso County, Texas, NA.

17. Capt. George B. McClellan claimed the McClellan saddle, which was recommended to replace the Grimsley saddle in 1859, was based on saddles he had observed during his tour of Europe and the Crimean War and was patterned on Prussian, Hungarian, and Russian models, as well as saddles he had seen in Mexico. In reality, the McClellan saddle was a far cry from the European saddles, especially the Hungarian hussar saddle. The saddle actually incorporated major features of the Grimsley, Campbell, and Hope models and made only minor modifications, such as having no leather covering on the seat. Stephen W. Sears, *George B. McClellan: The Young Napoleon* (New York: Ticknor and Fields, 1988), 47–48. Randy Steffen, *United States Military Saddles, 1812–1943* (Norman: University of Oklahoma Press, 1973), 63–65. See n. 77 for the Grimsley as well as the Hope and Campbell saddles.

18. Sgt. Richard Wall, thirty-five, a miner from Dublin, Ireland, had reenlisted in the Mounted Rifles at San Antonio for five years on Dec. 12, 1855. He reenlisted again, this time at Fort Marcy, New Mexico, on Dec. 11, 1860. Sergeant Wall was five feet, seven inches tall, with grey eyes, brown hair, and a ruddy complexion. Registers of Enlistments in the United States Army, 1798–1914, Vol. 51, 1855, Microcopy No. 233, AGO, NA.

19. Pennsylvania-born Charles Sutherland, thirty-two, was later sent to Fort Duncan. He went on to become a brigadier general of surgery in the Civil War and died on May 10, 1895. Heitman, *Historical Register*, 937; Eighth Census, Maverick County, Texas, NA.

20. John Hull Olmsted, younger brother of Frederick Law Olmsted, was with his brother on the well-known trip through Texas in 1855 and collaborated on their book *A Journey Through Texas; or, A Saddle-Trip on the Southwestern Frontier*. He was said to be dying from tuberculosis and looking for a better climate. Dr. Olmstead was first employed as a contract civilian surgeon for Fort Stockton in 1859 at eighty dollars per month. He was rehired on Apr. 6, 1860, and was discharged on June 6, 1860, and died later that year. House Executive Document No. 22, "War Department Contracts," 28; House Executive Documents No. 47, "Contracts of the War Department for 1860," 50; Thomas T. Smith to Jerry Thompson, July 29, 1999, Editor's file.

21. Called the *Laxas* (slack or feeble) or the San Pedro by early Spanish explorers, Devil's River, an intermittent stream, was allegedly renamed by Capt. John Coffee Hays of the Texas Rangers, who, after riding across a barren, rough, and arid country, came to the rugged river gorge. When Hays asked a Mexican guide the name of the river and was told it was the San Pedro, he remarked, "Saint Peter's, hell . . . it looks more like the devil's river to me." The river rises in northeastern Crockett County and flows southward for ninety-four miles through Schleicher, Sutton, and Val Verde counties to empty into the Rio Grande at what is today Lake Amistad near present-day Del Rio. "Devil's River," *NHT*, 2:612.

22. Seco Creek, just west of D'Hanis, rises in northwestern Medina County and flows southeast forty-five miles into Hondo Creek in northern Frio County.

23. "Wild Bill" Hazen had been wounded in a fight with Indians, probably

Kickapoos, on the headwaters of the Nueces River on May 20 and again on Sept. 30, 1859. San Antonio *Daily Herald*, May 31, Oct. 16, 1858; New Orleans *Daily True Delta*, Oct. 29, Dec. 16, 1859; Hazen to Jno. Withers, Dec. 20, 1858, LR, AGO, RG 94, NA; Hazen to R. B. Maclay, May 23, 1859, LR, AGO, RG 94, AGO; Thomas T. Smith, *Fort Inge: Sharps, Spurs, and Sabers on the Texas Frontier, 1849–1869* (Austin: Eakin Press, 1993), 117–18; Thompson, *Fifty Miles and a Fight*, 82–83.

24. Castroville, the "little Alsace" of Texas, twenty-five miles west of San Antonio, was founded by Henri Castro on Sept. 3, 1844, on the west bank of the Medina River. The Alsacian community boasted of several power and saw mills. Bobby D. Weaver, *Castro's Colony: Empresario Development in Texas, 1842–1865* (College Station: Texas A&M University Press, 1985), 40–56; Ruben E. Ochoa, "Castroville," *NHT*, 1:1,024.

25. Fort Pike (Fort Rigolets) was located thirty miles east of New Orleans. Named in honor of Gen. Zebulon Montgomery Pike, the fort guarded the nine-mile-long pass that connects Lake Pontchartrain with Lake Borgne. Fort Macomb (Fort Wood), only five miles from Fort Pike, was situated on the south bank of Chef Menteur Pass, which links Lake Pontchartrain and Lake Borge. The post, along with Fort Pike, was completed in 1827 and was designed to guard the major approaches to New Orleans. Battery Bienvenu was strategically located at the confluence of Bayou Bienvenu and Bayou Maxent (present-day Villere). Built in 1815, the battery was later enlarged and strengthened. Completed in 1830, Dupre Tower was located at the entrance to Bayou Dupre on the south shore of Lake Borge and was a two-story hexagonal structure designed to protect New Orleans's eastern approaches. Work on Fort Livingston (Fort at Barataria), at the mouth of Barataria Bay, was still underway in 1860. Robert B. Roberts, *Encyclopedia of Historic Forts: The Military, Pioneer, and Trading Posts of the United States* (New York: Macmillan, 1988), 330–47.

26. Capt. P. G. T. Beauregard, the Louisiana-born Creole, who in the 1850s ran unsuccessfully for mayor of New Orleans and who seriously considered resigning from the army to join the filibuster William Walker in Nicaragua, had also been placed in charge of the construction of the three-million-dollar New Orleans customhouse. After appointment as superintendent of West Point in January 1861, he was removed five days later because of his secessionist sentiments. After returning to New Orleans, he resigned on Mar. 1, 1861. T. Harry Williams, *P. G. T. Beauregard: Napoleon in Gray* (Baton Rouge: Louisiana State University Press, 1955), 44–48.

27. A lighthouse on Brand Point on the Louisiana side of the Sabine River estuary in southwestern Cameron Parish, Louisiana, just above its mouth on the gulf, had been completed by early summer 1857. The eighty-foot brick tower marked the entrance to Sabine Pass, the natural opening between Sabine Lake and the Gulf of Mexico. Down the coast, construction of a lighthouse on Harbor Island, a low-lying island just inside Aransas Pass between Saint Joseph and Mustang Island, was initiated in February 1856, and completed in early 1857. Lighthouse builder I. W. P. Lewis had first proposed erecting a screw-pile light to mark the pass, but District Lighthouse Inspector Lt. Walter H. Stevens recommended a prefabricated cast-iron tower. The Lighthouse Board, however, decided on masonry, and the lighthouse, the second oldest on the Texas coast today, was constructed as a tapered octagonal brick tower.

The small light at Timbalier Island on the Louisiana coast was built in 1857 on a low sand spit at the east end of the island and marked the entrance to Tambalier Bay, south of New Orleans. The screw-pile lighthouse that Mansfield mentions was on Ship Shoal in the Gulf of Mexico, ten miles off the Louisiana coast in thirteen feet of water. It was built in 1859 to replace a lightship that had marked Ship Shoal for ten years. When the town of Saluria was laid out in 1847 on the Texas coast on the northwestern corner of Matagorda Island, the government built a lighthouse nearby in 1852 to assist ships in passing through Cavallo Pass into Matagorda Bay and the bustling port of Indianola, the second busiest in Texas. Work began on a fifty-five-foot-tall iron tower on the extreme eastern tip of Matagorda Island in June 1852, and the structure was finished four months later. The site was exposed to beach erosion, however, and the tower was not tall enough. Consequently, the tower was extended upward twenty-four feet in 1858. A second lighthouse was completed on Halfmoon Reef, a mud and oyster shell shoal on the east side of Matagorda Bay by late 1858. The wooden superstructure was atop wrought-iron piles screwed into the shallow bottom of Matagorda Bay. The structure survived the September 1875 hurricane that ravaged Indianola but was abandoned following another hurricane in August 1886. Restored and reoccupied, the structure fell victim to another storm in 1942 and was abandoned before being later moved to Port Lavaca. There, the hexagonal building can be seen today on the east edge of the town.

The lighthouse at Pass Christian near Gulfport, Mississippi, was constructed in 1831 and was a short brick tower just twenty-eight feet high. Bolivar Lighthouse, near the west end of Bolivar Peninsula, was completed in December 1852. Five years later the cast iron tower was raised twenty-four feet and a more powerful lens installed. A lightship had been operating just inside the bar in Galveston Harbor since 1849. The vessel deteriorated so much that repairs were frequent, and, in the summer and fall 1859, beacons were placed on Pelican Spit, Bird Key, and in low water off Bolivar Point. A brick lighthouse was erected on the bluff at Corpus Christi in the winter of 1857. Two years later, however, the structure was reported as being "practically useless" and in disrepair. The structure was used by Confederate forces during the Civil War to store munitions and was damaged in the Federal bombardment of the village in 1863. What remained of the structure was destroyed in 1878. Corpus Christi Lighthouse File (mostly records from the Dept. of Commerce, RG 26, NA), courtesy of T. Lindsay Baker. Robert Wooster, "Sabine Pass," *NHT*, 5:745–46; Christopher Long, "Aransas Pass Light Station," *NHT*, 1:221; Art Leatherwood, "Matagorda Island," *NHT*, 4:560; A. Pat Daniels, "Bolivar Lighthouse," *NHT*, 1:626–27; George R. Putnam, *Lighthouses and Lightships of the United States* (Boston: Houghton Mifflin Company, 1933), 116–17; Francis Ross Holland, Jr., *America's Lighthouses: Their Illustrated History Since 1716* (Brattleboro, Vermont: Stephen Greene Press, 1972), 144–47; T. Lindsay Baker, *Lighthouses of Texas* (College Station: Texas A&M University Press, 1991), 23–27, 28–34, 35–39, 57–65, 71–79.

28. Fort McRee, frequently misspelled by Mansfield and others as Fort McRae, was located on a tongue of land overlooking the entrance to Pensacola Harbor. Named for Lt. Col. William M. McRee, a veteran of the War of 1812, the fort was completed in 1842 but never permanently occupied. Roberts, *Encyclopedia of Historic Forts*, 183.

29. Only three to five days by steamer from New Orleans, Indianola was a major depot for the transfer of supplies to the depots at Austin and San Antonio. The depot was located on the site of the German immigrant campsite, some three and one-half

miles southeast of Indianola, where the Powder Horn Lake connects with Matagorda Bay. In October 1853, Lieutenant Colonel Freeman reported the army was operating at Indianola five large buildings, a small blacksmith shop, and a stable, all constructed of rough lumber, as well as a 250-foot-long wharf. By the time of Mansfield's 1856 inspection, as many as forty-one citizens were employed at the depot. All supplies coming by sea for the principal depots at San Antonio and Austin were landed at Indianola. Crimmins, "W. G. Freeman's Report," 51:56–57; Brownson Malsch, "Indianola," *NHT*, 5:304; Smith, *U.S. Army and the Texas Frontier Economy*, 131; Brownson Malsch, *Indianola—Mother of Western Texas* (Austin: Shoal Creek, 1977), 43, 48, 88–89, 95–96.

Ever since the Mexican War, Brazos Santiago had been a major supply depot for the army in South Texas. Located on the north end of Brazos Island, across Brazos Santiago Pass from the south end of Padre Island, the supply depot had wharves on the lagoon side of the island. The port also handled commercial goods for Brownsville and Rio Grande towns such as Roma and Rio Grande City, as well as goods destined for Matamoros and towns in northeastern Mexico. Goods were offloaded at Brazos Santiago because the bars at the mouth of the Rio Grande were too shallow for ships capable of plying the Gulf of Mexico. At the beginning of the Mexican War, Richard King developed shallow-draft steamboats that could navigate the bars at the mouth of the Rio Grande. King's steamboats offloaded in the lee of Brazos Santiago, steamed down Brazos Island to the mouth of the river, and then made their way upstream. Art Leatherwood, "Brazos Santiago," *NHT*, 1:718.

30. Along with Duncan Charles Ogden, George Thomas "Tom" Howard ran the largest freighting operation in Texas prior to the Civil War. Howard had immigrated to Texas from Washington, D.C., in 1836 and rose to the rank of lieutenant colonel in the army of the Republic of Texas. A veteran of the Plum Creek fight, he was in both the Santa Fe and Somervell Expeditions, and, in 1850, he opened a mercantile store in San Antonio. The trading store functioned on personal vouchers, discounted promissory notes, land script, and general credit. When the United States government paid off one-half of the Texas public debt of ten million dollars in 1850, the state, in turn, paid its debtors in cash. Howard collected twenty-seven thousand dollars owed for services and supply to various Texas military adventures and promptly launched into a major business enterprise, expanding his San Antonio store and buying thousands of acres of land. In 1856, Howard and Ogden signed a one-year contract to supply all posts in the Department of Texas. They were said to have had eight hundred ox and mule teams on the road, mostly between Indianola and San Antonio, and averaged a profit of thirty thousand dollars to fifty thousand dollars per year. By 1860, Howard had 150,000 dollars in real and personal property, as well as nine slaves. During the Civil War, Howard supplied beef to the Confederate Army. He died in Washington, D.C., on Aug. 6, 1886. San Antonio *Daily Herald*, Mar. 12, 1859; Eighth Census (1860), Bexar County; Howard Lackman, "George Thomas Howard: Texas Frontiersman," (Ph.D. diss., University of Texas at Austin, 1954), 304; Howard Lackman, "George Thomas Howard," *NHT*, 3:744; St. Clair Griffin Reed, *A History of the Texas Railroads and of Transportation Conditions in Texas under Spain and Mexico and The Republic and The State* (Houston: St. Clair Publishing Company, 1941), 43–44;

Ralph A. Wooster, "Wealthy Texans, 1860," *Southwestern Historical Quarterly* 71 (October 1967): 163–80; Smith, *U.S. Army and the Texas Frontier Economy*, 53–54.

31. For a history of the post, see Martin L. Crimmins, ed., "W. G. Freeman's Report on the Eighth Military Department," *Southwestern Historical Quarterly* 53:71–77; Robert Wooster, *Soldiers, Sutlers, and Settlers: Garrison Life on the Texas Frontier* (College Station: Texas A&M University Press, 1987), 8–10, 68, 107, 118; Smith, *Fort Inge*, 64–65.

32. While at Fort Inge, Mansfield also compiled a list of the ordnance belonging to Co. C of the Second Cavalry. Mansfield Papers, MCHS.

33. South Carolina-born Robert Brodie is listed on the 1860 Census as twenty-eight and with personal property valued at five hundred dollars. Eighth Census (1860), Uvalde County, Texas, NA.

34. David Murphy, a resident of Victoria, not Daniel Murphy, also owned the land on which Fort Inge was located. On January 1, 1858, the army had leased the land for fifty dollars a month for five years. Smith, *Fort Inge*, 79; Smith, *U.S. Army and the Texas Frontier Economy*, 191; D. H. Vinton, "List of Property leased and rented by the U.S. Government in the Dept. of Texas," Jan. 21, 1861, Mansfield Papers, MCHS.

35. C. V. Fristoe is enumerated on the 1860 Census as thirty-two, a merchant born in Virginia with personal property valued at fifteen hundred dollars. A clerk, Texas-born Charles Johnson, sixteen, was employed by Fristoe. Eighth Census (1860), Uvalde County, Texas, NA.

36. San Lorenzo de la Santa Cruz Mission was established by Franciscans for the Lipan Apaches on Jan. 23, 1762. Situated about halfway between San Sabá and San Juan Bautista, the mission was also referred to as El Cañon. Garrisoned by twenty soldiers from the presidio at San Sabá, the mission was able to attract four hundred Indians within a week of its founding. Priests quickly perceived, however, that the Apaches had no real interest in conversion to Christianity, and, in October and November 1766, the mission came under attack by three hundred Comanches. Although two assaults were repulsed, in 1767 the Marqués de Rubì recommended the mission be abandoned. The official date of closure was set at June 21, 1771, although the actual date the mission was abandoned was sometime before then. Mansfield marks the site of the mission as on the northeast side of the post, near the bakery, housing for the laundresses, and the quarters for the commanding officer. Donald E. Chipman, "San Lorenzo de la Santa Cruz Mission," *NHT*, 5:865–66; Curtis D. Tunnell and William W. Newcomb, *A Lipan Apache Mission: San Lorenzo de la Santa Cruz* (Austin: Texas Memorial Museum, 1969).

37. Freschets refers to the sudden rise in the level of a stream, in this instance the Nueces River.

38. The conical Sibley tent was conceived and patented by Capt. Henry Hopkins Sibley of the Second Dragoons. Sibley, while stationed at Fort Belknap in north Texas during the winter of 1854–1855, visited a Comanche village, possibly that of Buffalo Hump, and observed the warmth and spaciousness of the Indian tepees. The Union Army used 47,541 Sibley tents during the Civil War. Other tents in use by the army at the time included the French Bell tent (18' x 6'), Kendrick tent (6'6" x 3'6"), and the Common tent (6'6" x 7'6"). Jerry Thompson, *Confederate General of*

the West: Henry Hopkins Sibley (College Station: Texas A&M University Press, 1996), 102–7; Jerry Thompson "Henry Hopkins Sibley: Military Inventor on the Texas Frontier," *Military History of Texas and the Southwest* 10 (No. 4, 1972): 227–48.

39. Nava, Mexico, was located some thirty miles southwest of Fort Duncan on the wagon road between San Fernando and Presidio del Rio Grande in the "bread-basket" of northern Coahuila.

40. Dead Man's Hole, or El Muerto, at the base of foreboding El Muerto Mountain, in the desert about thirty-two miles west of Fort Davis and about thirteen miles northeast of present-day Valentine, had been established as a stop on the San Antonio-El Paso mail route. It was raided a number of times before the Civil War by Comanches and Mescalero Apaches. Wayne R. Austerman, *Sharps Rifles and Spanish Mules: The San Antonio-El Paso Mail, 1851–1861* (College Station: Texas A&M University Press, 1985), 60–61.

41. Colonel Seawell, fifty-eight with personal property valued at five hundred dollars, is enumerated on the 1860 Census at the post along with two daughters, Louisiana-born Bullett, twelve, and Mary I., nine, born in California. Eighth Census (1860), Presidio County, Texas, NA.

42. Young had been the sutler at the post since 1856. At the time he also held a contract to supply Fort Davis with corn at $3.47 per bushel and wood at $13.00 per cord. The Pennsylvania-born sutler, forty, with real estate of two thousand dollars and personal property of two thousand dollars, is listed on the 1860 Census at "El Lympias." D. H. Vinton, "List of Contracts for Transportation, Forage of Wood made by the Gov't. with several Posts and Stations in the Department of Texas," Jan. 21, 1861, Mansfield Papers, MCHS; Eighth Census (1860), Presidio County, Texas, NA.

43. *Prosopis juliflora velutina* or velvet mesquite, a variety of mesquite with short-pubescent foliage and thorny twigs, is found in west Texas, southern New Mexico, and Arizona. Although the mesquite in the arid lowlands around Fort Quitman are small, the velvet mesquite can reach a height of fifteen to thirty feet and a width of twenty to forty feet. With a moderate growth rate, the velvet mesquite readily sprouts from the stump and is deep rooted, often capable of reaching water far below the surface and out of reach of many other plants, and not easily damaged by disease or insects. Because it was the only wood available at many forts, mesquite was used for charcoal, fuel, furniture, building blocks, posts, and, later, railroad crossties. Mesquite foliage and pods are eaten by livestock, and the seeds pass through the digestive tracts and grow where they fall. Mesquite beans also played an important part in the diet of Southwestern Native Americans. The mesquite remains one of the hardier plants in Texas. Robert A. Vines, *Trees, Shrubs, and Woody Vines of the Southwest* (Austin: University of Texas Press, 1960), 515–16.

44. Escondido Creek was formed by three springs, an upper (Tunas), middle, and lower springs, each about ten feet across. The lower spring, at which Mansfield evidently camped, was the first water that travelers found west of the Pecos River. All three springs had been favorite Comanche camping sites for decades. Austerman, *Sharps Rifles and Spanish Mules*, 40.

45. John D. Holliday, who was also the post sutler, was a forty-one-year-old freighter living at the post with his wife and three children. Holliday had acquired ownership of the land on which the post was built in 1859. A Council of Administration had

convened at Fort Stockton in June 1859 for the "purpose of recommending a suitable person to perform the duties as sutler of the post." The council, headed by Second Lt. John P. Sherburne, had recommended that Holliday and F. W. Green be appointed jointly. The same day, First Lt. Walter Jones, commanding the post, rejected the recommendation of the council. "Mr. Greene has been acting in the capacity as sutler at this post and has failed to give satisfaction, and his supply of goods is inadequate to the wants of the troops of the post," Jones wrote. The council reconvened but rejected Jones's recommendation. Jones then referred the matter to Department Headquarters, whereupon General David E. Twiggs upheld his recommendation and Holliday became the sole sutler at the post. Holliday also held a contract to supply the post with "mesquite roots" at thirteen dollars per cord. When the post was abandoned by the Confederates in June 1862, Holliday sold the land to George H. Giddings. The Kentucky-born Holliday returned to Fort Stockton, however, after the war. At Fort Stockton today, Holliday's sutler store is the only remaining building from the 1859 era. Clayton Williams, *Texas' Last Frontier: Fort Stockton and the Trans-Pecos, 1861–1895*, ed. Ernest Wallace (College Station: Texas A&M University Press, 1982), 64, 67, 73, 133; Eighth Census (1860), Presidio County, Texas, NA.; Vinton, "List of Contracts," Mansfield Papers, MCHS; Jones to Sherburne, Sherburne to Jones, Jones to Sherburne, Jones to John Withers, all June 23, 1859, and T. A. Washington endorsement on latter, June 24 [30], LR, AGO, RG 94, NA.

46. Howard Spring, a favorite watering stop on the San Antonio-El Paso Road, was located on Howard Creek near present-day Ozona in southern Crockett County and was named after Richard A. Howard, an ex-Texas Ranger from San Antonio who came upon the water in 1848 as part of the expedition of Col. John Coffee Hayes. Normally, the precious liquid had to be brought to the surface in buckets. John E. Hart, a soldier in the Sibley Brigade, wrote in 1861 that Howard Spring "was down in the channel of a dry creek. Here immense stone had been blasted or dug out, making a kind of stair-way down to the water, which could be reached by only one man at a time. Other men standing on this stair-way would hand [a] bucket to his comrade and so on to the thirsty men and animals." John E. Hart Diary, Hill College Museum, Hillsboro, Texas; James Collette, "The Bloody Legacy of Howard's Well," *Old West* 21 (spring 1985): 55–59; and Austerman, *Sharps Rifles and Spanish Mules*, 41.

47. Turnley cottages were designed by Capt. Parmenas Taylor Turnley, a quartermaster in the First Infantry. The structures, thirty by fifteen feet, were used by troops in New Mexico and Texas and were a compromise between the flimsy canvas tents and more permanent quarters that were required by army regulations to be constructed of stone or brick. The buildings were prefabricated in St. Louis and shipped west. The "kit" consisted of wood panels (ten feet by eight feet), glazed sashes, blinds, and doors that came complete with locks and keys. Sections of pine roofs were covered with asphalt paper and secured with battens. It usually took three men about four hours to erect and finish a single cottage. For a sketch of the Turnley cottages at Fort Lancaster, see *Harper's Weekly*, Apr. 13, 1861. Also, see Roy Eugene Graham, "Federal Fort Architecture in Texas during the Nineteenth Century," *Southwestern Historical Quarterly* 74 (October 1970): 183, 187–88; Parmenas Taylor Turnley, *Reminiscences of Parmenas Taylor Turnley: From the Cradle to Three-Score and Ten* (Chicago: Donohue and Henneberry, 1892), 127–29.

48. From Lancaster County, Pennsylvania, Sergeant Brenner, age forty, first enlisted in the Fifth Infantry at the age of twenty on May 24, 1839. Five feet, nine and three-fourth inches in height, with grey eyes, brown hair, and a fair complexion, Brenner had transferred to the Eighth Infantry in 1844, and became ordnance sergeant in 1853. He had reenlisted at Ringgold Barracks on Dec. 17, 1858. Serving as ordnance sergeant until February 1862, he was promoted to second lieutenant in the Fourth Infantry but was dismissed eight months later. Register of Enlistments, Vol. 53, AGO, NA; Heitman, *Historical Register*, 242.

49. California Springs, seven miles northeast of present-day Comstock at the headwaters of Evans Creek some sixteen miles north of Painted Caves, was another favorite campsite on the San Antonio-El Paso Road. Shallow wells had been dug at the springs to allow easy access to water. Early travelers frequently referred to California Springs as Yellow Banks. Gunnar Brune, *Springs of Texas*, (Fort Worth: Branch-Smith, 1981), 1:455; Kathryn S. McMillen, "The San Antonio-San Diego Mail Line in Texas, 1857–61" (Master's thesis, University of Texas at Austin, 1960), 120; Berndt Kuhn to Jerry Thompson, Sept. 19, 1999, Editor's files.

50. Surprisingly a large map of Fort Clark that Mansfield retained for his own records appears to be better than the map he submitted to the Adjutant General. Mansfield Papers, MCHS.

51. Mansfield is evidently using "landerstand" to indicate land that is occupied by individuals without authorization or a deed. The neighboring settlement of Las Moras had come into existence when Oscar Bernadotte Brackett, a New York-born merchant who had come to Texas in 1844 and established a supply village for the fort. The town's name was changed to Brackett in 1856 and later to Bracketville. Ben E. Pingenot, "Fort Clark," *NHT*, 1:1092.

52. "Esse's" cannot be identified with any certainty. A camp thirty-six miles south of Fort Duncan would have placed Mansfield in Mexico. He was certain to have been on the Rio Grande, approximately twenty-two miles downriver from present-day El Indio, on the north bank of the river in extreme northwestern Webb County.

53. Closson, twenty-nine, is listed on the 1860 Census at Fort Duncan, along with his Vermont-born, twenty-three-year-old wife, Olivia, and their two children, Henry, two, and their newborn daughter, Olivia, one month. The family had employed a twenty-year-old Irish nurse, Mary Telly, as a servant. Lieutenant Ramsay, twenty-nine, who was later killed at First Bull Run, was listed with personal property valued at one thousand dollars. Seven laundresses were also at the post along with Arkansas-born Virginia Harrison, twenty, who gave her occupation as "Officer's Lady." Eighth Census (1860), Maverick County, Texas, NA.

54. Ludovic Colquohn (Colquhoun, Coloquhoun), fifty-six, had represented Bexar in the Senate of the Republic of Texas and had been taken prisoner by Gen. Adrian Woll in 1842, imprisoned at Mexico City, and, later at Perote before his release in April 1845, held a contract to supply Fort Duncan with corn for $1.32 a bushel. He died sometime between April 1882 and April 1883. Ben E. Pingenot, ed., *Paso del Aguila: A Chronicle of Frontier Days on the Texas Border as Recorded in the Memoirs of Jesse Sumpter* (Austin: Encino Press, 1969), 98; Thomas W. Cutrer, "Ludovic Colquhoun," *NHT*, 1:231–32; San Antonio *Alamo Express*, Feb. 8, 1861; Seventh Census (1850), Bexar County, Texas; Eighth Census (1870), Atascosa County, Texas, NA: Vinton, "List of Contracts," Mansfield Papers, MCHS.

55. "Noria de los Federales" was probably Los Ojuelos, a few miles south of present-day Mirando City. As one of the few locations in the semiarid surroundings where surface water was dependable, Los Ojuelos had long been a favorite Comanche and Lipan campsite. Frequent Indian attacks had prevented any permanent settlement of the area. Capt. John S. Ford and a company of Texas Rangers, while attempting to police the wagon road between Laredo and Corpus Christi, had camped at the springs in 1850. In 1857, José María Guerra built an irrigation system and a chapel, as well as a stone enclosure to protect the springs and the small settlement from Indian raids. The only other springs in the general area are the Albercas de San Felipe or Pool Springs, some seven miles south of Los Ojuelos. Lea Anne Morrell, "Los Ojuelos," *NHT*; 4:296; Brune, *Springs of Texas*, 1:465–66.

56. Shouting "Death to the Americans" and "Viva Mexico," Juan Nepomuceno Cortina, with seventy-five raiders, had swept into Brownsville on Sept. 28, 1859, killing five citizens, including the city jailer. After evacuating the town, Cortina twice defeated the Texas Rangers before the Rangers, combined with the United States Army, crushed him at Rio Grande City on Dec. 27, 1859. In Mexico, Cortina rose to become governor of Tamaulipas and a general in the army of Benito Juárez. He died in Atzcapozalco, outside of Mexico City, on Oct. 30, 1894. Jerry Thompson, *Juan Cortina and the Texas-Mexico Frontier, 1859–1877* (El Paso: Texas Western Press, 1994).

57. Nuevo Laredo, Tamaulipas, had a population of approximately six hundred in 1860. The small community on the south bank, which had a variety of names at different times, was less exposed to Indian raids than Laredo, although it was more prone to flooding. The settlement had its origins almost from the time Laredo was founded by Tomás Sanchez de la Barrera y Garza in 1755. Travelers frequently referred to the settlement on the south bank as Monterey (not to be confused with Monterrey, Nuevo León). Lieutenant Colonel Freeman reported in 1853 that the Mexican government was maintaining a "small garrison" at Nuevo Laredo. A myth persists in Nuevo Laredo that the community was settled following the Treaty of Guadalupe Hidalgo in 1848, although the municipal government of the city does date from this period. Crimmins, "W. H. Freeman's Report," 53:351.

58. Major Trevitt had arrived from Fort Clark with Company F of the Eighth Infantry on Sept. 13, 1860. PR, Fort McIntosh, 1860, AGO, RG 393, NA.

59. Whistler, thirty-six, is listed on the 1860 Census at Fort Bliss, where he later transferred, along with his New York-born wife, Mary, thirty-five, and three children, Garland, thirteen, born in Texas, and Emma, nine, and Jane, seven, both born in New Mexico Territory. Whistler, thirty-seven, claimed personal property valued at one thousand dollars. He was also enumerated on the census at Fort Fillmore for Doña Ana County, New Mexico Territory. At the time of Mansfield's inspection of Fort McIntosh, Whistler was ill. Eighth Census (1860), El Paso County, Texas; Doña Ana County, New Mexico Territory, NA. PR, Fort McIntosh, 1860, AGO, RG 393, NA.

60. Major Sibley had previously been stationed at Albuquerque, New Mexico, where he was listed on the 1860 census as fifty-four with personal property valued at five hundred dollars. The Massachusetts-born major had brought his Michigan-born wife, Nancy, fifty, and their seven-year-old son, Frederick, to New Mexico. In Albuquerque, Sibley had hired two Irish-born servants, Frank and Ann Brown. Eighth Census (1860), Bernalillo County, New Mexico Territory, NA.

61. B. J. DeWitt, who is not listed on either the 1850 or 1860 Texas census, also held the contract to supply hay and corn to Camp Hudson at $19.00 per ton and $1.88 a bushel, respectively. Smith, *U.S. Army and the Frontier Texas Economy*, 206.

62. Enlistment records indicate that James Trumble reenlisted at Newport Barracks, Ky., on Apr. 9, 1855, listing his age as thirty-five and his occupation as a "soldier." This would have made Sergeant Trumble forty in 1860. He reenlisted again at Albuquerque on Mar. 6, 1860, prior to the Third Infantry being transferred to Texas. Trumble was five feet, eight inches in height, with blue eyes, light hair, and a fair complexion. An unsigned endorsement on Mansfield's report, presumably by Secretary of War John B. Floyd, observed, "Under the regulations governing such matters the transfer of the men to the Recruiting Service is impractical." Registers of Enlistments, Vol. 51, Microcopy No. 233, AGO, NA: Endorsement on J. K. F. Mansfield to Lorenzo Thomas, Dec. 13, 1860, LR. AGO, RG 94, NA.

63. Frederick Reynolds, thirty-five, and born in Richmond, Va., had reenlisted at Fort Fillmore on Oct. 19, 1855. Enlistment records indicate he was five feet, ten inches in height, with sandy hair a fair complexion and grey eyes, and was a musician. Reynolds was discharged on Aug. 20, 1860, but reenlisted for five years at Fort Clark. Registers of Enlistments, Vol. 50–51, AGO, NA.

64. Colonel Waite commanded Ringgold Barracks from Apr. 2, 1856, until Nov. 2, 1856. While Waite was in command, the widely publicized court-martial (six thousand pages) of Maj. Giles Porter for drunkenness was held at the post. The proceedings, which were attended by several high-ranking officers from all over the Department of Texas, assembled at Ringgold Barracks and later at Fort Brown. They included Lieutenant Colonels Robert E. Lee, Henry Bambridge, and Washington Seawell, Major George H. Thomas, and Captains Randolph Marcy, Daniel Ruggles, James V. Bombford, James Bradford, and Samuel Jones. When Ringgold Barracks served as the headquarters of the Eighth Infantry in the mid-1850s, as many as 492 men, including the regimental band, were present. By October 1856, thirty-three teamsters were employed at the post. PR, Ringgold Barracks, 1856, RG 393, AGO, NA; W. Eugene Hollond, *Beyond the Cross Timbers: The Travels of Randolph B. Marcy, 1812–1887* (Norman: University of Oklahoma Press, 1955), 146–47.

65. By orders of Gen. David E. Twiggs, Ringgold Barracks was abandoned in February 1859, not 1857. D. E. Twiggs to L. Thomas, Jan. 11, 1859, and General Order no. 1, Feb. 5, 1859. "Difficulties on the Southwestern Frontier." 36th Cong., 1st sess., 2–3.

66. Backus had assumed command of the post on Nov. 12, 1860, when Capt. Arthur T. Lee left with Company C of the Eighth Infantry for Fort Stockton. The post was abandoned by the army in March when Company C and E of the Third Infantry departed for Fort Brown. PR, Ringgold Barracks, 1860, AGO, RG 393, NA.

67. John B. McCluskey, a merchant born in Ireland, is listed on the 1860 census as thirty-six, with personal property of fifteen hundred dollars and real estate worth fifteen hundred dollars. At Ringgold Barracks, McCluskey employed a twenty-two-year-old clerk from New Orleans named John A. Mitchell. In 1857, he contracted with the army to supply Ringgold Barracks with 240 tons of hay at $11.30 per ton. On July 10, 1860, McCluskey again signed a contract for hay at $20.00 per ton. Eighth Census (1860), Starr County, Texas, NA; Smith, *U.S. Army and the Texas Frontier Economy*, 205; Vinton, "List of Contracts," Mansfield Papers, MCHS.

68. As Mansfield indicates, Sgt. Duncan McIntyre, thirty-nine, was a Mexican

War veteran. Listing his occupation as "soldier," he reenlisted at Albuquerque in January 1851 and again at Fort Thorn in January 1856. Born in Glasgow, Scotland, McIntyre was five feet, ten inches tall and had grey eyes, brown hair, and a dark complexion. Registers of Enlistments, Vol. 50, AGO, MC 233, NA.

69. Sgt. George Bromley, forty-seven, had served in the Mexican War and had re-enlisted at Philadelphia, Pa., on Christmas Day 1850, and again in August 1855. Born in New London, Conn., he is described on his enlistment record as five feet, seven and three-fourths inches tall and having grey eyes, light hair, and a fair complexion. Register of Enlistments in the United States Army, Vol. 49, AGO, MC 233, NA.

70. Mansfield would have been camped at or near the King Ranch on Santa Gertrudis Creek in present-day Kleberg County.

71. Mansfield was particularly nostalgic, perhaps because of his having been responsible some fourteen years earlier for the construction of the earthen works at the post.

72. In 1860, Edinburg, a small community on the Rio Grande at what is today Hidalgo, was the county seat of Hidalgo County.

73. In 1860, Point Isabel, which grew from the village of El Frontón de Santa Isabel, had a population of 211. From the time of the Mexican War, the community served as a major port and depot for the army in Texas. A lighthouse was constructed at the community in 1853 and by 1859, ten million dollars worth of cotton was being exported annually from the port. Alicia A. Garza, "Port Isabel," *NHT*, 5:278–80; Eighth Census (1860), Point Isabel, Cameron County, Tex.

74. Captain Hill had joined from detached service on Nov. 18, 1860, and assumed command from Captain Hunt, who had been given a sixty-day leave of absence. Mansfield was listed on the Post Returns for December 1860 as "Casually at Post . . . inspecting troops." A morning report of Light Co. M, Second Artillery, dated Jan. 2, 1861, survives in the Mansfield Papers. PR, Fort Brown, RG 393, AGO, RG 393, NA; Morning Report, Co. M, Second Artillery, Mansfield Papers, MCHS.

75. Many of the rough notes Mansfield compiled during his inspection of Major Cunningham's paymaster operation survive in the Mansfield Papers, MCHS.

76. Captain Bradfute shot Pvt. William Murray of the Second Cavalry in a confrontation at a place where "spiritious liquors" were consumed near Camp Cooper. Bradfute went on to command a brigade in the Confederate Army. Kenneth F. Neighbours, "Fort Belknap," *Frontier Forts of Texas* (Waco: Texian Press, 1966), 9.

77. In 1844, a patent was granted to Capt. Samuel Ringgold and the saddle adopted for general use during the Mexican War, but a new saddle that proved to be far more popular was made by Thornton Grimsley of St. Louis. This saddle, too, was used during the Mexican War and was highly praised, especially by Gen. Stephen Watts Kearny and his Army of the West. The tree of the Grimsley saddle was based on French and Spanish models and was clearly superior. The Grimsley saddle was also the first military saddle to be encased in wet rawhide and have a quilted seat. The saddle had two sets of skirts, one to protect the sides of the horse and an outer skirt to protect the rider's clothing from horse sweat. The saddle was light, with a strong tree that made it less susceptible to damage from the rigors of frontier use. In 1855, David Campbell patented a saddle with spring-steel arches that connected both the pommel and cantle to the sidebars. The sidebars on the Campbell saddle adjusted automatically so that the saddle always fit the horse's back. The saddle, which was issued to companies in the First and Second Cavalry, did not survive extreme field

testing, however, because it had a tendency to have a weak tree. Within a year it had been replaced by the more standard Grimsley saddle. The Hope or Texas saddle proved to be the favorite of Col. Joseph E. Johnston when he commanded the Second Cavalry in Texas, and in 1856, he wrote the secretary of war recommending the saddle for use by all officers. In 1857, 170 saddles were issued to two companies of the Second Cavalry. Manufactured by Rice and Childress of San Antonio, the Hope saddle had no skirts, and the tree had slots through which the stirrup leathers were hung. Today, Gen. Joseph E. Johnston's Hope saddle can be viewed at the Confederate Museum in Richmond, Va. For the McClellan saddle, see n. 17. Steffen, *United States Military Saddles*, 50–57, 64–65.

78. In the years preceding the Civil War, the U.S. Army occupied practically every building of any consequence in downtown San Antonio, including the Governor's Palace, the Alamo, the French Building, the Maverick Building, and a number of vacant lots and horse corrals. The buildings Mansfield refers to were first leased in 1856 from merchants James and William Vance for 446 dollars per month. They consisted of a large building for a troop barracks and a neighboring two-story stone house for the Department Headquarters. Both were located on what is today the site of the Gunter Hotel. By 1861, the army was also using a large arsenal at the 600 block of South Flores. Sam Woolford, ed., *San Antonio: A History for Tomorrow* (San Antonio: Naylor Company, 1963), 103; Smith, *U.S. Army and the Frontier Texas Economy*, 79.

79. Mansfield retained statements of public money disbursed in 1860 by Major Vinton, of public money in the hands of Vinton as of Jan. 21, 1861, and of outstanding debts and funds on hand as reported by the officers serving the Quartermaster Department at the various posts in the Department of Texas as of Dec. 31, 1861. In addition, he had lists of contracts for transportation, forage, and wood at the various posts, as well as a list of property leased and rented by the government in the Department of Texas. Mansfield Papers, MCHS.

80. For George Thomas Howard, see n. 30.

81. Gribeauval carriages were named for Gen. Jean Baptiste Gribeauval, a French general who, in 1835, developed the "flask" system for holding cannon for firing. Griveauval's improvements to field carriages included strengthening the members by reinforcing them with heavy iron straps in places of greatest stress and wear. An elevating screw for aiming that raised and lowered the platform on which the breech of the gun rested was also added. Because they were wooden, the carriages dissipated the shock of recoil and were convenient for transporting. First used by the United States Army in 1809, the carriages remained in use until 1835, when the army began replacing them with the stock-trail carriage. A few Gribeauval carriages, as indicated by Mansfield's report, remained in use until the time of the Civil War. The Gribeauval carriages had the reputation in the army for being the best for field artillery. Although mountain howitzer carriages followed the same design, they were smaller in size. Warren Ripley, *Artillery and Ammunition of the Civil War* (New York: Van Nostrand Reinhold and Company, 1970), 189–90; Harold L. Peterson, *Round Shot and Rammers: An Introduction to the Muzzle-Loading Land Artillery in the United States* (New York: Bonanza Books, 1959), 51–55, 74–76.

Conclusion

1. Quoted in Ralph A. Wooster, *Texas and Texans in the Civil War* (Austin: Eakin Press, 1995), 17–18. See also Russell Brown, "An Old Woman with a Broomstick: General David E. Twiggs and the U.S. Surrender in Texas, 1861," *Military Affairs* 48 (April 1984): 57–61.

2. C. A. Waite to E. D. Townsend, May 25, 1861, *OR*, I, 1:552–53. Other officers who surrendered in San Antonio included Maj. W. A. Nichols, assistant adjutant general; Surgeon E. H. Abadie and assistant surgeons J. R. Smith and E. P. Langworthy; Paymaster Daniel McClure; Maj. D. H. Vinton, who was in command of the Quartermaster Department; Capt. K, Garrard of the Second Cavalry; Lt. Col. W. Hoffman, Capt. J. T. Sprague, and Lts. E. L. Hartz and E. W. H. Read of the Eighth Infantry.

3. John C. Hesse to E. D. Townsend, Sept. 6, 1864, *OR*, I, 1:566–67.

4. Douglas Southall Freeman, *R. E. Lee, A Biography* (New York: Charles Scribner's Sons, 1934) 1:427.

5. Quoted in Ibid.

6. Samuel Peter Heintzelman Journal, Mar. 5, 25, 1861, LC.

7. I. V. D. Reeve to L. Thomas, June 18, 1861, *OR*, I, 1:571.

8. J. J. Bowden, *Exodus of Federal Forces from Texas, 1861* (Austin: Eakin Press, 1986), 111.

9. Reeve to L. Thomas, May 12, 1861 (two letters), *OR*, I, 1:567–68; Reeve to Thomas, June 18, 1861, *OR*, I, 1:568–70; Earl Van Dorn to S. Cooper, May 10, 1861, *OR*, I, 1:572–73.

10. Emily Van Dorn Miller, ed., *A Soldier's Honor* (New York: The Abbey Press, 1902), 52.

11. Bowden, *Exodus of Federal Forces from Texas*, 115.

12. C. C. Sibley to W. A. Nichols, *OR*, I, 1:534–35.

13. Malsch, *Indianola*, 150.

14. O. L. Shepherd to S. Cooper, Mar. 20, 1861, *OR*, I, 1:561.

15. Order No. 5, February 1861, *OR*, I, 1:537; James Thompson to L. G. Bailey, Feb. 22, 1861, *OR*, I, 1:537–58.

16. John Salmon Ford, *Rip Ford's Texas*, ed. Stephen B. Oates (Austin: University of Texas Press, 1963), 319.

17. Ibid., 321.

18. E. B. Nichols and H. B. Walter to R. H. Hill, Feb. 22, 1861, *OR*, I: 1:538.

19. E. Backus to S. Cooper, Mar. 30, 1861, *OR*, I, 1:560–61.

20. Ford, *Rip Ford's Texas*, 321.

21. Ibid., 321.

22. Quoted in Joseph H. Parks, *General Edmund Kirby Smith, C.S.A.* (Baton Route: Louisiana State University Press, 1982), 117. Also, see E. Kirby Smith to AAG, Mar. 1, 1861, *OR*, I, 1:559.

23. Ibid.

24. Thompson, *Confederate General of the West*, 201–10.

25. *Mesilla Times*, July 27, 1861; John R. Baylor to T. A. Washington, Sept. 21, 1861, *OR*, 1, 4:17–20; I. Lynde to Acting Assistant Adjutant General, July 26, 1861, *OR*, 1, 4:4–5; Lane, *I Married a Soldier*, 107–10; McKee, *Narrative of the Surrender of a Command*, 6–39.

26. Heitman, *Historical Register*, 623.
27. Ibid., 822.
28. Heitman, *Historical Register*, 813.
29. Ibid., 181.
30. Marvin E. Kroeker, "William B. Hazen," *Soldiers West: Military Biographies from the Military Frontier*, ed. Paul Andrew Hutton and Robert M. Utley (Lincoln: University of Nebraska Press, 1987), 193–221; William B. Hazen, *A Narrative of Military Service* (Huntington, W. Va.: Blue Acorn Press, 1933).
31. Ibid., 175–76.
32. Ibid., 403–4.
33. Heitman, *Historical Register*, 793–94.
34. Ezra F. Warner, *Generals in Blue: Lives of the Union Commanders* (Baton Rouge: Louisiana State University Press, 1972), 377.
35. Ibid., 414–15.
36. Heitman, *Historical Register*, 225.
37. Ibid., 378.
38. Warner, *Generals in Blue*, 363.
39. Ibid., 405–6.
40. Marion Cox Grinstead, *Destiny at Valverde: The Life and Death of Alexander McRae* (Socorro: Historical Society of New Mexico, 1993), 7–23.
41. Ed. R. S. Canby to Adjutant General, Mar. 1, 1862, *OR*, Ser. I, 9:492.
42. James C. MacRae to Jerry Thompson, Sept. 21, 1999, enclosing miscellaneous newspaper clippings, n. d., editor's files.
43. Miller, *Soldiers and Settlers*, 228–29.
44. Warner, *Generals in Blue*, 168–69.
45. Ibid., 161–62.
46. W. B. Franklin to S. Williams, Oct. 7, 1862, *OR*, I, 19, Pt. 1, 376–78.
47. James B. Mulligan to Robert Sutherland, Jan. 8, 1863, *OR*, I, 20, pt. 1, 405–6.
48. J. G. Barnard to J. C. Kelton, Sept. 4, 1863, *OR*, I, 29, Pt. 2, 154.
49. Heitman, *Historical Register*, 728.
50. Ibid., 873; Frazer, *Forts of the West*, 102–3.
51. Ezra F. Warner, *Generals in Gray: Lives of the Confederate Commanders* (Baton Rouge: Louisiana State University Press, 1970), 279.
52. For example, see various references to Ewell in Hammond, *Campaigns in the West*, 14, 15, 20–31, 34–36, 39.
53. Donald C. Pfanz, *Richard S. Ewell: A Soldiers Life* (Chapel Hill: University of North Carolina Press, 1998), 136–438.
54. Lowell Reidenbaugh, "James Edwin Slaughter," *Encyclopedia of the Confederacy*, 4:1432–33; Richard and James Owen, *Generals at Rest: The Grave Sites of the 425 Official Confederate Generals* (Shippensburg, Pa.: White Mane, 1997), 334.
55. William B. Hesseltine and Hazel C. Wolf, *The Blue and Gray on the Nile* (Chicago: University of Chicago Press, 1961), 113–14.
56. Thompson, *Fifty Miles and a Fight*, 60, 65, 71, 74, 85, 139, 144, 300, 302, 304.
57. Carolina Baldwin Darrow, "Recollections of the Twiggs Surrender," *Battles and Leaders of the Civil War*, 4 vols. (New York: Yoseloff and Co., 1956), 2:33–39; Warner, *Generals in Gray*, 312; M. L. Crimmins, "An Episode in the Texas Career of

General David E. Twiggs," *Southwestern Historical Quarterly* 41 (October 1937), 167–173; Utley, *Frontiersmen in Blue*, 128; and Jeanne Twiggs Heidler, "The Military Career of David Emanuel Twiggs," (Ph.D. diss., Texas Christian University, 1976).

58. Lesley Gordon-Burr, "John Breckenridge Grayson," *Encyclopedia of the Confederacy*, 2:710.

59. James G. Blunt to Samuel R. Curtis, Dec. 8, 1862, *OR*, I, 22, 1:69–70.

60. Symonds, *Joseph E. Johnston*, 93. Symonds's superb biography remains the definitive study of General Johnston.

61. Ibid., 94.

62. Ibid., 95–96.

63. Quoted in ibid., 96.

64. Richard M. McMurry, "Joseph E. Johnston," *Encyclopedia of the Confederacy*, 2:860.

65. Ibid.

66. Symonds, *Joseph E. Johnston*, 172.

67. Frank E. Vandiver, introduction, *Narrative of Military Operations During the Late War Between the States* (New York: Da Capo, 1959), xxvii.

68. Ibid., xxviii.

69. McMurry, "Joseph E. Johnston," 861.

70. Quoted in Symonds, *Joseph E. Johnston*, 380.

71. Sam R. Watkins, *"Co. Aytch": A Side Show of the Big Show* (New York: Collier Books, 1962), 171. Quoted in Symonds, *Joseph E. Johnston*, 381.

72. Thompson, *Fifty Miles and a Fight*, 281.

73. For example, at Fort Union John Van Dusen Du Bois, a second lieutenant in the Mounted Rifles, recorded "several very bitter political discussions." Du Bois went as far as to say that if an effort was made to "seduce my regiment from its allegiance," he "would assume command . . . & fight it out." Hammond, *Campaigns in the West*, 110.

74. Jeremiah Taylor, *Memorial of Gen. J. K. F Mansfield, United States Army, Who Fell in Battle at Sharpsburg, Md., Sept. 17, 1862* (Boston: T. R. Marvin and Son, 1862), 66.

75. J. K. F. Mansfield to John H. B. Latrobe, Feb. 19, 1861, Latrobe Papers, Maryland Historical Society. Two letters that Mansfield wrote to Latrobe are carefully examined in: Frank F. White, Jr., "A Soldier Views the Secession Crisis," *Military Affairs* 15 (winter 1951), 209–12.

76. White, "Soldier Views the Secession Crisis," 210.

77. Mansfield to Latrobe, Nov. 9, 1861, Latrobe Papers, MHS.

78. Ibid.

79. Ibid. Although a lifelong member of the American Colonization Society, Mansfield was far from being an abolitionist. "I regard slavery [as] a curse on the face of the earth & I believe that God has hardened the hearts of those slaveholders," he wrote Louisa on Jan. 24, 1862. Mansfield to Louisa Mansfield, Mansfield Papers, MCHS.

80. Mansfield to Lorenzo Thomas, Apr. 20, 1861, LR, AGO, NA.

81. Mansfield to Thomas, Apr. 22, 1861, LR, AGO, NA.

82. Benjamin Franklin Cooling III, *Symbol, Sword and Shield: Defending Washington During the Civil War* (Shippensburg, Pa.: White Mane, 1981), 33.

83. Margaret Leech, *Reveille in Washington: 1860-1865* (New York: Carroll and Graf, 1991), 105.

84. Mansfield to Louisa Mansfield, September 1861, Mansfield Papers, MCHS.
85. John A. Dix to Mansfield, Aug. 19, 1862, *OR*, Ser. II, 4:409.
86. Mansfield to Louisa Mansfield, Jan. 24, 1862, Mansfield Papers, MCHS.
87. Mansfield to Louisa Mansfield, July 21, 1862, Mansfield Papers, MCHS.
88. Mansfield to Louisa Mansfield, Nov. 3, 1861, Mansfield Papers, MCHS.
89. Leech, *Reveille in Washington*, 200.
90. Ibid.
91. Mansfield to Louisa Mansfield, Jan. 24, 1862, Mansfield Papers, MCHS.
92. Mansfield to Louisa Mansfield, July 21, 1862, Mansfield Papers, MCHS.
93. Mansfield to John Wool, Apr. 24, 1862, Mansfield Papers, USMA.
94. Mansfield to Louisa Mansfield, July 18, 1862, Mansfield Papers, MCHS. Samuel Mansfield went on to command the Twenty-fourth Connecticut Volunteers. He served in Louisiana and was in the bloody siege and assault on Port Hudson, Louisiana, in May through July 1863. After the war he made various examinations of harbors and rivers on both coasts and retired from the army as a brigadier general in 1903.
95. Mansfield to Sylvanus Thayer, Sept. 11, 1862, Mansfield Papers, MCHS.
96. Mansfield to Samuel Mansfield, Sept. 12, 1862, Mansfield Papers, MCHS.
97. J. H. Taylor to Mansfield, Sept. 16, 1862, Mansfield Papers, MCHS.
98. Stephen W. Sears, *Land-Scape Turned Red: The Battle of Antietam* (New Haven: Ticknor and Fields, 1983), 203.
99. Quoted in Diane Longley, "General Mansfield Slide Program," 1991, MCHS.
100. John Mead Gould, *Joseph K. F. Mansfield, Brigadier General of the U.S. Army: A Narrative of Events Connected with his Mortal Wounding at Antietam, Sharpsburg, Maryland, September 17, 1862* (Portland, Maine: Stephen Berry, Printer, 1895), 13.
101. Ibid., 17.
102. Statement of Capt. Clarence H. Dyer, Oct. 10, 1862, USMA.
103. Ibid.
104. Ibid.
105. Broadside, "Mansfield Memorial," Sept. 25, 1862, Mansfield Papers, MCHS.
106. Ibid.
107. *Antietam Valley Record*, May 24, 1900. Mary Louisa, General Mansfield's only daughter, died on June 22, 1863, at the age of twenty-two. Louisa Mather Mansfield lived on until February 1880, dying at the age of seventy-one. The Mansfield's youngest son, Henry, died at the age of seventy-two in 1918. Brig. Gen. Samuel Mansfield died in Boston in 1928 at the age of eighty-eight. All were buried next to their father and mother in the Indian Hill Cemetery in Middletown, Conn. Tombstone data, Indian Hills Cemetery.

Department Commanders

1. General Worth is listed as commander of both Military Department No. 8 and Military Department No. 9 as a result of the two departments being united by General Order No. 58 from Nov. 7, 1848 to Apr. 3, 1849, when they were again separated by General Order No. 21.
2. General Twiggs formally surrendered all military posts and property to the Texas authorities on Feb. 18, 1861.
3. General Kearny never formally assumed command. August 13, 1846, is the date of his Las Vegas, N.M., proclamation.
4. See n. 1.

BIBLIOGRAPHY

Primary Sources

Manuscripts and Archival Collections

Adjutant General's Office. National Archives, Washington, D.C.
- Letters Received, 1856–1860 (Main Series), Record Group 94
- Letters Sent, 1856–1860 (Main Series), Record Group 94

Department of New Mexico, Record Group 393
- Letters Received (1854–1865)
- Letters Sent (1854–1865)

Department of Texas, Record Group 393
- Letters Sent (1856–1858)

Ninth Military Department, Record Group 393
- Letters Received (1849–1853)
- Letters Sent (1849–1853)

Post Returns, Record Groups 94 and 393
- Camp Hudson, Texas
- Camp Verde, Texas
- Camp Wood, Texas
- Cantonment Burgwin, New Mexico
- Fort Bliss, Texas
- Fort Brown, Texas
- Fort Buchanan, New Mexico [Arizona]
- Fort Clark, Texas
- Fort Craig, New Mexico
- Fort Davis, Texas
- Fort Defiance, New Mexico [Arizona]
- Fort Duncan, Texas
- Fort Fillmore, New Mexico
- Fort Garland, Colorado
- Fort Inge, Texas
- Fort McIntosh, Texas
- Fort Marcy, New Mexico
- Fort Quitman, Texas
- Fort Stanton, New Mexico
- Fort Stockton, Texas
- Fort Union, New Mexico
- Post at Albuquerque, New Mexico
- Post at Los Lunas, New Mexico
- Ringgold Barracks, Texas

Regimental Returns (Infantry), Record Group 94 and 391
- Second Artillery
- Second Infantry
- Third Infantry
- Seventh Infantry

Eighth Infantry
Regimental Returns (Cavalry), Record Group 94 and 391
Second Cavalry
First Dragoons
Second Dragoons
Mounted Rifles
Bliss, Zenas R. Reminiscences. Center for the Study of American History, University of Texas at Austin, Austin, Texas.
Bureau of Indian Affairs, Record Group 75, Washington, D.C.
New Mexico Superintendency. Letters Received, 1859–1860.
Delafield, Richard. Papers. New York Historical Society. New York, New York.
Department of State, Record Group 59, Territorial Papers, New Mexico. Letters Received, 1859–1860.
Eighth Census (1860). National Archives, Washington, D.C.
Arizona County, New Mexico
Bernalillo County, New Mexico
Bexar County, Texas
Cameron County, Texas
Doña Ana County, New Mexico
El Paso County, Texas
Maverick County, Texas
Mora County, Texas
Presidio, County, Texas
San Miguel, New Mexico
Santa Fe County, New Mexico
Socorro County, New Mexico
Starr County, Texas
Taos County, New Mexico
Valencia County, New Mexico
Webb County, Texas

Gibbs, Alfred. Papers. Archives. United States Military Academy, West Point, New York.

Hartz, Edward L. Papers. Manuscript Division, Library of Congress, Washington, D.C.

Heintzelman, Samuel Peter. Papers. Manuscript Division, Library of Congress, Washington, D.C.

———. Papers. United States Military Academy Special Collections, West Point, New York.

Latrobe, John H. B. Papers. Maryland Historical Society, Annapolis, Maryland.

McClellan, George Brinton. Papers. Manuscript Division, Library of Congress, Washington, D.C.

Magoffin, James Wiley. Papers. Center for the Study of American History, University of Texas at Austin, Austin, Texas.

Mansfield, Joseph K. F. Papers. Middlesex County Historical Society, Middletown, Connecticut.

———. Papers. United States Military Academy Special Collections, West Point, New York.

Ritch, William G., Papers. Manuscript Department. Huntington Library, San Marino, California.

Secretary of War. Record Group 107. National Archives, Washington, D.C. Letters Received (1856–1860).

Seventh Census (1850). National Archives, Washington, D.C.

Bexar County, Texas

Simonson, John Smith., Papers. Center for the Study of American History, University of Texas at Austin.

United States Congress. House of Representatives.

30th Cong., 1st Sess., Executive Document 5. Report of the Secretary of War.

30th Cong., 1st Sess., Executive Document 41. William S. Emory, Notes of a Military Reconnaissance.

31st Cong., 1st Sess., Executive Document 1. Report of the Secretary of War.

32d Cong., 1st Sess., Executive Document 112. Rio Grande Frontier.

32d Cong., 2d Sess., Executive Document 1, II. Report of the Secretary of War.

33d Cong., 1st Sess., Executive Document 1, II. Report of the Secretary of War.

34th Cong., 3d Sess., Executive Document 1. Report of the Secretary of War.

36th Cong., 1st Sess., Executive Document 52. Difficulties on the Southwestern Frontier.

36th Cong., 1st Sess., Executive Document 81. Troubles on Texas Frontier.

United States Congress. Senate.

31st Cong., 1st Sess., Executive Document 12. Marcy and Simpson Reports, 1850.

31st Cong., 1st Sess., Executive Document 64. Reports on routes from San Antonio to El Paso, 1850.

32d Cong., 1st Sess., Executive Document 1, Report of the Secretary of War.

33d Cong., 1st Sess., Executive Document 1, Report of the Secretary of War.

34th Cong., 1st Sess., Executive Document 96. Statistical Report on the Sickness and Mortality in the Army of the United States, 1839–1855.

36th Cong., 1st Sess., Executive Document 32. Message from the President.

36th Cong., 1st Sess., Executive Document 52. Statistical Report on the Sickness and Mortality in the United States Army, 1855–1860.

Books

Abel, Annie Heloise, ed. *The Official Correspondence of James S. Calhoun While Indian Agent at Santa Fe and Superintendent of Indian Affairs in New Mexico.* Washington: Government Printing Office, 1915.

———. *Expedition to the Southwest: An 1845 Reconnaissance of Colorado, New Mexico, Texas, and Oklahoma*. Lincoln: University of Nebraska Press, 1999.

Abert, James William. *Abert's New Mexico Report, 1846–'47*. Albuquerque: University of New Mexico Press, 1962.

Altshuler, Constance Wynn. *Latest from Arizona: The Hesperian Letters, 1859–1861*. Tucson: Arizona Pioneers' Historical Society, 1969.

Averell, William Woods. *Ten Years in the Saddle: The Memoir of William Woods Averell, 1851–1862*. Edited by Edward K. Eckert and Nicholas J. Amato. San Rafael, Calif.: Presidio Press, 1978.

Bailey, L. R., ed. *A. B. Gray Report: Survey of a Route on the 32nd Parallel for the Texas Western Railroad, 1854*. Los Angeles: Westernlore Press, 1963.

Bartlett, John Russell. *Personal Narrative of Exploration and Incidents in Texas, New Mexico, California, Sonora, and Chihuahua*. Chicago: Rio Grande Press, 1865.

Benham, Henry Washington. *Recollections of Mexico and the Battle of Buena Vista, Feb. 22 and 23, 1847, by an Engineer Officer, on its Twenty-Fourth Anniversary*. Boston: n.p., 1871.

Bennett, James A. *Forts and Forays: A Dragoon in New Mexico, 1850–1856*. Edited by Clinton E. Brooks and Frank D. Reeves. Albuquerque: University of New Mexico Press, 1996.

Brackett, Albert G. *History of the United States Cavalry: From the Formation of the Federal Government to the 1st of June 1863*. Freeport, N.Y.: Books for Libraries Press, 1970.

Cazneau, Mrs. William L. *Eagle Pass or Life on the Border*. Edited by Robert Crawford Cotner. Austin: Pemberton Press, 1966.

Chance, Joseph E., ed. *My Life in the Old Army: The Reminiscences of Abner Doubleday from the Collection of the New York Historical Society*. Fort Worth: Texas Christian University Press, 1998.

Coker, Caleb, ed. *The News from Brownsville: Helen Chapman's Letters from the Texas Military Frontier, 1848–1852*. Austin: Texas State Historical Association, 1992.

Dillon, Richard H., ed. *A Cannoneer in Navajo Country: Journal of Private Josiah M. Rice*. Denver: Old West Publishing Co., 1970.

Edwards, Frank S. *A Campaign in New Mexico with Colonel Doniphan*. Philadelphia: Carey and Hart, 1847.

Emory, William H. *Lieutenant Emory Reports*. Edited by Ross Calvin. Albuquerque: University of New Mexico Press, 1951.

Ford, John Salmon. *Rip Ford's Texas*. Edited by Stephen B. Oates. Austin: University of Texas Press, 1963.

Frazer, Robert W., ed. *Mansfield on the Condition of the Western Forts, 1853–54*. Norman: University of Oklahoma Press, 1963.

———, ed. *New Mexico in 1850, A Military View: Colonel George Archibald McCall*. Norman: University of Oklahoma Press, 1968.

Giese, Dale F. *James E. Farmer, My Life with the Army in the West:* Santa Fe: Stagecoach Press, 1967.

Gould, John Mead. *Joseph K. F. Mansfield, Brigadier General of the U.S. Army: A Narrative of Events Connected with his Mortal Wounding at Antietam, Sharpsburg, Maryland, September 17, 1862*. Portland, Maine: Stephen Berry, Printer, 1895.

Hammond, George P., ed. *Campaigns in the West, 1856–1861: The Journal and Letters of Colonel John Van Deusen Du Bois with Pencil Sketches by Joseph Heger*. Tucson: Arizona Pioneers Historical Society, 1949.

Hammond, John Fox. *A Surgeon's Report on Socorro, New Mexico, 1852*. Santa Fe: Stagecoach Press, 1966.

Hinton, Harwood P., ed. *Afoot and Alone: A Walk from Sea to Sea by the Southern Route, Adventures and Observations in Southern California, New Mexico, Arizona,*

Texas, etc. Austin: Book Club of Texas, 1995.

Hood, John Bell. *Advance and Retreat: Personal Experiences in the United States and Confederate States Armies.* New Orleans: G. T. Beauregard, 1880.

Hunter, J. Marvin. *Old Camp Verde, the Home of the Camels: A Romantic Story of Jefferson Davis' Plan to Use Camels on the Texas Frontier.* Bandera: Frontier Times, 1936.

Johnson, R. W. *A Soldier's Reminiscences in Peace and War.* Philadelphia: J. B. Lippincott, 1886.

Johnston, Joseph E. *Narrative of Military Operations During the Civil War.* New York: Da Capo Press, 1959.

Lane, Lydia Spencer. *I Married a Soldier or Old Days in the Old Army.* Albuquerque: Horn and Wallace, 1974.

McKee, James Cooper. *Narrative of the Surrender of a Command of U.S. Forces at Fort Fillmore, New Mexico in July, a.d., 1861.* Houston: Stagecoach Press, 1960.

McNitt, Frank, ed. *Navajo Expedition: Journal of a Military Reconnaissance from Santa Fe, New Mexico, to the Navaho Country, Made in 1849 by Lieutenant James H. Simpson.* Norman: University of Oklahoma Press, 1864.

Marcy, Randolph B. *Border Reminiscences.* New York: Harper and Brothers, 1872.

Maury, Dabney Herndon. *Recollections of a Virginian in the Mexican, Indian, and Civil Wars.* New York: Charles Scribner's Sons, 1894.

Memorial of Gen. J. K. F. Mansfield, United States Army, Who Fell in Battle at Sharpsburg, Md., Sept. 17, 1862. Boston: Press of T. R. Marvin and Son, 1862.

Miller, Darlis, ed. *Above a Common Soldier: Frank and Mary Clarke in the American West and Civil War, 1847–1872, From their Letters.* Albuquerque: University of New Mexico Press, 1977.

Miller, Emily Van Dorn, ed. *A Soldier's Honor.* New York: The Abbey Press, 1902.

Mills, Anson. *My Story.* Edited by C. H. Claudy. Washington, D.C.: Press of Byron S. Adams, 1921.

Mills, W. W. *Forty Years at El Paso, 1858–1898.* El Paso: Carl Hertzog, 1962.

Olmsted, Frederick Law. *A Journey Through Texas; Or, A Saddle-Trip on the Southwestern Frontier.* New York: Dix, Edwards & Co., 1857.

Pingenot, Ben E., ed. *Paso Del Águila: A Chronicle of Frontier Days on the Texas Border as Recorded in the Memoirs of Jesse Sumpter.* Austin: Encino Press, 1969.

Remley, David, ed. *Adios Nuevo Mexico: The Santa Fe Journal of John Watts in 1859.* Las Cruces: Yucca Tree Press, 1999.

Taylor, Jeremiah. *Memorial of Gen. J. K. F. Mansfield, United States Army, Who Fell in Battle at Sharpsburg, Md., Sept. 17, 1862.* Boston: T. R. Marvin and Son, 1862.

Tevis, James H. *Arizona in the '50s.* Albuquerque: University of New Mexico Press, 1954.

Thian, Raphael P., comp. *Notes Illustrating the Military Geography of the United States, 1813–1880.* Edited by James M. Carroll. Austin: University of Texas Press, 1979.

Thomas, W. Stephen. *Fort Davis and the Texas Frontier: Paintings by Captain Arthur T. Lee, Eighth U.S. Infantry.* College Station: Texas A&M University Press, 1976.

Thompson, Jerry D., ed. *Into the Far Wild Country: True Tales of the Old Southwest by George Wythe Baylor.* El Paso: Texas Western Press, 1996.

———, ed. *Fifty Miles and a Fight: Major Samuel Peter Heintzelman's Journal of Texas and the Cortina War*. Austin: Texas State Historical Association, 1998.

Turnley, Parmenas Taylor. *Parmenas Taylor Turnley: From the Cradle to Three-Score and Ten*. Chicago: Donohue and Henneberry, 1892.

Vielé, Teresa Griffin. *Following the Drum: A Glimpse of Frontier Life*. Lincoln: University of Nebraska Press, 1984.

War of the Rebellion: A Compilation of the Official Records of the Union and Confederate Armies. 128 vols. Washington: U.S. Government Printing Office, 1880–1901. Series I: Vol. 2, 4, 9, 11. 12, 18, 19 (Pt. 1), 19 (Pt. 2), 50, 51; Series II: Vol. 1, 2, 4.

Watkins, Sam R. *"Co. Aytch": A Side Show of the Big Show*. New York: Collier Books, 1962.

Whipple, A. W., *The Whipple Report: Journal of an Expedition from San Diego California, to the Rio Colorado, from September 11 to December 11, 1849*. Los Angeles: Westernlore Press, 1961.

Articles

Clary, David A, ed. "'I Am Already Quite a Texan': Albert J. Myer's Letters from Texas, 1854–1856." *Southwestern Historical Quarterly* 82 (July 1978): 25–76.

Crimmins, Martin L., ed. "Colonel Robert E. Lee's Report on Indian Combats in Texas." *Southwestern Historical Quarterly* 39 (July 1935): 21–32.

———, ed. "Colonel J. K. F. Mansfield's Report of the Inspection of the Department of Texas in 1856." *Southwestern Historical Quarterly* 42 (October 1938): 122–48; 42 (January, 1939): 215–57; 42 (April, 1939): 351–87.

———, ed. "W. G. Freeman's Report on the Eighth Military Department." *Southwestern Historical Quarterly* 51 (July 1946): 54–58; 51 (October 1947): 167–74; 51 (January 1948): 252–58; 51 (April 1948): 350–57; 52 (July 1948): 100–108; 52 (October 1948): 227–33; 52 (January 1949): 349–53; 52 (April 1949): 444–47; 53 (July 1949): 71–77; 53 (October 1949): 202–8; 53 (January 1950): 308–19; 53 (April 1950): 443–73; 53 (October 1950): 204–18.

Lazelle, Henry M. "Puritan and Apache: A Diary," ed. Frank D. Reeve. *New Mexico Historical Review* 23 (October 1948): 269–301; 24 (January 1949): 12–53.

Miller, Nyle H., ed. "Surveying the Southern Boundary Line of Kansas: From the Private Journal of Col. Joseph E. Johnston." *Kansas Historical Quarterly* 18 (February 1932): 104–39.

Moore, John Hammond, ed. "Letters from a Santa Fe Army Clerk, 1855–1856." *New Mexico Historical Review* 40 (April 1965): 141–64.

Pingenot, Ben E. "Jack Woodland: Forgotten Frontiersman." *The Journal of Big Bend Studies* 8 (1996): 51–60.

Roland, Charles P. and Richard P. Robbins, eds. "The Second Cavalry Comes to Texas: The Diary of Eliza (Mrs. Albert Sidney) Johnston." *Southwestern Historical Quarterly* 60 (April 1957): 463–500.

Whilden, Charles E., ed. "Letters from a Santa Fe Army Clerk, 1855–1856," ed. John Hammond Moore. *New Mexico Historical Review* 40 (1965): 141–64.

Secondary Sources

Books

Alexander, David V. *Arizona Frontier Military Place Names, 1846–1912.* Las Cruces: Yucca Tree Press, 1998.

Altshuler, Constance Wynn, ed. *Latest from Arizona.* Tucson: Arizona Historical Society, 1969.

———. *Chains of Command, Arizona and the Army, 1856–1875.* Tucson: Arizona Historical Society, 1981.

———. *Starting With Defiance, Nineteenth Century Arizona Military Posts.* Tucson: Arizona Historical Society, 1983.

Arrott, James W. *Arrott's Brief History of Fort Union.* Las Vegas, N.M.: Highlands University Rodgers Library, 1962.

Aston, B. W., and Donathan Taylor. *Along the Texas Forts Trail.* Denton: University of North Texas Press, 1997.

Austerman, Wayne R. *Sharps Rifles and Spanish Mules: The San Antonio-El Paso Mail, 1851–1861.* College Station: Texas A&M University Press, 1985.

Baker, T. Lindsay. *Lighthouses of Texas.* College Station: Texas A&M University Press, 1972.

Black, Art. *Fort Lancaster State Historic Site, Crockett County, Texas: Archeological Excavations.* Austin: Texas Parks and Wildlife Department, 1975.

Bowden, J. J. *The Exodus of Federal Forces from Texas, 1861.* Austin: Eakin Press, 1986.

Brandes, Ray. *Frontier Military Posts of Arizona.* Globe: Dale Stuart King Publishers, 1960.

Brune, Gunnar. *Springs of Texas.* Vol. 1. Fort Worth: Branch-Smith, 1981.

Clark, John W., Jr. *Archeological Investigations at Fort Lancaster State Historic Site, Crockett County, Texas.* Texas Archeological Salvage Project Research Report No. 12. Austin: University of Texas at Austin, 1972.

Clary, David A., and Joseph W. A. Whitehorne. *The Inspectors General of the United States Army, 1777–1903.* Washington, D.C.: Office of the Inspector General and Center of Military History, United States Army, 1987.

Coffman, Edward M. *The Old Army: A Portrait of the American Army in Peacetime, 1784–1898.* New York: Oxford University Press, 1986.

Conger, Roger N., et al. *Frontier Forts of Texas.* Waco: Texian Press, 1966.

Cooling, Benjamin Franklin III. *Symbol, Sword and Shield: Defending Washington During the Civil War.* Shippensburg, Pa.: White Mane, 1981.

Corder, Jim W. *Hunting Lieutenant Chadbourne.* Athens: University of Georgia Press, 1993.

Couchman, Donald Howard. *Cooke's Peak—Pasaron Por Aqui: A Focus on United States History in Southwestern New Mexico.* Las Cruces: Bureau of Land Management, 1988.

Delo, David Michael. *Peddlers and Post Traders: The Army Sutler on the Frontier.* Salt Lake City: University of Utah Press, 1992.

Descendants of Richard and Gillian Mansfield who Settled in New Haven, 1639, With Sketches of some of the Most Distinguished. New Haven: H. Mansfield, 1885.

Emmett, Chris. *Texas Camel Tales; Incidents Growing up Around an Attempt by the War Department of the United States to Foster an Uninterrupted Flow of Commerce through Texas by the Use of Camels.* San Antonio: Naylor Company, 1932.

———. *Fort Union and the Winning of the Southwest.* Norman: University of Oklahoma Press, 1965.

Exploring the American West, 1803–1879. Washington, D.C.: Division of Publications, National Park Service, 1982.

Faragher, John Mack, et al. *Drawing the Borderline: Army Explorers of the U.S.—Mexico Boundary Survey.* Albuquerque: Albuquerque Museum, 1996.

Francell, Lawrence John. *Ft. Lancaster State Historic Park, Crockett County, Texas.* Austin: Texas Parks and Wildlife Department, 1969.

———. *Fort Lancaster: Texas Frontier Sentinel.* Austin: Texas State Historical Association, 1999.

Frazer, Robert W. *Forts of the West: Military Forts and Presidios and Posts Commonly Called Forts West of the Mississippi River to 1898.* Norman: University of Oklahoma Press, 1965.

———. *Forts and Supplies: The Role of the Army in the Economy of the Southwest, 1846–1861.* Albuquerque: University of New Mexico Press, 1983.

Freeman, Douglas Southall. *R. E. Lee, A Biography.* Vol. 1. New York: Charles Scribner's Sons, 1934.

Giese, Dale F. *Forts of New Mexico: Echoes of the Bugle.* Silver City, N.M.: n.p., 1991.

Gluckman, Arcadi. *United States Muskets, Rifles and Carbines.* Buffalo: Otto Ulbrich, 1948.

———. *United States Martial Pistols and Revolvers.* Harrisburg: Stackpole Company, 1960.

Goetzmann, William H. *Exploration and Empire: The Explorer and the Scientist in the Winning of the American West.* New York: W. W. Norton, 1978.

———. *Army Exploration in the American West, 1803–1863.* Lincoln: University of Nebraska Press, 1979.

Govan, Gilbert Eaton, and Livingood, James W. *A Different Valor: The Story of General Joseph E. Johnston, C.S.A.* Indianapolis: Bobbs-Merrill, 1956.

Greene, Jerome A. *Fort Davis: National Historic Site, Texas.* Washington, D.C.: United States Department of the Interior, 1986.

Gregg, Andrew K. *New Mexico in the Nineteenth Century: A Pictorial History.* Albuquerque: University of New Mexico Press, 1968.

Grinstead, Marion Cox. *Life and Death of a Frontier Fort: Fort Craig, New Mexico, 1854–1885.* Socorro: Historical Society of New Mexico, 1973.

———. *Destiny at Valverde: The Life and Death of Alexander McRae.* Socorro: Historical Society of New Mexico, 1993.

Hart, Herbert H. *Old Forts of the Southwest.* Seattle: Bonanza Books, 1964.

———. *Old Forts of the Far West.* Seattle: Superior Publishing Company, 1965.

———. *Pioneer Forts of the West.* Seattle: Superior Publishing Company, 1967.

Hartje, Robert G. *Van Dorn: The Life and Times of a Confederate General.* Nashville: Vanderbilt University Press, 1967.

Hays, T. R., and Edward B. Jelks. *Archeological Explorations at Fort Lancaster, 1966: A Preliminary Report.* Austin: Texas Historical Commission, 1966.

Hazen, William B. *A Narrative of Military Service.* Huntington, W.Va.: Blue Acorn Press, 1933.

Heitman, Francis B. *Historical Register and Dictionary of the United States Army, From its Organization, September 29, 1789, to March 2, 1903*, 2 vols. Washington D.C.: Government Printing Office, 1903.

Hendricks, Rick, and W. H. Timmons. *San Elizario: Spanish Presidio to Texas County Seat*. El Paso: Texas Western Press, 1998.

Hesseltine, William B. and Hazel C. Wolf. *The Blue and Gray on the Nile*. Chicago: University of Chicago Press, 1961.

Holland, Francis Ross. *America's Lighthouses: Their Illustrated History Since 1716*. Battleboro, Vt.: Stephen Greene Press, 1972.

Hollon, W. Eugene. *Beyond the Cross Timbers: The Travels of Randolph B. Marcy, 1812–1887*. Norman: University of Oklahoma Press, 1955.

Horn, Calvin. *New Mexico's Troubled Years: The Story of the Early Territorial Governors*. Albuquerque: Horn and Wallace, 1963.

Hosley, William. *Colt: The Making of an American Legend*. Amherst: University of Massachusetts Press, 1996.

Hughes, Robert Morton. *General Johnston*. New York: Appleton, 1893.

Hutton, Paul Andrew, and Robert M. Utley, eds. *Soldiers West: Biographies from the Military Frontier*. Lincoln: University of Nebraska Press, 1987.

Johnson, Bradley Tyler. *A Memoir of the Life and Public Service of Joseph Eggleston Johnston*. Baltimore: Woodward, 1891.

Keleher, William A. *Turmoil in New Mexico, 1846–1868*. Santa Fe: Rydal Press, 1952.

Knight, Oliver. *Life and Manners in the Frontier Army*. Norman: University of Oklahoma Press, 1978.

Lash, Jeffrey N. *Destroyer of the Iron Horse: General Joseph E. Johnston and Confederate Rail Transport, 1861–1865*. Kent, Ohio: Kent State University Press, 1991.

Leech, Margaret. *Reveille in Washington: 1860-1865*. New York: Carroll and Graf, 1991.

McMaster, Richard Keith. *Musket, Saber and Missle: A History of Fort Bliss*. El Paso, 1962.

McMurry, Richard M. "Joseph E. Johnston." In *Encyclopedia of the Confederacy*, ed. Richard N. Current. New York: Simon & Schuster, 1993.

McNitt, Frank. *Navajo Wars: Military Campaigns, Slave Raids, and Reprisals*. Albuquerque: University of New Mexico Press, 1972.

Malsch, Brownson. *Indianola–Mother of Western Texas*. Austin: Shoal Creek, 1977.

Mansfield, E. D. *Personal Memories: Social, Political, and Literary with Sketches of Many Noted People, 1803–1841*. Cincinnati: Robert Clarke and Co., 1879.

Metz, Leon C. *Fort Bliss: An Illustrated History*. El Paso: Mangan Books, 1981.

———. *Desert Army: Fort Bliss on the Texas Border*. El Paso: Mangan Books, 1988.

Miller, Darvis A. *Soldiers and Settlers: Military Supply in the Southwest, 1861–1885*. Albuquerque: University of New Mexico Press, 1989.

Miller, Ray. *Texas Forts: A History and Guide*. Austin: Texas Parks, 1985.

Myers, Lee C. *Fort Stanton, New Mexico: The Military Years, 1855–1896*. Lincoln, N.M.: Lincoln County Historical Society, 1983.

———. *Fort Stanton, New Mexico: The Military Years, 1855–1896*. Lincoln, New Mexico: Lincoln County Historical Society, 1988.

Nelson, George S. *Preliminary Archaeological Survey and Testing of Fort Inge, Texas.* Uvalde, Tex.: Uvalde County Historical Commission, 1981.

Ness, George T., Jr. *The Army on the Eve of the Civil War.* Manhattan: Sunflower University Press, 1983.

Newton, Steven H. *Joseph E. Johnston and the Defense of Richmond.* Lawrence: University of Kansas Press, 1998.

Norris, L. Davis, et al. *William H. Emory: Soldier-Scientist.* Tucson: University of Arizona Press, 1998.

Owen, Richard and James. *Generals at Rest: The Grave Sites of the 425 Official Confederate Generals.* Shippensburg, Pa.: White Mane, 1997.

Parks, Joseph H. *General Edmund Kirby Smith, C.S.A.* Baton Rouge: Louisiana State University Press, 1982.

Peterson, Harold L. *Round Shot and Rammers: An Introduction to the Muzzle-Loading Land Artillery in the United States.* New York: Bonanza Books, 1959.

Pfanz, Donald C. *Richard S. Ewell: A Soldier's Life.* Chapel Hill: University of North Carolina Press, 1998.

Prince, Bradford L. *Old Fort Marcy, Santa Fe, New Mexico; historical sketch and panoramic view of Santa Fe and its vicinity.* Santa Fe, New Mexican Printing Company, 1912.

Prucha, Francis Paul. *The Sword of the Republic: The United States Army on the Frontier, 1783–1846.* New York: Macmillan Company, 1969.

Putnam, George R. *Lighthouses and Lightships of the United States.* Boston: Houghton Mifflin Company, 1933.

Raab, James W. *W. W. Loring, "Old Blizzards": Florida's Forgotten General.* Manhattan: Sunflower University Press, 1996.

Raht, Carlysle G. *The Romance of the Davis Mountains and Big Bend Country.* Odessa: Rahtbooks Company, 1963.

Reed, St. Clair Griffin. *A History of the Texas Railroads and of Transportation Conditions in Texas under Spain and Mexico and The Republic and The State.* Houston: St. Clair Publishing Company, 1941.

Reidenbaugh, Lowell. "James Edwin Slaughter." In *Encyclopedia of the Confederacy*, ed. Richard N. Current. New York: Simon & Schuster, 1993.

Rickey, Don. *Forty Miles a Day on Beans and Hay: The Enlisted Soldier Fighting the Indian Wars.* Norman: University of Oklahoma Press, 1963.

Ripley, Warren. *Artillery and Ammunition of the Civil War.* New York: Van Nostrand Reinhold and Company, 1970.

Risch, Erna. *Quartermaster Support of the Army: A History of the Corps, 1775–1939.* Washington, D.C.: U.S. Government Printing Office, 1962.

Rister, Carl Coke. *Robert E. Lee in Texas.* Norman: University of Oklahoma Press, 1946.

Roberts, Robert B. *Encyclopedia of Historic Forts: The Military, Pioneer, and Trading Posts of the United States.* New York: Macmillan, 1988.

Robinson, Charles M., III. *Frontier Forts of Texas.* Houston: Lone Star Books, 1986.

Robinson, Willard B. *American Fortress: Architectural Form and Function.* Urbana: University of Southern Illinois Press, 1977.

Roland, Charles P. *Albert Sidney Johnston: Soldier of Three Republics.* Austin: University of Texas Press, 1964.

Ryan, John P. *Fort Stanton and its Community, 1855–1896*. Las Cruces: Yucca Tree Press, 1998.

Scobee, B. *Fort Davis, Texas, 1583–1960*. El Paso: Hill Printing Company, 1963.

Sears, Stephen W. *Land-Scape Turned Red: The Battle of Antietam*. New Haven: Ticknor and Fields, 1983.

———. *George B. McClellan: The Young Napoleon*. New York: Ticknor and Fields, 1988.

Simmons, Marc. *Albuquerque, A Narrative History*. Albuquerque: University of New Mexico Press, 1982.

Simpson, Harold B. *Cry Comanche: The 2nd U.S. Cavalry in Texas, 1855–1861*. Hillsboro, Texas: Hill Junior College Press, 1979.

Skelton, William B. *An American Profession of Arms: The Officer Corps, 1784–1861*. Lawrence: University of Kansas Press, 1992.

Smith, Thomas T. *Fort Inge: Sharps, Spurs, and Sabers on the Texas Frontier, 1849–1869*. Austin: Eakin Press, 1993.

———. *The U.S. Army and the Texas Frontier Economy, 1845–1900*. College Station: Texas A&M University Press, 1999.

———. *The Old Army in Texas: A Research Guide to the U.S. Army in Nineteenth-Century Texas*. Austin: Texas State Historical Association, 2000.

Sonnichsen, C. L. *Pass of the North, Four Centuries on the Rio Grande*. El Paso: Texas Western Press, 1968.

Stanley, F. [Father Stanley Crocchiola], *Fort Union, New Mexico*. Denver: The World Press, 1953.

———. *The Fort Conrad, New Mexico, Story*. Dumas, Tex., 1961.

———. *The Fort Fillmore, New Mexico, Story*. Pantex, Tex., 1961.

———. *Fort Craig*. Pampa, Tex.: Pampa Print Shop, 1963.

———. *Fort Stanton*. Pampa, Tex.: Pampa Print Shop, 1964.

———. *E. V. Sumner: Major General, United States Army (1797–1863)*. Borger, Tex.: Jim Hess Press, 1969.

Steffen, Randy. *United States Military Saddles, 1812–1943*. Norman: University of Oklahoma Press, 1973.

Strickland, Rex W. *Six Who Came to El Paso: Pioneers of the 1840s*. El Paso: Texas Western Press, 1963.

Symonds, Craig L. *Joseph E. Johnston: A Civil War Biography*. New York: W. W. Norton, 1992.

Thomlinson, Matthew H. *The Garrison of Fort Bliss, 1849–1916*. El Paso: Hertzog and Resler, 1945.

Thompson, Jerry. *Sabers on the Rio Grande*. Austin: Presidial Press, 1974.

———. *Desert Tiger: James "Paddy" Graydon and the Civil War in the Southwest*. El Paso: Texas Western Press, 1992.

———. *Juan Nepomuceno Cortina and the Texas-Mexico Frontier, 1859–1877*. El Paso: Texas Western Press, 1994.

———. *Confederate General of the West: Henry Hopkins Sibley*. College Station: Texas A&M University Press, 1996.

———. *A Wild and Vivid Land: An Illustrated History of the South Texas Border*. Austin: Texas State Historical Association, 1997.

Tiller, Veronica E. Velarde. *The Jicarilla Apache Tribe: A History, 1846–1970*. Lincoln: University of Nebraska Press, 1983.

Toulouse, James R. *Pioneer Posts of Texas*. San Antonio: Naylor Press, 1936.

Tunnell, Curtis D., and William W. Newcomb. *A Lipan Apache Mission: San Lorenzo de la Santa Cruz*. Austin: Texas Memorial Museum, 1969.

Tyler, Ron, et al. *New Handbook of Texas*. 6 vols. Austin: Texas State Historical Association, 1996.

Utley, Robert M. *Fort Union: National Monument, New Mexico*. Washington, D.C.: National Park Service, 1962.

———. *Fort Davis National Historic Site, Texas*. Washington, D.C.: United States Department of the Interior, 1965.

———. *Frontiersmen in Blue: The United States Army and the Indian, 1848–1865*. New York: Macmillan Company, 1967.

———. *Fort Union and the Santa Fe Trail*. El Paso: Texas Western Press, 1989.

Utley, Robert M., and J. U. Salvant, eds. *If These Walls Could Speak: Historic Forts of Texas*. Austin: University of Texas Press, 1991.

Vines, Robert A. *Vines, Trees, Shrubs, and Woody Vines of the Southwest*. Austin: University of Texas Press, 1960.

Warner, Ezra F. *Generals in Gray: Lives of the Confederate Commanders*. Baton Rouge: Louisiana State University Press, 1970.

———. *Generals in Blue: Lives of the Union Commanders*. Baton Rouge: Louisiana State University Press, 1972.

Weaver, Bobby D. *Castro's Colony: Empresario Development in Texas, 1842–1865*. College Station: Texas A&M University Press, 1985.

Wilkinson, J. B. *Laredo and the Rio Grande Frontier*. Austin: Jenkins Company, 1975.

Williams, Clayton. *Texas' Last Frontier: Fort Stockton and the Trans-Pecos, 1861–1895*. Edited by Ernest Wallace. College Station: Texas A&M University Press, 1982.

Williams, T. Harry. *P. G. T. Beauregard: Napoleon in Gray*. Baton Rouge: Louisiana State University Press, 1955.

Woolford, Sam, ed. *San Antonio: A History for Tomorrow*. San Antonio: Naylor Company, 1963.

Wooster, Ralph A. *Texas and Texans in the Civil War*. Austin: Eakin Press, 1995.

Wooster, Robert. *Soldiers, Sutlers, and Settlers: Garrison Life on the Texas Frontier*. College Station: Texas A&M University Press, 1987.

———. *History of Fort Davis, Texas*. Santa Fe: Department of the Interior, 1990.

———. *Fort Davis: Outpost on the Texas Frontier*. Austin: Texas State Historical Association, 1996.

Articles

Ashcraft, Allan C. "Fort Brown, Texas, in 1861." *Texas Military History* 3 (winter 1963): 243–47.

Ball, Durwood. "Fort Craig, New Mexico, and the Southwest Indian Wars." *New Mexico Historical Review* 73 (April 1998): 153–73.

Barrett, Arrie. "Western Frontier Forts of Texas, 1845–1861." *West Texas Historical Association Year Book* 7 (June 1931): 115–39.

Barrett, Leonora. "Transportation, Supplies, and Quarters for the West Texas Frontier under the Federal Military System, 1848–1861." *West Texas Historical Association Year Book* 5 (June 1929): 87–99.

Bender, A. B. "The Soldier in the Far West, 1848–1860." *Pacific Historical Review* 8 (June 1939): 159–78.

———. "Frontier Defense in the Territory of New Mexico During the Territorial Period." *New Mexico Historical Review* 17 (October 1942): 281–87.

Bloom, John P. "New Mexico Viewed by Anglo Americans, 1846–1849." *New Mexico Historical Review* 34 (July 1959): 165–98.

Breeden, James O. "Health of Early Texas: The Military Frontier." *Southwestern Historical Quarterly* 80 (April 1977): 357–98.

Brown, Russell. "An Old Woman with a Broomstick: General David E. Twiggs and the U.S. Surrender in Texas, 1861." *Military Affairs* 48 (April 1984): 57–61.

Clark, John W., Jr. "The 'Digs' at Fort Lancaster, Texas, 1966 and 1971." *Military History of Texas and the Southwest* 12 (1974): 284–99.

Collette, James. "The Bloody Legacy of Howard's Well." *Old West* 21 (spring 1985): 55–59.

Connelly, Thomas L. "The American Camel Experiment: A Reappraisal." *Southwestern Historical Quarterly* 69 (April 1966): 442–62.

Crimmins, M. L. "Fort Fillmore." *New Mexico Historical Review*, No. 6 (1931): 327–33.

———. "An Episode in the Texas Career of General David E. Twiggs." *Southwestern Historical Quarterly* 41 (October 1937): 167–73.

———. "Old Fort Duncan: A Frontier Post." *Frontier Times* (June 1938): 161–71.

Darrow, Carolina Baldwin. "Recollections of the Twiggs Surrender." *Battles and Leaders of the Civil War*, 2:33–39.

Dewey, George Harmon. "The United States Indian Policy in Texas, 1845–1860." *Mississippi Valley Historical Review* 17 (December 1930): 377–403.

Field, William T. "Fort Duncan and Old Eagle Pass." *Texas Military History* 6 (summer 1967): 160–71.

Fletcher, Henry T. "Old Fort Lancaster." *West Texas Historical and Scientific Society Bulletin* 44 (December 1932): 33–34.

Franz, Joe B. "The Significance of Frontier Forts to Texas," *Southwestern Historical Quarterly* 74 (October 1970): 204–5.

Frazer, Robert W. "Fort Butler: The Fort That Almost Was." *New Mexico Historical Review* 43 (October 1968): 253–70.

———. "The Army and New Mexico Agriculture, 1848–1861." *El Palacio* 47 (July 1972): 25–29.

———. "Purveyors of Flour to the Army: Department of New Mexico, 1849–1861." *New Mexico Historical Review* 47 (July 1972): 213–38.

———. "Army Agriculture in New Mexico, 1852–53." *New Mexico Historical Review* 50 (October 1975): 313–34.

Graham, Roy Eugene. "Federal Fort Architecture in Texas during the Nineteenth Century." *Southwestern Historical Quarterly* 74 (October 1970): 165–88.

Hutchins, James S. "Bald Head Ewell, Frontier Dragoon." *Arizoniana: The Journal of Arizona History* (spring 1962): 18–23.

McMaster, Richard K. "Records and Reminiscences of Old Fort Bliss." *Password* 8 (spring 1963): 18–32.

Miller, Darlis A. "Military Supply in Civil War New Mexico." *Military History of Texas and the Southwest* 16, No. 3 (1982): 177–97.

———. "Los Pinos, New Mexico: Civil War Post on the Rio Grande." *New Mexico Historical Review* 62 (January 1987): 1–31.

Mozer, Corinne C. "A Brief History of Fort Fillmore, 1851–1862." *El Palacio* (summer 1967): 5–18.

Murphy, Lawrence R. "The United States Army in Taos, 1847–1852." *New Mexico Historical Quarterly* 48 (January 1972): 32–48.

———. "The United States Army in Taos, 1847–1852." *New Mexico Historical Review* 47 (1972): 33–48.

———. "Cantonment Burgwin, New Mexico, 1852–1860." *Arizona and the West* 15 (spring 1973): 22–46.

Myers, Lee. "Fort Webster on the Mimbres River." *New Mexico Historical Review* 41 (1966): 47–57.

———. "Military Establishments in Southwestern New Mexico: Stepping Stones to Settlement." *New Mexico Historical Review* 43 (January 1968): 5–48.

Neighbours, Kenneth F. "Fort Belknap." *Frontier Forts of Texas*. Waco: Texian Press, 1966.

Ruhlen, George. "Quitman's Owners: A Sidelight on Frontier Reality." *Password* 5 (April 1960): 54–64.

———. "Fort Quitman: 'The Worst Post at Which I Ever Served.'" *Password* 11 (fall 1966): 107–26.

Sacks, B. "The Origins of Fort Buchanan: Myth and Fact." *Arizona and the West* 7 (autumn 1965): 207–26.

Scheips, Paul J. "Albert James Myer, an Army Doctor in Texas, 1854–1857." *Southwestern Historical Quarterly* 82 (July 1978): 1–24.

Taylor, Morris. G. "Campaign Against the Jicarilla Apache, 1854." *New Mexico Historical Quarterly* 44 (1969): 269–91.

———. "Campaign Against the Jicarilla Apache, 1855." *New Mexico Historical Quarterly* 45 (1970): 119–36.

Thompson, Jerry D. "Henry Hopkins Sibley: Military Inventor on the Texas Frontier." *Military History of Texas and the Southwest* 10 (1973): 227–48.

Thompson, Jerry, ed. "With the Third Infantry in New Mexico, 1851–1853: The Lost Diary of Private Sylvester W. Matson." *Journal of Arizona History* 31 (winter 1990): 349–404.

Timmons, W. H. "The Merchants and the Military, 1849–1854." *Password* 27 (summer 1982).

Utley, Robert M. "Fort Union and the Santa Fe Trail." *New Mexico Historical Review* 36 (1961): 36–48.

White, Frank F. "A Soldier Views the Secession Crisis." *Military Affairs* 15 (winter 1951): 209–12.

Wilson, John P. "Excavations at Fort Fillmore." *El Palacio* (summer 1967), 27–41.

———. "Why the Fort Fell Down: Fort Fillmore, 1851–1869." *La Frontera* (1999): 105–213.

Wooster, Ralph A. "Wealthy Texans, 1860." *Southwestern Historical Quarterly* 71 (October 1967): 163–80.

Newspapers

Antietam: *Antietam Valley Record*
Brownsville: *American Flag, Bandera Americana, Daily Ranchero, Fort Brown Flag*
Corpus Christi: *Ranchero*
Clarksville: *Northern Standard*
Galveston: *Galveston News*; *Tri-Weekly News*
Mesilla: *Mesilla Times*
New York: *Harper's Weekly*
San Antonio: *Alamo Express, Daily Herald, Ledger*
Santa Fe: *Santa Fe Weekly Gazette*
Tubac: *Weekly Arizonian*
Victoria: *Victoria Advocate*

Unpublished Material

Ball, Larry Durwood. "The United States Army on the Interwar Frontier, 1848–1861." Ph.D. diss., University of New Mexico, 1994.

Barrett, Arrie. "Federal Military Outposts in Texas, 1846–1861." Master's thesis, University of Texas, 1927.

Christian, Garna Loy. "Sword and Plowshare: The Symbiotic Development of Fort Bliss and El Paso, Texas, 1849–1918." Ph.D. diss., Texas Tech University, 1977.

Downs, Alan Craig. "Gone Past All Redemption?: The Early War Years of General Joseph Eggleston Johnston." Ph.D. diss., University of North Carolina, 1991.

Gamble, Richard Dalzell. "Garrison Life at Frontier Military Posts, 1830–1860." Ph.D. diss., University of Oklahoma, 1956.

Giese, Dale F. "Soldiers at Play, A History of Social Life at Fort Union, New Mexico, 1851–1891." Ph.D. diss., University of New Mexico, 1969.

Hays, Kelly R. "Fort Stanton: A History of its Relationship with the Mescalero Apaches." Master's thesis, New Mexico State University, 1988.

Heidler, Jeanne Twiggs. "The Military Career of David Emanuel Twiggs." Ph.D. diss., Texas Christian University, 1976.

Lackman, Howard. "George Thomas Howard, Texas Frontiersman." Ph.D. diss., University of Texas at Austin, 1954.

McLaughlen, Thomas J. "History of Fort Union, New Mexico. Master's thesis, University of New Mexico, 1952.

McMillen, Kathryn S. "The San Antonio-San Diego Mail Line in Texas, 1857–61." Master's thesis, University of Texas at Austin, 1960.

Marcum, Richard T. "Fort Brown, Texas: A History of the Border Post." Ph.D. diss., Texas Tech University, 1964.

Sellers, Roseola A. "The History of Fort Duncan, Eagle Pass, Texas." Master's thesis, Sul Ross College, 1960.

INDEX